ARMENIANS BEYOND DIASPORA

Alternative Histories: Narratives from the Middle East and Mediterranean

Series Editor: Sargon Donabed

This series provides a forum for exchange on a myriad of alternative histories of marginalised communities and individuals in the Near and Middle East and Mediterranean, and those of Middle Eastern or Mediterranean heritage. It also highlights thematic issues relating to various native peoples and their narratives and – with particular contemporary relevance – explores encounters with the notion of 'other' within societies. Often moving beyond the conventional state-centred and dominant monolithic approach, or reinterpreting previously accepted stories, books in the series examine and explain themes from inter-communal relations, environment, health and society, and explore ethnic, communal, racial, linguistic and religious developments, in addition to geopolitics.

Editorial Advisory Board

Professor Ali Banuazizi
Dr Aryo Makko
Professor Laura Robson
Professor Paul Rowe
Professor Hannibal Travis

Books in the series (published and forthcoming)

Sayfo – An Account of the Assyrian Genocide
'Abd al-Masih Nu'man of Qarabash
Translated and annotated by Michael Abdalla and Łukasz Kiczko

Tunisia's Andalusians: The Cultural Identity of a North African Minority
Marta Dominguez Diaz

Armenians Beyond Diaspora: Making Lebanon their Own
Tsolin Nalbantian

The Art of Minorities: Cultural Representation in Museums of the Middle East and North Africa
Edited by Virginie Rey

Shia Minorities in the Contemporary World: Migration, Transnationalism and Multilocality
Edited by Oliver Scharbrodt and Yafa Shanneik

Protestants, Gender and the Arab Renaissance in Late Ottoman Syria
Deanna Ferree Womack

edinburghuniversitypress.com/series/ahnme

ARMENIANS BEYOND DIASPORA

MAKING LEBANON THEIR OWN

Tsolin Nalbantian

EDINBURGH
University Press

To my families:
The ones I was born into,
made and joined,
and the one I have
created with Cyrus.

Edinburgh University Press is one of the leading university presses in the UK. We publish academic books and journals in our selected subject areas across the humanities and social sciences, combining cutting-edge scholarship with high editorial and production values to produce academic works of lasting importance. For more information visit our website: edinburghuniversitypress.com

© Tsolin Nalbantian, 2020, 2021

Edinburgh University Press Ltd
The Tun – Holyrood Road
12 (2f) Jackson's Entry
Edinburgh EH8 8PJ

First published in hardback by Edinburgh University Press 2020

Typeset in 11/15 Adobe Garamond by
Servis Filmsetting Ltd, Stockport, Cheshire

A CIP record for this book is available from the British Library

ISBN 978 1 4744 5856 6 (hardback)
ISBN 978 1 4744 5857 3 (paperback)
ISBN 978 1 4744 5858 0 (webready PDF)
ISBN 978 1 4744 5859 7 (epub)

The right of Tsolin Nalbantian to be identified as author of this work has been asserted in accordance with the Copyright, Designs and Patents Act 1988 and the Copyright and Related Rights Regulations 2003 (SI No. 2498).

CONTENTS

Acknowledgements | vi
List of Figures | x

Introduction | 1
1 Repositioning Armenians in Newly Post-colonial Nation-states: Lebanon and Syria, 1945–1946 | 44
2 The Homeland Debate, Redux: The Political–Cultural Impact of the 1946–1949 Repatriation to Soviet Armenia | 84
3 Cold War, Bottom-up: The 1956 Catholicos Election | 126
4 Making Armenians Lebanese: The 1957 Election and the Ensuing 1958 Conflict | 167
Conclusion | 196

Bibliography | 205
Index | 221

ACKNOWLEDGEMENTS

This book would not have been written without the support of many individuals and institutions. I want to thank the Netherlands Organisation for Scientific Research (NWO), the European Commission and the Marie Curie Career Integration Grant, Columbia University and its Department of Middle Eastern, South Asian and African Studies, the Clara and Krikor Zohrab Fellowship, the Gorvetzian Family fund, the Fulbright–Hayes Programme, the Wenner-Gren Foundation and Leiden University for giving me the opportunity to conduct and present this research. I also want to thank the Catholicosate of the Cilician See and its library staff for the extensive use of their archives, the American University of Beirut and the staff of its Jafet Library, Haigazian University and the staff of its Derian Armenian library, the Department of History at the Massachusetts Institute of Technology, the University of Chicago and its Department of Near Eastern Languages and Civilisations and the Dumanian Armenian Studies Fund. In particular, I would like to thank Lila Abu-Lughod, Anny Bakalian, Léon Buskens, Maghiel van Crevel, Vera Gosdanian, Rashid Khalidi, Archbishop Dirayr Panossian, Ara Sanjian, Vahé Tachjian, Erik-Jan Zurcher and my students and colleagues at the Leiden Institute of Area Studies and its Department of Middle East Studies. I continue to feel the encouragement of Sossie

Kasbarian, along with the participants of the Contextualising Community – Diasporas of the Modern Middle East workshop, especially Mezna Qato and Andrew Arsan. I am indebted to Knarik Avakian and Verjine Svazlian, who provided me with the pictures documenting repatriation that were taken by their late father and husband, Karnik Svazlian. Finally, I am grateful for all of the support received from Edinburgh University Press, especially Nicola Ramsey and Sargon Donabed.

While the research for this book began in 2007 during my Ph.D. studies, its preliminary questions germinated when I first started visiting my family in Beirut after the end of the Lebanese Civil War. I had grown up hearing about them and their city, and was confused by the stories of transformations that had taken place. Yet, throughout all those wartime and postwar changes, with their shifting political allegiances and boundary (re)makings, one thing did not change: my family's presence. I once asked my late great-uncle Sarkis why he never moved – even within the space of the city. He looked at me as if he didn't understand my question, and responded in turn with a rhetorical question of his own: 'Why would I?'

By the time I started this work, Sarkis had passed away, but I continued to spend hours at my family's house. By then they had changed neighbourhoods from Zokak al-Blat to nearby Zarif. Their landlord had sold the old Ottoman-style house in which they lived on the top floor to develop a high rise in its place. Although change had come, their move was also a mark of continuity for Beirut. Their new apartment was owned by a Jewish family living in France, a family that had left Beirut, but did not want Beirut to leave them. My family's presence facilitated this bond, and, in turn, their new home enabled my family to remain in a familiar neighbourhood.

And so I came to observe and become a part of their daily life in between Zokak al-Blat and Zarif. I made my own experiences as I moved between Beirut's spaces as well: from the libraries of the American University of Beirut and Haigazian University, to the archives of *Aztag*, *Zartonk* and *Ararad*, the Armenian dailies; from the archives of the Prelacy of the Armenian Church in Bourj Hamoud to those housed at the Catholicosate of Cilicia in Antelias. I immersed myself in their daily news, their 'main stories' and behavioural counsels, travel and product advertisements, foreign news, film debuts, telegrams and personal correspondences. And then, I would leave the 1940s and

1950s behind – or so I thought – and enter the world of my family, who had lived through those very years and were part of the 'news' I was now studying, and who, in a way, represented its continued relevance and presence in the everyday life of Beirut and its people. Thank you to Shakeh Artin, Mako Oundjian, Seta Hadichian, Serge Artin, Dalida Adjemian, Gassia Artin, Vicken Baghdassarian, Dani Shukri, Sonia Wartanian and to those who have passed on, Sosse and Sarkis Oundjian. Thank you also to Sandra Habchi and Alain Bifani, Lara Anawati, Cynthia Habchi and Mado Anawati.

Wonderfully, luckily, my family is not limited to lineage, or limited by geography and time.

My own time in Beirut grew full with my own extended friendship circle that exhibited all I love about family. Thank you to the wolves and villagers, and to Ramla Khalidi, Lina Mikdashi, Marc Sirois, Jim Quilty, Nazha Merabi, May Farah, Kiki Ghossainy and Cynthia Zaven.

Thank you to my friends who morphed into family as we embarked on similar journeys in graduate school: Dina Ramadan, Yasmine Ramadan, Shane Minkin, Linda Sayed, Haytham Bahoora, Naomi Schiller, Elizabeth Johnston and Andrea Stanton. And to my students who have become colleagues and friends and have inspired me to continue that journey as a professor: Mariam Taher, Eftychia Mylona, Margot van der Heide and Farah Bazzi.

For warmly welcoming me I thank Christine and Masud Schayegh and Leila Schayegh Saraga and Daniel Saraga. I owe much gratitude to my friends who allowed me to make Leiden my home. Thank you for grounding and nurturing me: Nira Wickramasinghe, Sanjukta Sunderason, Limin Teh, Nell Crawford, Carrie Nakamura, Tom Aldrich, Crystal Ennis, Ra'id Al-Jamali, Jue Wang, Anne-Isabelle Richard, Rawan Ziadeh, Emre and Nihal Erol and Denise Sommers.

Then there are those friends that moved, like me, from place to place, making it delightfully difficult for me to connect them to a particular place. These friendships are the family I too take with me from place to place: Bedross Der Matossian, Hocine Dimerdji, Ghenwa Hayek, Maha Jweied, Vanya Dugalic, Christian Henderson, Tamar Boyadjian, Lara Manoukian, Sara Scalenghe, Sonya Meyerson Knox, Kevin Martin, Lina Mounzer, Waleed Hazbun, Michelle Woodward, Karin van der Tak, Nadya Sbaiti, Hiba Qaraman and Nader Uthman.

In many ways, my moves have echoed my family's past journeys. While we have often crisscrossed geographies, our love has only strengthened our connections. My parents, Michel and Sonia Nalbantian; my sisters, Barig Nalbantian and Lorig Buckley; my gaggle of nieces and nephews, Adené, Aramayis, Ocean, Thomas, Achilles and Endza; the members of the WhatsApp group 'Tuhbzfvcfipv Fgyujkmncxdj', Taleen Moughamian, Natasha Khoury and Dalita Khoury; my grandmother, Jeannette Oundjian; and my late grandparents, Stephan and Lily Nalbantian and Meroujan Oundjian.

Finally, I dedicate this book to the one with whom I created our own family: Cyrus Schayegh. You make it all ok. And fun. How we have combined the two, I'm not sure, but I figure Rosdom's resounding 'Ya!' when I tell him that he is a manifestation of our love ('*Tun mer sern es*') affirms we're doing lots of things right. And I'm just sure that Nazani will agree, once she becomes more verbal!

While I stand on the shoulders of so many, any faults of the work are my own.

FIGURES

1.1	President Bechara Khoury in Anjar	50
1.2	Front page of *Ararad* commemorating the ASSR	67
2.1	The first caravan departure from Beirut	86
2.2	Armenians aboard the first repatriation ship	93
2.3	Soviet Armenian National University Students	104
2.4	Well-wishers gathered at the Port of Karantina	108
2.5	Comparing Lebanon to ASSR	109
3.1	Crowds at the airport to welcome Vasken	133
3.2	Crowds beside the road from the airport	134
3.3	Crowds lining the roads to the Cilician See	134
3.4	Chamoun meeting Vasken at the presidential palace	137
3.5	Zareh I after his election	139
3.6	The Cilician See monastery complex on election day	140
3.7	Zareh and Chamoun in the presidential palace	142
3.8	Zareh with the recovered *ach*	147
3.9	Crowds celebrating the return of the *ach*	148
3.10	Zareh performing the consecration of holy chrism	150
4.1	*The Daily Star*'s coverage of Chamoun	168
4.2	Page in *Ayk* celebrating Edde's 'miraculous operation'	186

INTRODUCTION

This book, *Armenians Beyond Diaspora: Making Lebanon their Own,* is a post-genocide history of Armenians and of what *was*. It is not a history of absence, or of what should or could have been. Rather than a history of loss or simple rebirth, two interlinked viewpoints omnipresent in writings on modern Armenian history, it is a history of power – often of manipulating and managing loss and renewal, in this case in early post-colonial, Cold War Lebanon, centred on Beirut. The absence of a national homeland accepted by all and the absence of an official state did not mean that Lebanon's Armenians lacked a real, and really momentous, political life. Despite the genocide and even after it, Armenians still knew thriving political, social, cultural, ideological and ecclesiastical centres. This book gives a case in point: an often-surprising story of Armenian sociopolitical life in one such centre, Lebanon.

At the same time, this book asks: what can we learn about Lebanon, and the Arab world more broadly, by looking at it through the lens of everyday Armenian sociopolitics? This analysis of Armenians in Lebanon does not, then, only contribute to the study of Armenians. As a matter of fact, *Armenians Beyond Diaspora* is not principally concerned with demonstrating how something 'Armenian' was created. Rather, it shows how Armenians in Lebanon experienced politics everyday, and what those experiences can teach us about interlinked national and global events. By examining changing aspects of belonging, and by exploring how these concepts travel over time and space, *Armenians Beyond Diaspora* simultaneously challenges the supremacy of the nation-state and the role of state power in regional and Cold War histories.

By demonstrating how Armenian experiences in Lebanon informed Lebanese, Middle Eastern and Cold War histories and vice versa, this book also illustrates that there is no single narrative of the modern Middle East. This argument builds on recent studies of the history of the modern Middle East that focus on hitherto ignored or lesser-known actors, and helps to move marginalised segments of society centre-stage.[1] This move is particularly crucial for studies of Lebanon, where scholars struggle to include, within a dominant narrative, members of society who have been excluded from power by design as a retort to Lebanon's sectarian formation. *Armenians Beyond Diaspora* registers Lebanon as a space of both Armenian fashioning and belonging, and challenges the tendency to read Middle Eastern history through the lens of dominant (Arab) nationalisms.

Historical Outline

While the Armenian Genocide condemned surviving Armenians to a life outside of Anatolia and destroyed Istanbul as the primary centre of Armenian economic and cultural life, it also had other effects.[2] For one, in Lebanon, and specifically in Beirut, the remnants of Armenian communities hailing from myriad points all across Anatolia, with the vast majority from Cilicia, gathered in a single space.[3] The geography of Anatolia was radically compressed into one city. Sectors in Beirut's Armenian refugee camps and later quarters in permanently-built neighbourhoods were named after their inhabitants' points of origin, for instance Marash, Hajin and Sis.[4] While back in 'real' Cilicia, residents of Marash and Sis were hundreds of miles apart, in Beirut they shared the selfsame refugee camps like Qarantina, and from the 1920s they lived in the same neighbourhood of Bourj Hamoud, where they found each other across the street and soon started to mix and mingle. And even when some started to move into other neighbourhoods, they still lived within the confines of a single city. In Beirut, the Armenian Genocide and post-genocide era had forced migrations from the Ottoman Empire, which brought Armenians from across the empire into extreme proximity to one another.

This had far-reaching sociopolitical and cultural effects. What had been multiple Armenian commun*ities* back in the Ottoman Empire's vast lands grew into a single communi*ty* in Beirut. The teaching of Western Armenian, rather than Turkish or village dialects, made Beirut (and Lebanon itself) a site of 'Armenianisation'.[5] The community was not homogeneous, though. Quite the opposite: it was extremely heterogeneous – and in a much more high-energy, involved, boisterous, vociferous and indeed conflict-ridden way than Anatolia's Armenian communities had been. Beirut was the largest urban concentration of Armenians in the Arab world, with over 70,000 Armenians (out of a population of over 1.1. million) in Lebanon by 1944.[6] As important, the Arab East's most thriving city from the mid-nineteenth century provided an energising environment for political parties, church institutions, newspapers and eventually radio stations and lay people to interact in the everyday in unprecedented ways.[7]

Early on after World War I, this process was facilitated by France, Lebanon's Mandate ruler from 1918 to 1946.[8] A key event in this regard came in 1924, when the French included Armenian inhabitants of Lebanon in the new Mandate citizenship law.[9] That particular French act had a 'negative' effect, as it were. It legally nixed, or at least drastically reduced, the chance that Armenians would return to their former homes back in Anatolia.[10] After all, they now were citizens of another national space. Coming on the heel of the consolidation of Kemal Ataturk's power, the Turkish National Movement's victory in the Turkish war of independence and the Treaty of Lausanne (1923) that formalised Allied recognition of the Ottoman successor state, France's Lebanese Mandate citizenship law including Armenians happened to contribute to Turkey's Turkification.[11] The citizenship act also had a 'positive', constructive effect. It created the legal and, by extension, political framework for re-centring much of Armenian life in and on Lebanon.[12]

After Lebanon gained full independence in 1946, the country's postcolonial sectarian structure, which was firmly grounded in the Mandate period and late Ottoman times, helped to re-energise Armenian life in Lebanon, especially in Beirut.[13] This most directly and immediately profited Armenian political parties, the nationalist Dashnaks and two leftist organisations, the

Hnchaks and Ramgavars. Their presence in Lebanon marked a distinct continuity with late Ottoman times. All three were rooted in the ideologies of the late Ottoman liberal reform period, and were concerned with the Armenians' condition in the Empire's peripheries, most notably Anatolia.[14] Many survivors of those party organisations and their descendants made their way to Lebanon, and there reestablished these parties. The three parties mentioned above, as well as the Armenian communist party, which entertained close relations with Lebanon's and Syria's communist parties, modified their political platforms and adjusted to the new political theatre of Lebanon. Given this country's sectarian system, after independence Armenians were guaranteed political power, and these four parties jockeyed with one another to this end.

From the 1940s onwards, the ideologies of these Armenian organisations and institutions mirrored the ideological positions of the Cold War superpowers. Basically, the Ramgavar, Hnchak and Communist parties supported the Armenian Socialist Soviet Republic (ASSR), whilst the nationalist Dashnak Party did not. This alignment held true even though the Ramgavar Party's position opposed communism, the Hnchak Party was more socialist than communist in rank and ideology and the late nineteenth-century founders of the Dashnak Party had been strident socialists. In addition, at specific moments, such as the first year of the 1946–1949 repatriation movement to the ASSR, about which more below, the Dashnak Party did not oppose the exodus of many of its members. These complexities notwithstanding, the significant ideological split between Armenian nationalists, principally the Dashnaks, and leftists faciliated US and Soviet attempts to pull Armenians around the world into their ideological corner. But at the same time, as this book shows, Armenians in Lebanon at certain moments used super powers and their alignment with those powers to articulate their own agency in intra-Armenian struggles. These struggles were played out locally within the Armenian community, but they also affected the Lebanese political sphere and even transcended that country's borders: In a regional and transnational turn, Armenian political parties headquartered in Lebanon, along with the Catholicosate of Cilicia (also known as the Cilician See), one of two surviving Armenian ecclesiastical institutions that had moved to Lebanon in 1930, vied for authority over Armenian communities in different countries in the Middle East and the Americas.[15] They also used Cold War ideological bifurcations here to distinguish themselves from their opposition and to garner support from either power.

In the field of politics, Armenian ecclesiastical authorities played an important role. Most central here was the Cilician See, far and away the most powerful Armenian church organisation in Lebanon. It had been headquartered at Sis, in the Ottoman province of Adana (present-day Kozan), before the genocide. Thereafter, like many of its surviving congregants it resettled in Lebanon. It set up its new headquarters in 1930 in Antelias, just north of Beirut, on land donated by the US Near East Relief Foundation.[16] Politically, by the mid-1950s most Armenians saw it as an ally of the Dashnak Party. With the crystallisation of Cold War politics, this identification took on an additional significance. The Dashnak Party was seen as a supporter of the Eisenhower administration, the Baghdad Pact and Lebanon's President Camille Chamoun, and as hostile to Arab nationalism, Egypt's popular president Gamal Abdel Nasser, socialism and the Soviet Union. The Cilician See was likewise seen as an extension of these Dashnak positions by its political rivals. But the See certainly was not an arm of the Dashnaks. It also manipulated and used that party. Indeed, it used the political factionalisation within Armenian communities to expand its power. Moreover, the post-genocide move to Lebanon expanded the Cilician See's regional influence. It now became in a clear-cut fashion the spiritual head of Armenian churches throughout the Middle East. And due to tensions among Armenians supporting and opposing the Dashnak Party in the United States of America, it even became a transnational power across the Atlantic, establishing churches in America under its jurisdiction after World War II.

The Cilician See was likewise a crucial focus of collective life, also beyond politics in Lebanon. This was a quite extraordinary reversal of developments dating back to the late Ottoman period. Istanbul's nineteenth-century *tanzimat* reforms had challenged the control of religious authorities by removing them as mediators. Citizens and the state had communicated much more directly. While this act had removed a layer of protection for some inhabitants, it was likewise celebrated by non-religious elites, for many of them gained a much more unmediated access to the Armenian population.

These *tanzimat* changes punctured the relationship between congregant and religious authority amongst all *millets*.[17] But whereas the authority of the

Greek and Jewish religious authorities never entirely recovered, the Armenian case differed. The French extension of citizenship to Lebanon's Armenians, the Cilician See's re-establishment in Antelias and the Lebanese state's sectarian structure allowed for, and indeed encouraged, ecclesiastic authorities to re-establish their presence in the Armenian community.[18] The Cilician See emerged strongly empowered. In 1929, the Jerusalem Patriarchate ceded its authority over the Armenian communities of Damascus, Latakia and Beirut, including their monasteries, churches and schools, to the Cilician See.[19] By the 1940s, the Armenian Catholicosate of the Great House of Cilicia, its formal name, had established Armenian elementary and high schools, numerous churches and a seminary, and published journals. Furthermore, it acted as a key community intermediary to the Lebanese government. By the same token, Armenians who otherwise could or would never have gotten involved in church politics now had the occasion to do so.

In sum, the post-genocide story of Armenians in Lebanon was, to be sure, a story of loss, and the ingathering of very diverse populations within a small urban area of Beirut was extraordinary to say the least. But, as this book shows, this process also helped to refashion Armenian identity and power. The Lebanese case thus demonstrates that the Armenian Genocide also had – in a most traumatic and tremendously tragic way, to be certain – regenerative consequences. The genocide ended up being more than exclusively a source of trauma and victimhood.

Historians, therefore, do not need to treat the genocide solely as an epistemological break and an end. Rather, they can discern in it – and in what followed – new starts and continuities as well as breaks for the Armenian populations hailing from the Ottoman Empire.

Outline of Chapters

Chapter 1, 'Repositioning Armenians in Newly Post-colonial Nation-states: Lebanon and Syria, 1945–1946', begins our journey by following the issues that the Armenian print media in Lebanon saw as noteworthy by in the 1940s. These often-ideologically-opposed newspapers, the leftist *Ararad*, the communist *Joghovourti Tzain*, the capitalist supporter of the ASSR *Zartonk* and the firmly right-wing nationalist Dashnak *Aztag*, reflected the issues of interest of the day. As chronicled in these newspapers, Armenians in Lebanon re-situated themselves and re-imagined their place in that Middle Eastern country and in the world more broadly during a sensitive, transitional time of change, i.e. the early post-colonial period. I dig deep into the manifold triangulations and balancing acts constitutive of Lebanese Armenians' changing views of their place in and vis-à-vis the complex making of the Lebanese state, its wider Arab environment, as well as the ASSR.

The chapter examines four main themes. One is the Armenians' position in and vis-à-vis the Lebanese polity, as well as Syria. The second concerns language, specifically the multiple roles of Arabic. The third has to do with the ambiguities of spaces relevant for Armenians in and beyond Lebanon. And the last is the fascinating political positioning of the church that, although conservative, at moments felt forced to support communist Armenia and the USSR as the ASSR's protector.

By tracing recurring news items and community concerns, this chapter provides a rich understanding of the activities of the Armenian inhabitants in Lebanon. The establishment, proliferation and continuation – many of the dailies profiled are still in publication – of an active Armenian press in Lebanon reveals the enthusiasm of such ventures and indicates the high level of literacy amongst Armenians.[20] This examination also shows how the Armenian press categorised events – as local, regional and/or international – and how these events were presented to Armenians. The coverage also demonstrates how writers and readers engaged with these items and how related concerns played out amongst Armenians and non-Armenians alike. What emerges is a complex, not at all homogeneous picture. Newspaper consumers and producers were also political party members, parliamentary members, church officials, businessmen, students, school officials and parents – a diversity that informed the different ways in which Beirut's Armenians engaged with a variety of issues in their city, in Lebanon and beyond. Last but not least, through the pages of those newspapers Armenians emerge not as passive objects of history but as active subjects, and in this sense as members of the Lebanese nation-state that carried a certain weight, even power, in it.

Chapter 2, 'The Homeland Debate, Redux: The Political–Cultural Impact of the 1946–1949 Repatriation to Soviet Armenia', studies the 1946–1949 repatriation movement, an organised Soviet drive to collect all worldwide Armenians and 'return' them to the ASSR. The story itself of the repatriation drive has been told before, by historians and in memoirs.[21] Rather than rehashing the details, then, this chapter focuses on Lebanese Armenian political–cultural understandings of repatriation. This examination uses Armenian and Lebanese history to engage with Cold War history and – the other side of the coin – to problematise diasporic understandings of Armenians. Constructing and capitalising on the diasporic dimension of Armenian life, the Soviet Union's repatriation drive was highly successful in Lebanon. For that very reason, however – that is, because of the massive departure of Armenians friendly to the USSR – it somewhat paradoxically helped political parties opposed to the ASSR and the USSR to consolidate their power. Initially an aspect of an internal community power struggle, this new configuration mirrored Cold War power bifurcations. Lebanon's Armenians both manipulated these understandings *and* became proxy forces in that global power struggle. At the same time, Armenians' engagement in the repatriation movement formed part of, and illustrated, a broader endeavor to fashion a homeland of sorts: to find and build a final solution to prior occasions and experiences of victimhood.

This chapter explores how that initiative formed a chapter of Lebanese (and other Middle Eastern) Armenians' renegotiation of national belonging in early post-colonial times.[22] Although about a third of all Armenian repatriates travelled via Beirut (including residents of Syria and Lebanon), I also look at those who remained in Lebanon and in other countries in the Middle East. The emerging Cold War was more than simply a backdrop to the repatriation story. Moscow's initiative made repatriation possible in the first place. It was the USSR that announced the initiative to unite Armenians from around the world in the ASSR; that organised the transport of tens of thousands of Armenians to the USSR and that allowed them to enter the country; and that housed them in the ASSR, making them Soviet citizens. Also, the Soviet initiative was a victory vis-à-vis the USSR's rivals: At a time of peace, citizens of some countries voluntarily sold their belongings and moved to become part of the motherland of state socialism. But most importantly, the escalating Cold War – and the very divergent readings of, and responses to, the repatriation initiative among Lebanese Armenians – reinforced tensions between Armenian rightists and leftists. The Lebanese example shows that Armenians' response to repatriation did not simply reflect their extant political–cultural positions. Rather, repatriation sharpened those positions.

In thinking through these issues, Chapter 2 specifically broaches three themes. First, it shows how responses to repatriation echoed issues involved with the changing Lebanese/Syrian/Armenian identity complex at the dawn of the post-colonial nation-state. Second, it examines how responses to repatriation included a retelling and a reconstitution of the history of the tragedy of the genocide. Relatedly, three decades after the genocide, the initiative automatically triggered questions about the location and nature of the Armenian homeland. And thirdly, it demonstrates how repatriation added fuel to the division between Dashnaks and Armenian leftists, foreshadowing their confrontation in the form of active debates in the press and violent conflict.

Chapter 3, 'Cold War, Bottom-up: The 1956 Catholicos Election', takes the 1956 Cilician See's catholicos election in Lebanon to illuminate Cold War understandings of the Middle East, and vice versa.[23] While in the later 1940s the excitement of the repatriation movement was a public relations victory for the USSR, supported by local Armenian institutions and assisted by Lebanese and Syrian governments, this election became a site of contestation by Cold War powers and by their state and non-state allies and proxies in the Middle East. Lebanon, staunchly pro-Western and pro-American under President Camille Chamoun, was indeed not the only state directly involved in that election. So were Egypt and Jordan, among other Middle Eastern states, as well as the Soviet Union, principally through Vasken, the catholicos of the Echmiadzin See, headquartered in the ASSR. The United States and key European states like France and Britain also made appearances in the story. Even so, it was the Armenians who were this story's main protagonists – Armenians of different, if not diametrically opposed, political convictions.

During the 1946–1949 ASSR repatriation initiative, leftists had wielded considerable power in the Armenian community of Beirut and beyond; and the repatriation initiative further boosted their influence at that juncture. But as noted in passing above, a decade later the situation had changed. Ironically, the very success of the leftist repatriation drive, i.e. the emigration to the ASSR, depleted the leftists' ranks in Lebanon and other repatriation 'donor' countries. In consequence, from the late 1940s the rightist Dashnak

Party became more preponderant, certainly in Beirut. What is more, the Cold War was much more heated by the mid-1950s than it had been in the late 1940s.

The 1956 catholicos election thus allows us to look at the Cold War in the Middle East not from the top down, through the eyes of Washington or Moscow (or Lebanon's or Egypt's state authorities, for that matter), and not through the lens of famous flashpoints like the US and Soviet reactions to the Tripartite Aggression against Egypt in 1956 or the 1958 US armed intervention in Lebanon. Rather, in the 1956 election, Armenians made use of Cold War tensions to designate a leader of the Armenian church who was seen to suit the community's interests.[24] That story also expands historians' understanding of Lebanon's Armenians: from refugees and outsiders in national politics to true participants, whose own internal politics, moreover, were also of interest to Lebanon's authorities, and who by now felt free to invade and use public spaces beyond their own neighbourhoods to express themselves politically.

I tell this story while keeping an eye on three analytical aspects. One is the overlap between the global Cold War and regional Middle Eastern inter-state competition.[25] Another is the mutual use, if not exploitation, of state actors and Armenian actors. And a third is a fascinating duality of states' approaches to the Armenian issue: both nation-state-bound and transnational. States sought to assert their sovereignty vis-à-vis ecclesiastical Armenian matters that happened on their territory; thus, the Lebanese state, and in particular President Chamoun, was involved politically and symbolically in the 1956 catholicos election. But states also tried to use Armenian issues and religious Armenian bodies, whose authority was non-secular and whose reach was not quite bound by nation-state borders (to say the least), to affect third countries' politics. The foremost example in the present case was the Soviet attempt to meddle in the 1956 election through Vasken.

In taking this approach to the 1956 election, 'Cold War, Bottom-up' continues to addresses lacunae in the secondary literature on Armenians in the Middle East and especially Lebanon, and reflects on how their case can shine a light on larger topics. Power struggles, political differences and alignments among Armenians have long been ignored in the historiography of modern Lebanon, which has described the Armenian population as a coherent community. The Cold-War-related nature of inner-Armenian events and their place within the broader history of Lebanon and the Middle East has been ignored accordingly.

The fourth and final chapter, 'Making Armenians Lebanese: The 1957 Election and the Ensuing 1958 Conflict', explores Armenian participation in the 1957 elections and in the 1958 mini-civil war, both in the 'general' Lebanese and the intra-Armenian elections.[26] These events illustrated Armenian involvement in both local Beiruti and national Lebanese settings, yet in a way different from that of the previous year, in 1956. In telling this story, I make three interrelated points. First, coming a good decade after the 1946 transition from the French Mandate to post-colonial independence, Armenians were now firmly part of, and ensconced in, Lebanese politics. Armenians' (re)-positioning vis-à-vis Lebanon's imminent post-colonial independence in the mid-1940s included a fair share of double-entendres, tensions and contrasts. But already at that point it was clear that Armenians in Lebanon were indeed part of that country – and wished to remains so as well. This was shown in the clearest (and most painful) fashion possible in 1957 and 1958. Lebanese Armenians were divided along the right–left faultlines that divided Lebanese politics and society in general at that point: they were Lebanonised, one may say. Secondly, and at the same point, the Lebanese state was somehow Armenianised. It started to pay more attention to Armenian matters than before, intervening directly and by military force in Armenian neighbourhoods by December 1958 in order to finally end the internecine Armenian confrontation. Thirdly, while Armenians were Lebanonised, they also, more than other confessions in Lebanon, were very strongly – and by 1958 indeed mortally – internally divided along political lines. This division was not new, of course. It dated back to before World War II, and had been manifest in the 1946–1949 repatriation and in the 1956 catholicos election. But it came to a boil in 1958. This was the case not only because of the general Lebanese context, i.e. the accentuating right–left political polarisation that at this point in time mapped roughly, though by no means perfectly, onto the country's Muslim–Christian confessional landscape. It was the case also because the Cold War – a global constentation between left-wing versus right-wing politics and ideologies – was felt with particular acuity in the Armenian case. This was for the simple reason that the Soviet Union included the ASSR, that is, that Armenia formed part of one Cold War superpower. In turn, this meant that leftist, and especially communist, Armenians had an especially direct connection to the Soviet Union. Vice versa, it was of supreme importance for right-wing Armenians to criticise that connection, to reject the 1920 Sovietisation of Armenia, which had been an independent republic from 1918 to 1920, and to assert the right to speak for Armenians despite the existence of Soviet Armenia.

My analysis demonstrates that Armenian parties participated in, and contributed to, the considerable political tensions in Lebanon. Simultaneously, they used their position within the Lebanese political system to jostle for power within the Armenian community – a development that turned violent and came to a close only in December 1958, almost two months *after* the Lebanese mini-civil war had ended, when the Lebanese army intervened. These tensions and violent confrontations between Armenian parties and their armed men had a crucial spatial effect: they unprecedentedly territorialised parts of Beirut. To be sure, parts of Lebanon were already organised by sects and classes. By relative contrast, it was according to political party affiliation that in 1957–1958 many Armenians of the neighbourhoods of Mar Mikael, Sin el-Fil, Bourj Hamoud and Corniche al-Nahr were re-sorted and relocated, often by force.

As *Armenians Beyond Diaspora* situates Armenians in Lebanon within a network of daily local, regional and transnational actors and events, it engages with key bodies of literature.

Armenian Studies

Scholarly works on Armenians have traditionally been found within two overlapping fields: Armenian Studies and Diaspora Studies. Within Armenian Studies, works are further divided, focusing on Armenians as a diaspora, or as the victims of genocide.[27] Both groupings assume an Armenian collectivity, regardless of lived experiences, locality or historical context. Armenian historians paint Armenians, practically regardless of their location, as lost tribes of a singular Armenian nation.[28] They assume this nation to have a known homeland, whether real or imagined. This limits understandings of daily life and their engagement within a given locality and its population, assuming that Armenians live and conceive of themselves only within an Armenian frame. In addition, this construction fails to consider when Armenians may or may not use such a collectivity, its associated 'homeland', or a diasporic identification to articulate their agency and exercise power in local contexts, often in a bid to claim power transnationally as well.

This 'understood' homeland, without a clear location, distracts from how Armenians actually used the term *erkir*, homeland, in a variety of specific circumstances. An ambiguous term, *erkir* is flexible and differs in meaning depending on time and space: presenting, in fact, a good opportunity to appreciate an Armenian heterogeneity. Nineteenth-century economic migrants from Eastern Anatolia, seeking employment in Istanbul, used *erkir* to denote their place of origin.[29] As Hagop Barsoumian writes, these migrants 'reminded' wealthier urban Armenians of the disenfranchised status of Eastern Anatolian Armenians.[30] By invoking *erkir*, they nurtured an emotional attachment to a place that housed a substantial marginalised Armenian population, which depended on remittances from urban centres. At the same time, by representing the *erkir* to wealthier Armenians, migrant Armenians in turn validated their presence in the city. They acted to bridge the centre and periphery, even if to reinforce the dominance of the centre.

This portrayal of Armenian inhabitants as organised communities throughout the world *and* as part of one larger Armenian diaspora connected through a singular traumatic event and to one 'known' *erkir*, encourages historians to represent Armenians as perennial victims. Richard Hovannisian's edited volumes, *The Armenian People from Ancient to Modern Times*, for example, impressively profile practically every Armenian populated area, an incredibly diverse range of places and experiences.[31] The Introduction, however, seeks a common thread, constructing Armenians as one collective – and, to boot, all as victims.[32] In addition, it considers the eleventh-century kingdom of Cilicia as 'expatriate', as if national constructions of belonging were already created and spatially clearly set and demarcated.[33] Hovannisian's second volume, which focuses on the fifteenth through the twentieth centuries, adopts a similar tone. For example, Krikor Maksoudian's labelling of Armenians of Eastern Europe as 'assimilated' enables him to link them to Armenians in the Americas.[34] In fact, he claims that the shared attribute of 'assimilation' can aid in the understanding of both communities.[35] While I am not writing against comparative studies, which have the potential to bring together even the most divergent experiences, I am cautious.[36]

What is particularly problematic in these depictions is that the authors provide an otherwise detailed history on particular Armenian communities and their achievements. For example, Armenians established a military organisation in Vienna, numerous merchant guilds in Poland and the Ukraine, and monasteries in Moldavia.[37] Still, whenever possible, the author stresses a connection between the Armenian communities living in Eastern Europe and those present in the Ottoman Empire.[38] It is a fact, of course, that Armenians indeed did arrive from Istanbul or from further east, for instance from Van. But I beg to differ from the author's assumption that this demonstrates that Armenians in Crimea are more authentic to the Armenian nation because of their location or that a worldwide affinity *and underlying, irreducible, indelible similarity* exists between Armenians worldwide despite their most variant locations, experiences and backgrounds.

One of the notable exceptions in Hovannisian's volumes is Ronald Grigor Suny's contribution 'Eastern Armenians under Tsarist Rule'.[39] Unlike some of his colleagues, his analysis on Armenian national awareness considers issues of class and social experience.[40] He accounts not only for territorial dispersion and its associated differences but also, more importantly, for the social divisions between peasants and urban dwellers.[41] And he couples these issues with the activity of the Russian state, which was constructing its own identity and power. He examines Armenians living in the Caucasus, their intellectual engagement with German idealist philosophies and tensions with Armenian church authorities; Armenian revolutionaries' attempts to use class issues to subvert the national; and the Armenian bourgeoisie that, growing tired with revolutionaries, 'made their peace with tsarism'.[42] He does this without engaging in how these Armenians shared a national affinity with Armenians living elsewhere. The activities, participation, achievements, failures and tragedies of Armenians under Tsarist rule are represented on their own terms.

Even more recent scholarship has continued in a similar vein, such as Razmik Panossian's *The Armenians: From Kings and Priests to Merchants and Commissars*. While he notes in the Introduction that 'various sources of Armenian identity formulation were quite different from one another', he closes the same paragraph by stating, 'it also became apparent that Armenians were developing a sense of identity as part of *one* nation despite the objective differences and the historical as well as sociological divisions', thereby (re)constructing a singular national history.[43] I am not, of course, denying that mass migration due to military interventions or economic processes happened. But I am wary of connecting and reducing historical moments to one Grand Lachrymose History of Armenians worldwide as perpetual victims who all long for one and the same clearly defined homeland.

Studies of specific Armenian communities are uncommon, yet growing in number. It is important to note that such studies do not isolate Armenians from either other Armenians and/or communities and networks. Rather, they consider, paying special attention to, what *else* is going on in the community. It is in this space, I argue, that one can discern multiple power struggles, engagements and fashioning (and refashioning) of belonging and identification. In her work on Armenians in Cyprus, for example, Sossie Kasbarian does not argue against Armenian co-option within Greek nationalism.[44] Through an examination of the shared sense of belonging based in daily experience, the author demonstrates how minorities in Cyprus have and can continually impact the 'vision of the nation', and exercise 'a significant degree of autonomy in cultural and social matters'.[45] And yet, the author firmly places the Armenians of Cyprus within a worldwide diaspora and follows a shift in diasporic identity 'from exilic weakness to one of transnational resourcefulness'.[46]

While works that profile 'singular' Armenian communities can challenge the tendency to position Armenians solely in relation to other Armenians, they may (still) reinforce the separation between Armenians and other locals. James Barry's rich work on Iranian Armenians begins with the separation of Armenians from others in Iran, categorising 'two groups' of Iranian citizens: one 'excluded', the other 'mainstream'.[47] These classifications inevitably lead to a focus on the 'challenges' faced by the marginalised Armenian community, often ending with the 'threat of a loss of culture and identity', often connected to emmigration.[48] In his profile on the Armenians in Northern Iraq, Darren L. Logan adopts a similar approach to describe the challenges faced by the Armenians there. Descriptions including 'decline', 'fading' and 'remnant', not only fail to attribute any power to the Armenian population, representing them as victims, but also juxtapose their presence with a bygone era of glory and power (that may or may not have existed, the article does not elaborate).[49] Its tone of defeat culminates in the final sentence of the article, that simultaneously typifies a warning: 'In the long run, without this protection [of the Kurdistan Regional Government] it is likely the Armenian remnant in Northern Iraq will fade away'.[50]

Other works that profile individual Armenian communities take the Armenian Genocide as a temporal and social starting point. In doing so, they thread trauma throughout their analyses of Armenian experiences and activities in their new locales. Simon Payaslian's work on Armenians in Syria states that it was Armenian Genocide survivors who 'exercised considerable command over the cognative development of the next generations'.[51] While this indeed may be the case, I wonder what else can be gained by this identification besides linking Armenian activities in this period to the violence and collective trauma of the genocide. In addition, the author's constant reference to their 'marginalisation', 'inferior status', connected to their being an involuntary diaspora (again, a reference to the Armenian Genocide), and 'decline', distracts from the activities and innovative structures carried out by these very same Armenians.[52] Even when Payaslian does cite evidence of a construction of local, Syrian Armenian institutions, the author refers to these actions as a 'tortuous task'.[53]

These understandings of Armenian life in Syria also present a linear understanding of history, forwarding an evolutionary model (refugees to diasporisation) with Armenians finally becoming 'sedentary' in the '*spyurk* (diaspora)'.[54] Viewing Armenians as sedentary within the rubric of a diaspora fails to consider Armenians in Syria on the own terms. What were the dynamics within this population? Instead of engaging with the daily lives of Armenians in Syria, Payaslian therefore almost has no choice but to view their presence through the macro-actions of the Syrian state. While this is certainly one way of studying Armenians in Syria, it prevents our access to their everyday, and separates Armenians from their Syrian co-nationals. In addition, it fails to conceive of Armenians personifying the Syrian state, even as Payaslian mentions that Armenians gained seats in the Syrian parliament.[55] It is almost as if such authors wish to draw attention to either the legacy of the Armenian Genocide and/or to transnational connections, that they have no choice but to ignore or minimise their experiences of belonging to or being part of that very nation-state.

The Literature on the Armenian Genocide

Armenian historiography's disregard for the possibility of multiple homelands and hierarchical centres is a very powerful reflex to a singular act of violence: the Armenian Genocide.[56] This defensive construction flattens profound differences between specific communities around the world that have enjoyed incredibly variant histories and experiences throughout the century following the genocide. At the same time, it (re)connects Armenians worldwide to a singular understanding of *erkir*, generating a corollary. It homogenises the genocide as, in an effort to interconnect Armenians, the genocide's totality is stressed. Individual experiences become indiscernible. In addition, the creation of this monolith collapses different phases of extermination into each other, into a single whole.[57] But perhaps most important for this book, studies that centre on, and ultimately always return to, the genocide as the ultimate uniting factor for any and every Armenian neglect the formation of political, social, cultural, ideological and ecclesiastical centres of Armenian life post-genocide.

The historiography of the Armenian Genocide also often maintains the representation of Armenians as perennial victims of oppression, disregarding Armenian agency and power. Armenians indeed *were* victims of genocide. But this is not, I would argue, a continuous state for all Armenians. It makes no sense to call all Armenians worldwide 'genocide survivors': what of the distinctions between them? Moreover, many works treat 1915 as an epistemological break for both Armenians and Armenian historiography. I question the totality of this break and the resulting lack of distinction between the experiences of a segment of the Armenian population who were the targets of genocide and Armenian historiography in its entirety. In Hovannisian's volumes, for example, Christopher J. Walker's contribution on the Armenian Genocide begins and ends with the author proving that genocide occurred.[58]

Perhaps this is an understandable consequence of (admittedly fewer and fewer) politicians and academics' denial of the genocide or their attempt to justify mass deportation. It may even be necessary. Nevertheless, it also lends itself to distractions. Works on Armenians mention the genocide even if they treat pre-genocide events or concern a population that was little or not at all affected by these tragic events and/or their survivors. Thus, the genocide has been used to explain (away) the economic superiority of the Iranian Armenians – they were not its victims – and the assimilation and lack of engagement with constructing an Armenian national home amongst the Armenians in Ukraine and Poland.[59] With regard to Armenians in Iran, this can be particularly egregious, as it concurrently denies that those inhabitants experienced hardship during the Russo-Persian War (1826–1828), World War I and the Soviet invasion of Iran in 1941.[60] Surviving the Armenian Genocide 'explained' the miserable conditions of Armenians living in Egypt, Lebanon, Syria and Palestine in its wake, and not the stipulations placed upon them by French and British mandate powers, such as preventing Armenians from moving out of organised camps until 1923, or the lack of facilities made available and provided for by British occupation forces.[61]

Bedross Der Matossian profiles the more recent historiographic trends of Armenian Genocide scholarship and how it has begun to engage with new methodologies and approaches. The growing use of Armenian sources, Raymond Kévorkian's contention of the 'second phase of the genocide', which targeted the survivors of the deportation in Syria and Upper Mesopotamia, Ronald Grigor Suny's focus on the fear of a 'crumbling empire' as an important factor in leading to genocide, Donald Bloxham's contention of a nationalist genocide and Fuat Dündar's, Uğur Ümit Üngör's, and Taner Akçam's emphases on demographic engineering as a compelling factor of the genocide have all contributed to our grasp of the Armenian Genocide.[62] The ensuing debates have likewise broadened our understandings of its premeditation, contigency, continuum and motives.[63]

And yet, because scholars of the Armenian Genocide seem compelled to address the policy of disavowal by successive Turkish governments, the institutions of state ideology and national historiographic discourse, they inevitably turn into prosecutors seeking a flawless indictment against decades of denial. They construct the field as the lone possibility to pierce this discourse and correct this injustice. While I do not take further issue with this position, leaving it up to individual scholars to qualify their interventions, I am concerned that we may miss the productive and creative elements that Armenians engaged in in the wake of the genocide. This, even in cases when authors themselves are interested in revealing such fashioning. Take Melissa Bilal's 'Lullabies and the Memory of Pain: Armenian Women's Remembrance of the Past in Turkey', as one such example.[64] In exploring how lullabies 'intervene against the ordinariness of forgetfullnes', and 'from the margins of memory' they have been pushed to, Bilal's work also demonstrates how these women's everyday performances *produce* historical knowledge.[65] In addition, these songs and their singing are said to simultaneously 'establish bridges between generations in a family' and challenge the 'grand fissure' narrative of the Armenian Genocide.[66] While unexpected, these melancholic songs have the capacity to create – and act as conduits not only between generations, as Bilal states, but also between time and space. And yet, Bilal's work is more often categorised solely as being part of the 'growing work on Armenians in post-genocide Turkey'.[67]

Lebanese Historiography

By studying such actions, *Armenians Beyond Diaspora* also challenges the historiography of Lebanon. Recent works on Lebanon have called into question histories that left out ethnic and religious minorities which did not support particular understandings of Lebanon. These had constructed Lebanon as an abnormal state – as if there was a natural or standardised form to follow – and depicted its political system, population composition and nation-state borders as reasons why the state was bound to fail or breakdown. This tautological construction only confined Lebanon and paralysed its historiography.[68] It has encouraged scholars to view Lebanon through the lens, solely, of conflict and of its corollary, sectarianism. This is evidenced by the overabundance of works on the 1975–1991 Lebanese Civil War and by the dearth of studies on the periods before and after this period.[69] To be sure, there have been exceptions in the field of history, for example Max Weiss' *In the Shadow of Sectarianism: Law, Shi'ism, and the Making of Modern Lebanon*, Linda Sayed's study on how the Shi'i community in Jabal Lubnan both used and circumvented the sectarian structure to assert itself, and Ussama Makdisi's classic *The Culture of Sectarianism: Community, History, and Violence in Nineteenth-Century Ottoman Lebanon*.[70] Some of the most important interventions have been by anthropologists. Lara Deeb's *An Enchanted Modern: Gender and Public Piety in Shi'i Lebanon* and Joanne

Nucho's *Everyday Sectarianism in Urban Lebanon: Infrastructures, Public Services and Power* challenge familiar notions, focusing on how the Lebanese use state and power structures to exercise their own power in everyday interactions.[71] Together, these historical and anthropological works shift our focus to marginalised inhabitants of Lebanon and narrate additional stories of that country.

The need to explain Lebanon's so-called propensity for violence also directs works dedicated to minority populations, such as the Druze.[72] At the same time, influential histories that focus on Lebanon's violence have ignored populations that have not played a substantial role in propagating or maintaining conflict. This is certainly true for the Armenian inhabitants of the country. A celebrated history of Lebanon, Kamal Salibi's *A House of Many Mansions*, mentions the Armenians five times, always as outliers and outsiders, failing to consider their presence or contributions as active members of Lebanese society.[73] Salibi claimed Armenians did not share Arabic as a 'common language' or 'an Arab way of life', as if substantiating his own refusal to consider Armenians as active members of Lebanese society.[74] While he identified Armenians as a non-Arab and therefore non-local refugee population, relegating them as present yet absent from making any meaningful impact onto the country's history, another classic, Fawwaz Traboulsi's *A History of Modern Lebanon*, failed to mention Armenians at all.[75] This is doubly problematic as his history consciously seeks to address the gaps of previous historical scholarship on Lebanon.[76]

In sum, even when Armenians are mentioned by historians of Lebanon, they are solely viewed as a refugee population, as outsiders. In a fascinating but problematic twist, this reinforces Armenian historiography's construction of Armenians in the region as a victimised population apart. These two historiographies, the Lebanese and the Armenian, therefore treat Armenians in a complementary way. As a result, both historiographies impose an exclusively diasporic reading of Armenian history, never quite considering Armenians, regardless of their present *locale*, as being really linked with and belonging to anywhere other than the imagined homeland. This fails to consider the contribution of Armenians in and to Lebanon, apart from and in addition to a larger Armenian diasporic community. It also strips Armenians in Lebanon of their agency, failing to consider their presence in the country beyond being victims of the genocide – and all of this despite the fact that the French Mandate government extended citizenship rights to the Armenians in 1926, meaning that Armenians were allocated rights and restrictions as an official Lebanese sect.

While this book explores Lebanese Armenians, its ultimate aim is not to insert an Armenian story within a national Lebanese one, let alone to lionise the contributions Armenians have made to Lebanon.[77] I do not seek to merely include yet another ethno-religious group within the history of Lebanon. *Armenians Beyond Diaspora* does not attempt to make the Lebanese history fuller, or more complete. Rather, I contend that scholars have hitherto ignored *everyday engagements* amongst Lebanese, including Armenians, focused as they have been on exploring, and viewing, Lebanon as a conflict-prone state. My study of how Armenians lived in Lebanon in the 1940s and 1950s challenges these *overall* conceptions about Lebanon. As important, it advances additional methods for viewing the inhabitants of Lebanon, Armenians and non-Armenians alike, and expanding our understandings of Lebanon, diaspora and the Cold War in the Middle East. These interrelated analyses offer new ways to narrate these fields of study, not only by bringing marginalised groups into the fore, but also by looking at notions of power articulated in everyday life. When and where *Armenians Beyond Diaspora* considers state power, it does so while focusing on everyday struggles for power. These actors both used state power and circumvented it, established local institutions that often engaged in transnational activities, and were at once targets of Cold War proxy warfare and able to exploit the competition amongst the superpowers to claim their authority amongst other inhabitants.

As this discussion demonstrates, the fields of Armenian studies and Lebanese historiography do not consider that Armenians 'fit' their subjects. So – where and how *do* Armenians fit? Again, I am not seeking to pry open a field in order to insert Armenian actors into it, thus rendering it more 'complete'. *Armenians Beyond Diaspora* contends that there is no idealised history that is to be pursued. Moreover, it cautions against so-called 'corrective histories' that buttress nationalist understandings of a community's contributions. Armenians in Lebanon created and participated in an active political life that has never been represented in scholarship on its own terms without being connected to a story of victimhood, a real or imagined faraway homeland or other Armenian communities. This presents a valuable opportunity to challenge these representations and perhaps more significantly, to enhance our understandings of early post-colonial, Cold War Lebanon and the inhabitants who engaged with local, regional and transnational powers during this period, and in so doing, articulated an agency of their own. Considering these histories necessarily frees Armenians from the marginalised periphery of history books, diasporic accounts and nationalist renderings. It likewise helps us understand Armenians not simply as victims but, rather, as actors, irrespective of their tragic past, statelessness and shallow historical footprint in Lebanon. And it advances the notion that Lebanon, and Beirut more specifically, was simultaneously an Armenian centre as much as it has been understood as an Arab and Lebanese one. In this way, these findings contribute to and complicate existing studies of Lebanon, Beirut and the Middle Eastern region more broadly.

Cold War Histories

In an effort to locate missing histories during the Cold War era, recent trends in international history have pointed to the Middle East, where a fascinating array of actors engaged with Cold War superpowers below and beyond the state level. These local and transnational histories have produced additional ways to understand how the Cold War affected and was used by regular people.[78] These encounters add to the more familiar stories of the region that focus on Gamal Abdel Nasser, the non-Alignment movement and how Egypt's president engaged with Western powers and the USSR. They also contribute to stories that centre on the overthrow and public execution of the Iraqi King Faisal II in 1958, the establishment of the United Arab Republic that same year and its fall in 1963, and how the governments of Jordan and Lebanon attempted to dissipate the ensuing tension in 1958 and after.[79]

Still, these newer works continue to view the period as a contest for supremacy between local, regional and international *powers*, and not necessarily amongst the inhabitants of the region, or amongst the more marginal members of society.[80] And even though these revisions have at least resulted in Lebanon being considered more of a player in this period than in the past (and linked Lebanon to transnational studies on the global drug trade), they continue in the worn vein of attempting to understand the 'inevitable' breakdown of civil society in the 1975 civil war.[81] Unsurprisingly, no attention has been paid to how Armenian inhabitants of the region, already ignored in national historiographies, engaged with the tension enacted by Cold War powers and became Cold War players themselves. *Armenians Beyond Diaspora* contributes to studies on the interface between the Cold War and the region by addressing exactly this issue: by demonstrating how marginal actors – in this particular case Armenians – used and were used by the state and greater powers in their local struggles for power.

Diaspora Studies

Finally, a word is due about Diaspora Studies. This scholarly field has adapted to focus on the multiple attachments displayed and experienced by populations both transnationally and locally.[82] These innovative studies recognised how Armenians inhabited both local and transnational spaces – often simultaneously – moving away from the more rigid associations of traumatic dispersal and expanding beyond the Jewish, Armenian and Greek 'ideal types'.[83] And yet, viewing Armenians in Lebanon as *solely* a diasporic community misses additional power dimensions articulated by members of this community.[84] As *Armenians Beyond Diaspora* demonstrates, Beirut – as well as Lebanon – was an especially salient node for intra-Armenian struggles for power and informed local, regional and global experiences. This particularity allowed Armenians to make Lebanon an Armenian global centre, partly due to the historical role Beirut enjoyed from the late nineteenth century onward, along with the configuration of the Lebanese state that recognised Armenians as one of the seventeen sects and therefore privileged their confessional elites. Accordingly *Armenians Beyond Diaspora* demonstrates the categorisation of the Armenian diasporic community, something that is often occluded in studies of diaspora. This story therefore challenges the homogenising aspect of 'diaspora' as an experience and study, while contributing to studies that highlight the plurality of diasporas and the struggle to move diaspora theory 'forwards'.[85]

In drawing attention to how Armenians in Lebanon imagined and constructed a categorisation of Armenian communities worldwide, marking themselves as *the* source of authority, *Armenians Beyond Diaspora* also reveals new sites of power and power struggles, challenging the positionality of historic centres of Armenian authority, such as Istanbul and even the Armenian Republic.[86] Istanbul had served as the centre of Armenian power due to its existence as the imperial capital, the power afforded by the Ottoman state upon the Armenian Patriarchate, how that institution exercised power and its historic connection to the Armenian provinces and population in Anatolia, the remnants of a historic Armenia.[87] Reorienting the centre for Armenian life from its historic centre in the Ottoman Empire, Istanbul, to Beirut, in the Lebanese nation-state, also questions the scholarly categorisations in works on Armenians.[88]

Understanding the power struggles profiled in *Armenians Beyond Diaspora* transforms histories of Lebanon, Armenians and the greater Middle East. They demonstrate that the creation and maintenance of Beirut as the centre for Armenian power was not just a consequence of the Ottoman defeat in World War I and the Armenian Genocide. Rather, it was a reflection of how Armenian individuals, institutions, political parties, as Lebanese citizens, state officials and political actors made it so. In addition, such an understanding begs the question of why one should analyse the activities of Armenians in Lebanon through the activity of Armenians in other locales? This positioning both reifies the nation-state and fixes the identification of Armenians, thus divorcing them from individual activities, their locales or transnational and global concerns.

Almost always connecting Armenians to an external homeland, whether real or imagined, Diaspora Studies flatten the experiences of Armenians in Lebanon and homogenise them, connecting them to a larger Armenian community that exists beyond Lebanon.[89] Situating Armenians exclusively within Diaspora Studies almost by necessity ignores, or at least smoothens, differences amongst Armenians within a particular location. They posit a more unified experience amongst Armenians, indeed helping to textually produce that experience. But they fail to consider Armenians' everyday engagements, entanglements and confrontations, for instance in Lebanon where they became part of local life.[90] They also assume that Armenians in Lebanon do not meaningfully interact with, and create long-term relationships with, non-Armenians. In this sense, studies of Armenians as a diaspora treat their subject in a self-referential way. They assume that an internally-developed Armenian identity trumps all. Interrelations with others, here

Lebanese, come to matter only by way of background, not as a central dimension of Armenian life.

Moreover, many works in Diaspora Studies push us to understand Armenians as sharing, fundamentally, a *singular* experience, as if identifying or being identified as an ethnic group guarantees a shared experience irrespective of specific history, location and agency.[91] I am not denying the connections between Armenians in Lebanon and elsewhere, of course. The transnational nature of certain Armenian institutions in Lebanon helped them claim power outside of the nation-state's borders, in effect challenging the authority of the nation-state.[92] But we cannot simply view Armenians' experiences in Lebanon solely through the lens of a diasporic connection, for this approach by itself limits the historical lessons we can draw from their experiences.[93] Exclusively diasporic understandings of Armenians also render the lives of those included within the categorisation as one of tension: being in one place, but thinking of another.[94] It is quite ironic that, were we to focus on Lebanese Armenians' connections to other Armenian communities worldwide, we would in fact narrow our understanding of them.

By searching for connections to a homeland or to other Armenians – and being built on the assumption that those connections are *the* most fundamental trait of an ethnic group – Diaspora Studies can fail to consider when and why Armenians in Lebanon leveraged their diasporic identity as a political power tool vis-à-vis internal rivals, regional ones and larger global powers.[95] In this way, Armenians in Lebanon, articulated a diaspora identity that was neither oppressed nor alienated within the hostland.[96] In fact, *Armenians Beyond Diaspora* demonstrates that at certain moments, they manoeuvred the socio-political sphere in Lebanon to the extent that they dominated it. These tactics used the rhetoric of the homeland and of the Armenian nation to mark and increase power. But this does not mean that either were present as a presumably 'natural' unit. Rather, time and again, they were used and constructed in very specific contexts.

Notes

1. See for example, Orit Bashkin, *New Babylonians: A History of Jews in Modern Iraq* (Stanford, CA: Stanford University Press, 2012); Julia Phillips Cohen, *Becoming Ottomans: Sephardi Jews and Imperial Citizenship in the Modern Era* (New York:

Oxford University Press, 2014); Bedross Der Matossian, *Shattered Dreams of Revolution: From Liberty to Violence in the Late Ottoman Empire* (Stanford, CA: Stanford University Press, 2014); Lerna Ekmekçioğlu, *Recovering Armenia: The Limits of Belonging in Post-Genocide Turkey* (Stanford, CA: Stanford University Press, 2016); Heather Sharkey, *A History of Muslims, Christians, and Jews in the Middle East* (Cambridge: Cambridge University Press, 2017); Talin Suciyan, *The Armenians in Modern Turkey: Post-genocide Society, Politics and History* (London: I. B. Tauris, 2016); and Max Weiss, *In the Shadow of Sectarianism: Law, Shi'ism, and the Making of Modern Lebanon* (Cambridge, MA: Harvard University Press, 2010).

2. For works on the history of the Armenian Genocide see, amongst others, Raymond H. Kévorkian, *The Armenian Genocide: A Complete History* (London: I. B. Tauris, 2011); Ronald Grigor Suny, *'They Can Live in the Desert but Nowhere Else': A History of the Armenian Genocide* (Princeton: Princeton University Press, 2015); and Ronald Grigor Suny, Fatma Müge Goçek, and Norman M. Naimark, eds, *Question of Genocide: Armenians and Turks at the End of the Ottoman Empire* (Oxford: Oxford University Press, 2011).

3. For works that profile the arrival of the two waves of Armenian refugees to Lebanon, the first at the end of World War I and the second when the French government ceded the Alexandretta *Sanjak* to Turkey, see Hratch Bedoyan, 'The Social, Political, and Religious Structure of the Armenian Community in Lebanon', *The Armenian Review* 32 no. 2 (1979): 119–30; Vahe Sahakyan, 'Between Host-Countries and Homeland: Institutions, Politics and Identities in the Post-Genocide Armenian Diaspora (1920s to 1980s)' (Ph.D. diss., University of Michigan, 2015), 121–41; Nicola Schahgaldian, 'The Political Integration of an Immigrant Community into a Composite Society: The Armenians in Lebanon, 1920–1974' (Ph.D. diss., Columbia University, 1979), 49–62; Vahé Tachjian, 'Des camps de réfugiés aux quartiers urbains: processus et enjeux', in *Les Arméniens 1917–1939: La quête d'un refuge*, eds Raymond Kévorkian, Levon Nordiguian, and Vahé Tachjian (Paris: Réunion des musées nationaux, 2007), 113–45; and Vahé Tachjian, 'L'établissement définitif des réfugiés arméniens au Liban dans les années 1920 et 1930', in *Armenians of Lebanon: From Past Princesses and Refugees to Present-Day Community*, ed. Aïda Boudjikanian (Beirut: Haigazian University Press, 2009), 59–94.

4. For a map that demonstrates these proximities, see Vahé Tachjian, 'Des camps de réfugiés', 120.

5. Joanne Randa Nucho, *Everyday Sectarianism in Urban Lebanon: Infrastructures, Public Services and Power* (Princeton: Princeton University Press, 2016), 16.
6. Nicola Migliorino, *(Re)constructing Armenia in Lebanon and Syria: Ethno-cultural Diversity and the State in the Aftermath of a Refugee Crisis* (Oxford: Berghahn Books, 2008), 89. These numbers are based on Albert Hourani, *Syria and Lebanon: A Political Essay* (London: Oxford University Press, 1946), Appendix B, Table II, 386. In terms of sheer numbers, Syria had the largest population of Armenians, with approximately 121,000 out of 2.8 million people in 1943. The vast majority of Armenians living in Syria and Lebanon (and the Greater Levant for that matter) came as a direct result of the Armenian Genocide. By 1925, there were approximately 52,000 Armenians in Lebanon (approximately 2,000 of whom were native) and 120,000 in Syria (approximately 20,000 of whom were native). Migliorino, *(Re)constructing Armenia*, 32–4. Richard Hovannisian's 1974 article is still used a benchmark for Armenian population figures in the Middle East. He puts the number of Armenian refugees in 1925 in Iran at 50,000, adding to the substantial number of Armenians historically living there, and in Egypt at 40,000. Richard G. Hovannisian, 'The Ebb and Flow of the Armenian Minority in the Arab Middle East", *Middle East Journal* 28, no. 1 (1974), 20. For more on Armenians in Iran, including their participation in the political realm, see Houri Berberian, *Armenians and the Iranian Constitutional Revolution of 1905–1911: The Love for Freedom Has No Fatherland* (Boulder: Westview Press, 2001), 34–66.
7. For more on the intellectual construction of Beirut, see Jens Hanssen, *Fin de Siècle Beirut: The Making of an Ottoman Provincial Capital* (Oxford: Oxford University Press, 2005); and Cyrus Schayegh, *The Middle East and the Making of the Modern World* (Cambridge, MA: Harvard University Press, 2017).
8. Of course, one could date the relationship between Cilician Armenians and the French (and British) government earlier than the establishment of the Lebanese Mandate with the discussions and debates surrounding the formation of the Légion d'Orient. The blend of the expectations of the Armenian elite and of the French government with French and British imperial ambitions resulted in the creation and use of the legion, though not in the lands where the Armenians had imagined. See Susan Pattie, *The Armenian Legionnaires: Sacrifice and Betrayal in World War I* (New York: I. B. Tauris, 2018); and Andrekos Varnava, French and British Post-War Imperial Agendas and Forging an Armenian Homeland after the Genocide: The Formation of the Légion d'Orient in October 1916',

The Historical Journal 57, no. 4 (2014): 997–1025. For more on the history of Middle East mandates see Cyrus Schayegh and Andrew Arsan, eds, *The Routledge Handbook of the History of the Middle East Mandates* (New York: Routledge, 2015); Nadine Meouchy and Peter Sluglett, eds, *The British and French Mandates in Comparative Perspectives/Les Mandats français et anglais dans une perspective comparée* (Leiden: Brill, 2004); Idir Ouahes, *Syria and Lebanon under the French Mandate: Cultural Imperialism and the Workings of Empire* (New York: I. B. Tauris, 2018); and Elizabeth Thompson, *Colonial Citizens: Republican Rights, Paternal Privilege, and Gender in French Syria and Lebanon* (New York: Columbia University Press, 1999). Specifically on the French mandate rule in Syria, see Philip S. Khoury, *Syria and the French Mandate: The Politics of Arab Nationalism, 1920–1945* (Princeton: Princeton University Press, 1987) and Benjamin Thomas White, *The Emergence of Minorities in the Middle East: The Politics of Community in French Mandate Syria* (Edinburgh: Edinburgh University Press, 2011).

9. Migliorino, *(Re)constructing Armenia*, 54–5. In the nineteenth century, Ottoman citizenship had been extended to all imperial subjects with the *Tanzimat* reforms of 1839, culminating in the constitutional era of 1876. For more on how these reforms impacted the Empire's minorities see Cohen, *Becoming Ottomans*, and Der Matossian, *Shattered Dreams of Revolution*.

10. With the Ottoman Empire's defeat in the World War, the survivors of the Armenian Genocide had hoped and lobbied to be able to return to Anatolia. For example, in 1918, 50,000 Armenians in Aleppo held a rally and articulated their demands to Boghos Nubar Pasha, head of the Armenian Delegation in Paris, including the 'rapid repatriation of deportees'. See Vahram Shemassian, 'The Repatriation of Armenian Refugees from the Arab Middle East, 1918–1920', in *Armenian Cilicia*, eds Richard Hovannisian and Simon Payaslian (Costa Mesa: Mazda, 2008), 422–3. Despite difficulties in transportation, safety, and bureaucracy, Armenians did return. On the short-lived French polity in Cilicia and its subsequent fall to Kemal Ataturk's forces, see Garabet K. Moumdjian, 'Cilicia Under French Administration: Armenian Aspirations, Turkish Resistance, and French Stratagems', in *Armenian Cilicia*, eds Richard Hovannisian and Simon Payaslian (Costa Mesa: Mazda, 2008), 457–89. On the hasty withdrawal of the French and its consequences for the repatriated Cilician Armenians, see Richard G. Hovannisian, 'The Postwar Contest for Cilicia and the 'Marash Affair'', in *Armenian Cilicia*, 495–518. On the strategies and failings of French and British policies in repatriating Armenians to Cilicia see Vahé Tachjian,

'The Cilician Armenians and French Polity, 1919–1921', in *Armenian Cilicia*, 539–55.

11. While I am not suggesting that French actions of conferring citizenship matched – for the surviving Armenians of the now former Ottoman Empire – the devastating effects of the Treaty of Lausanne, the combination of the French and Kemalist actions solidified, at least for that moment, the Armenian presence in Lebanon. For more detail on how Armenians in Turkey reacted to the treaty, different goals of the participants of the conference, the impact of the lack of state-representation for the Armenians, and the attempts to support and oppose the Armenian delegation, see Ekmekcioğlu, *Recovering Armenia*; Hakem al-Rostom, "Rethinking the 'Post-Ottoman': Anatolian Armenians as an Ethnographic Perspective', in *A Companion to the Anthropology of the Middle East*, ed. Soraya Altorki (Oxford: Wiley Blackwell, 2015), 452–79; and Suciyan, *The Armenians in Modern Turkey*. This, even though the Treaty of Lausanne never even mentioned Armenia and the Armenians: Ekmekcioğlu, *Recovering Armenia*, 97; and al-Rostom, 'Rethinking the 'Post-Ottoman', 467.

12. In investigating citizenship under the Syrian and Lebanese mandates, Elizabeth Thompson, *Colonial Citizens*, explores the tensions between those who used citizenship to claim agency and the Lebanese elites and French mandate officials who aimed to uphold patriarchal standards. On the extension of citizenship for Armenian inhabitants of Syria and Lebanon see Migliorino, *(Re)constructing*, 89–109. For an analysis of how this process was strengthened by France using some Armenians as subaltern colonial administrators, including as soldiers, see Keith David Watenpaugh, *Bread from Stones: The Middle East and the Making of Modern Humanitarianism* (Berkeley: University of California Press, 2015), 279–98.

13. Within the past twenty years, scholarship has questioned the epistemological break between Lebanon under Ottoman rule and the French mandate. Ussama Makdisi, *The Culture of Sectarianism* (Berkeley: University of California Press, 2000) explored ruptures and continuities between Ottoman and mandate rule in the realm of sectarianism. See also, for political environmental history, Graham Auman Pitts, 'Fallow Fields: Famine and the Making of Lebanon' (Ph.D. diss., Georgetown University, 2016), and Elizabeth Rachel Williams, 'Cultivating Empires: Environment, Expertise, and Scientific Agriculture in Late Ottoman and French Mandate Syria' (Ph.D. diss., Georgetown University, 2015).

14. For more on the history of the Hnchak, Dashnak and Ramgavar parties, as well as the preceding Armenagan Party, see Razmik Panossian, *The Armenians:*

From Kings and Priests to Merchants and Commissars (New York: Columbia University Press, 2006), 200–27. In addition, by the early twentieth century, the Dashnak Party had become directly involved in the Iranian constitutional movement. As described by David N. Yaghoubian, its 'loose socialist ideals and goal of Armenian liberation were deemed compatible with the Iranian movement's progressive, antiautocratic aims'. Yaghoubian, *Ethnicity, Identity, and the Development of Nationalism in Iran* (Syracuse: Syracuse University Press, 2014), 127. For more on the involvement of the Dashnak Party in Iran see also Berberian, *Armenians and the Iranian Constitutional Revolution of 1905–1911*.

15. On the move and establishment of the Cilician See in Lebanon, see Simon Payaslian, 'The Institutionalization of the Catholicosate of the Great House of Cilicia in Antelias', in *Armenian Cilicia*, 557–92. *Armenian Cilicia* is the most comprehensive volume on Cilician Armenia and the interrelated political, social, economic and religious roles of the Catholicosate.

16. Payaslian, 'The Institutionalization of the Catholicosate of the Great House of Cilicia in Antelias', 557–92.

17. For more on how the minority groups, including the Armenians, engaged and were affected by the Tanzimat reforms and subsequent constitutional period, see Der Matossian, *Shattered Dreams of Revolution*.

18. It should also be noted that this is not limited to Armenian religious institutions and that British authorities also pursued a similar policy of readdressing power 'back' to the clergy. As Bedross Der Matossian notes 'The British were further aware (as the Ottomans had been) that it was easier to deal with the religious hierarchies, and consequently vested full authority in them as the main representatives of Palestine's religious groups'. Bedross Der Matossian, 'The Armenians of Palestine 1918–1948', *Journal of Palestine Studies* 41, no. 1 (Autumn 2011): 28.

19. Avedis Sanjian, *The Armenian Communities in Syria Under Ottoman Domination* (Cambridge, MA: Harvard University Press, 1965), 141.

20. This is in contrast to neighbouring Syria where seventeen printing houses were established during the Mandate Period, but most were closed within the first fifteen years of independence. Simon Payaslian, 'Diasporan Subalternities: The Armenian Community in Syria', *Diaspora: A Journal of Transnational Studies* 16, no. 1/2 (Spring/Fall 2007): 108–11. The hostile publishing environment of Syria was Lebanon's gain. The migration of Armenian intellectuals to Beirut reinforced the city as a literary hub. Migliorino, *(Re)constructing Armenia*, 122–24. For more on the history of publishing houses in Syria see Vayk Parikian

and Hovnan Varzhapetian, *Patmut'iwn Surioy hay tparanneru* [The History of Syrian Armenian Printing Houses] (Syria: Bibliothèque Violette Jébéjian-UGAB, 1973).

21. For more on the repatriation movement more generally and from the perspective of the USSR and Soviet Studies see, Joanne Laycock, 'The Repatriation of Armenians to Soviet Armenia, 1945–49', in *Warlands Population Resettlement and State Reconstruction in the Soviet-East European Borderlands, 1945–50*, eds Peter Gatrell and Nick Baron (London: Palgrave Macmillan, 2009), 140–62; Joanne Laycock, 'Armenian Homelands and Homecomings, 1945–1949', *Cultural and Social History* 9, no. 1 (2012): 103–23; Panossian, *The Armenians*, 358–65; Susan Pattie, 'From the Centres to the Periphery: "Repatriation" to an Armenian Homeland in the 20th Century', in *Homecomings: Unsettling Paths of Return*, eds Fran Markowitz and Anders H. Stefansson (Oxford: Lexington Books, 2004), 109–24; Farid Shafiyev, *Resettling the Borderlands: State Relocations and Ethnic Conflict in the South Caucasus* (Montreal: McGill-Queen's University Press, 2018), 43–95; Ronald Suny, *Looking Towards Ararad* (Indianapolis: Indiana University Press, 1993), 163–69; and Sevan Nathaniel Yousefian, 'The Postwar Repatriation Movement of Armenians to Soviet Armenia, 1945–1948' (Ph.D. diss., University of California, Los Angeles, 2011). On the possessions brought to (and often confiscated by) the USSR, see Joanne Laycock, 'Belongings: People and Possessions in the Armenian Repatriations 1946–1949', *Kritika* 18, no. 3 (2017): 511–38. On memoirs, Joanne Laycock, 'Soviet or Survivor Stories? Repatriate Narratives in Armenian Histories, Memories and Identities', *History and Memory* 28, no. 2 (2016): 123–51, and Hagop Touryantz, *Search for a Homeland* (New York: issued privately, 1987).

22. Repatriation was a matter of concern even in locales where it did not actually take place. For example, Talin Sucijan writes about how 'various accounts and news items show that no Armenians from Turkey immigrated in 1946–1948, despite the fact that, according to the sources, hundreds of people, if not thousands, had registered'. The local Turkish press used repatriation, along with Soviet and Armenian territorial claims for Kars and Ardahan to (re)invoke anti-Armenian sentiment throughout the repatriation period. This anti-Armenian upsurge prompted the local Armenian press to respond to the Turkish press and to governments that embraced these campaigns. Suciyan, *The Armenians in Modern Turkey*, 157–68.

23. This chapter builds upon my article 'Articulating Power Through the Parochial', *Mashriq and Mahjar* 2, no. 1 (2013): 41–72.

24. Cold War tensions manifested in other Armenian religious sites as well, most notably in Istanbul (1944–1950) and Jerusalem (1948–1960). While the context of the Cold War can thread these crises, the Cilician See in Beirut was the only ecclesiastical power that played an active role in all three episodes, demonstrating both its authority and importance. For more on the patriarchal election crisis in Turkey see Suciyan, *The Armenians in Modern Turkey*, 161–97. For more on the crisis in Jerusalem see Bedross Der Matossian, 'The Armenians of Jerusalem in the Modern Period: The Rise and Decline of a Community', in *Routledge Handbook on Jerusalem*, eds Suleiman A. Mourad, Naomi Koltun-Fromm, and Bedross Der Matossian (New York: Routledge, 2019), 396–407.
25. On how the United States attempted to influence the events surrounding the Jerusalem Patriarchate and its elections, see James R. Stocker, 'The United States and the Struggle in the Armenian Patriarchate of Jerusalem, 1955–1960', *Jerusalem Quarterly* 71, no. 2 (2017): 19–21. On an analysis of both direct and indirect interventions of the United States in Armenian affairs see Stocker, 'The United States and the Armenian Community in Lebanon, 1943–1967', in *Armenians of Lebanon (II) Proceedings of the Conference (14–16 May 2014)*, ed. Antranik Dakessian (Beirut: Haigazian University Press, 2017), and 'An Opportunity to Strike a Blow? The United States Government and the Armenian Apostolic Church, 1956–1963', *Diplomacy & Statecraft* 29, no. 4 (2018): 590–612.
26. Very few works on Armenian involvement in the 1958 mini-civil war exist. Those that do position the tension and violence solely as an 'Armenian' affair. See, for example, Seta Kalpakian, 'The Dimensions of the 1958 Inter-Communal Conflict in the Armenian Community in Lebanon' (MA thesis, American University of Beirut, 1983). For more on Armenian involvement in Lebanese politics, see Schahgaldian, 'The Political Integration of an Immigrant Community into a Composite Society'; on their involvement specifically in Lebanese parliamentary elections see Zaven Messerlian, *Armenian Participation in the Lebanese Legislative Elections 1934–2009* (Beirut: Haigazian University Press, 2013). On the so-called 'third voice', an attempt to bridge the ideologically opposed Armenian parties, see Yeghia Tashjian, 'The Origin, Success and Failure of the Lebanese-Armenian "Third Force" during the Intra-communal Cold War (1956–1960)', in *Armenians of Lebanon (II)*, 181–98.
27. Of course understanding Armenians through particular fields is not unique to Armenian historiography or Armenians for that matter. Comparisons can also be made, for example, with Palestinian historiography. According to Jamil Hilal,

Palestinian historiography can largely be divided into two narratives: 'one that adopts a vocabulary of surrender and defeat, and a second that highlights heroism and resistance'. Armenian historiography largely ignores stories of defiance, opting instead to construct a singular nation, disrupted by forced migration and genocide. Jamil Hilal, 'Reflectons on Comptemporary Palestinian History', in *Across the Wall: Narratives of Israeli-Palestinian History*, eds Ilan Pappé and Jamil Hilal (New York: I. B. Tauris, 2010), 177.

28. See for example, George Bournoutian, *A History of the Armenian People*, vol. I: *Pre-History to 1500 AD* (Costa Mesa: Mazda, 1993); Bournoutian, *A History of the Armenian People*, vol. II: *1500 AD to the Present* (Costa Mesa: Mazda, 1994); Richard Hovannisian, ed., *The Armenian People from Ancient to Modern Times (Volume 2) From Dominion to Statehood: The Fifteenth Century to the Twentieth* (London: Macmillan 1997); David Marshall Lang, *The Armenians: A People in Exile* (London: Unwin Hyman, 1988); Simon Payaslian, *History of the Armenian People* (Costa Mesa: Mazda, 1993); Christopher Walker, *Armenia: Survival of a Nation* (New York: St Martin's Press, 1980). Sebouh David Aslanian laments that many Armenian Studies scholars have demonstrated a lack of interest in connected, global histories leaving the field 'rather insular and reluctant to engage in constructive self-criticism': Aslanian, 'From "Autonomous" to "Interactive" Histories: World History's Challenge to Armenian Studies', in *An Armenian Mediterranean: Words and Worlds in Motion*, eds Kathryn Babayan and Michael Pifer (London: Palgrave Macmillan, 2018), 83.

29. Hagop Barsoumian, 'The Eastern Question and the Tanzimat Era', in *The Armenian People from Ancient to Modern Times (Volume 2) From Dominion to Statehood: The Fifteenth Century to the Twentieth*, ed. Richard Hovannisian (London: Macmillan 1997), 191.

30. Ibid. And while *erkir* denoted Eastern Anatolia for the migrant Armenians in urban centres, the same term referred to both the urban and provincial areas of the Ottoman Empire for Russian Armenian intellectuals. Razmik Panossian, *The Armenians*, 155. Albeit for different reasons, this understanding of the homeland seems to be consistent with the editor-in-chief of *Marmara*, the Istanbul Armenian language daily, who stated, 'The Armenians of Istanbul do not belong to *Spiurk* [diaspora]. *Spiurk* is made up of people who have left the homeland. We have not'. Ulf Björklund, Armenians of Athens and Istanbul: the Armenian Diaspora and the "Transnational" Nation', *Global Networks* 3, no. 3 (2003): 345.

31. Richard Hovannisian, *The Armenian People from Ancient to Modern Times, volume I: The Dynastic Periods: From Antiquity to the Fourteenth Century*; volume II: *From Dominion to Statehood: The Fifteenth Century to the Twentieth* (London: Macmillan 1997). *The History of the Armenian People* is but one example of a work that brings together an impressive array of contributors while continuing what Sebouh Aslanian has called 'a general pattern' of relying on secondary source literature, and more significantly for *Armenians Beyond Diaspora*'s intervention, relying 'upon a linear narrative to chart the unfolding of the Armenian national subject in History'. Aslanian, 'From "Autonomous" to "Interactive", 94–5.
32. Richard Hovannisian, 'Introduction', in *The Armenian People from Ancient to Modern Times, Volume 2*, vii–xi. The authors of the first volume, which focuses on the pre-modern period and ends in the fourteenth century, all reference loss and victimhood, usually in connection with a forced migration or enemy conquest. Richard Hovannisian, ed., *The Armenian People from Ancient to Modern Times, volume I*.
33. Richard Hovannisian, 'Introduction', in *The Armenian People from Ancient to Modern Times, Volume 2*, viii.
34. Krikor Maksoudian, 'Armenian Communities in Eastern Europe', in *The Armenian People from Ancient to Modern Times, Volume 2*, 51–2.
35. Ibid.
36. For Maksoudian, his branding suggests that Armenians in Eastern Europe by necessity relate or connect to Armenians elsewhere. The effort to connect Armenians in Eastern Europe to those living elsewhere is even demonstrated in their admitted *lack* of connection. Maksoudian also mentions the 'isolation' of Armenians in Poland to 'explain' a purported distance from Armenian life. In doing so however, he concurrently links Armenians in Poland who may or may not have been aware of Armenians in the provinces of the Ottoman Empire. And if so, it is unclear if they identified as 'belonging' to a national framework of some sort. For the reader, however, a connection has already been created. Ibid, 65–6.
37. Ibid., 63–4, 75.
38. Ibid., 65.
39. Richard Grigor Suny, 'Eastern Armenians Under Tsarist Rule', in *The Armenian People from Ancient to Modern Times, Volume 2*, 109–37.
40. Ibid., 116.
41. Ibid., 121–6.

42. Ibid., 137.
43. Razmik Panossian, *The Armenians*, 3. (Emphasis added.)
44. In addition, Kasbarian delves into how the Greek Cypriot administered sector differentied between experiences of victimhood, essentially treating Armenians 'as second- class citizens whose loss is not (worth) the same as the 1974 [majority Greek] losses' thereby categorising its own citizenship. Sossie Kasbarian, 'Between Nationalist Absorption and Subsumption: Reflecting on the Armenian Cypriot Experience', in *Cypriot Nationalisms in Context*, eds Thekla Kyritsi and Nikos Christofis (New York: Palgrave Macmillan, 2018), 178, 191.
45. Ibid., 178.
46. Ibid., 183, 188.
47. James Barry, *Armenian Christians in Iran: Ethnicity, Religion, and Identity in the Islamic Republic* (Cambridge: Cambridge University Press, 2019), 1–2.
48. Barry, *Armenian Christians in Iran*, 246–58.
49. Darren L. Logan, 'A Remnant Remaining: Armenians amid Northern Iraq's Christian Community', *Iran & the Caucasus* 14, no. 1 (2010): 143, 152, 153, 154, 155.
50. Logan, 'A Remnant Remaining', 156.
51. Payaslian, 'Diasporan Subalternities', 101.
52. Ibid., 92, 93, 97, 98, 99, 102, 104, 111, 113, 119, and 122.
53. It should be noted here that it was not considered tortuous due to any impediments put forth by the Mandate Syrian government at that time. In fact, this is once again not only a reference to the Genocide, but also to the collective memory of the 1894–1896 massacres. Ibid., 102.
54. Ibid., 93.
55. Ibid., 108.
56. Sebouh David Aslanian also observes in what he terms the 'post-genocide fixation' a 'precluded interest in other kinds of histories and identities in which Armenians in the past have also engaged". 'From 'Autonomous' to 'Interactive' Histories", 102.
57. It is not only different phases of the Armenian Genocide that are stitched together. Other incidents of aggression against Armenians in the Ottoman Empire are configured as additional episodes in grand narrative of violence perpetrated by Turks against Armenians. For example, the Adana Massacres of 1909 are seen either as a precursor to the genocide or its start, without considering the differences (and similarities, for that matter) in time and the political and economic environments. See for example, Raymond Kévorkian, *The Armenian*

Genocide: A Complete History (New York: I. B. Tauris, 2011), 71–118. This minimises the experience of violence for the victims, homogenises perpetrators, and likewise discourages the individual examination of such events, which, when analysed, lead to a greater understanding of the living and working conditions in Adana and its environs, and of the repercussions of the 1908 Revolution outside of the centre of Istanbul. One of the notable exceptions to the homogenised reading is Der Matossian, *Shattered Dreams*, 149–72.

58. Christopher Walker, 'World War I and the Armenian Genocide', in *The Armenian People from Ancient to Modern Times, Volume 2*, 239–74.
59. On the exceptionalism of Iran see, for example, Anthonie Holslag, *The Transgenerational Consequences of the Armenian Genocide: Near the Foot of Mount Ararat* (New York: Palgrave Macmillan, 2018), 70. Houri Berberian's work is an exception to this. She argues that the majority of Iranian Armenians in the mid-twentieth century did not have direct links to Armenia (and to Armenian nationalism for that matter). Berberian, *Armenians and the Iranian Constitutional Revolution of 1905–1911*, 187. On Armenian 'assimilation' in the Ukraine and Poland see Maksoudian, 'Armenian Communities in Eastern Europe', 68–9.
60. For example, through a social biography of Lucik Moradiance, Yaghoubian, *Ethnicity, Identity, and the Development of Nationalism*, 175–185, traces how local and regional historical events including these wars and hardships shaped the lives of the Armenian population in Iran.
61. A stark exception to this reading is Der Matossian, 'The Armenians of Palestine 1918–1948', 30. In addition to describing the chaos in Jerusalem during the war, the influx of surviving Armenian refugees, and the changes and tension that manifested within the Armenian community with their arrival, Der Matossian delves into how British policy manifested in Armenian affairs, especially with regards to the affairs of the Jerusalem Patriarchate.
62. Bedross Der Matossian, 'Explaining the Unexplainable: Recent Trends in the Armenian Genocide Historiography', *Journal of Leventine Studies* 5, no. 2 (Winter 2015), 150–55.
63. Ibid., 156.
64. Melissa Bilal, 'Lullabies and the Memory of Pain: Armenian Women's Remembrance of the Past in Turkey", *Dialect Anthropology* (2018):18. https://doi.org/10.1007/s10624-018-9515-8. Bedross Der Matossian, 'The Armenians of Palestine 1918–1948', is another example. Der Matossian analyses how refugee Armenians 'infused' a dynamic new element into the community, demonstrating growth in this period. While Der Matossian does not shy away

from the hardship the refugees experienced, it is important to note his focus upon the relationship amongst the Armenian inhabitants of Palestine along with their active processes of community building (even if this manifested in intra-Armenian tension as details). Ibid., 34–39. Such a story is often relegated to studies on refugees that profile the activity of international aid organisations (instead). See for example, Laura Robson, 'Refugees and the Case for International Authority in the Middle East: The League of Nations and the United Nations Relief and Works Agency for Palestinian Refugees in the Near East Compared', *International Journal of Middle East Studies* 49, no. 4 (2017): 628.

65. Ibid., 18.
66. Ibid., 2.
67. See for example, al-Rostom, 'Rethinking the 'Post-Ottoman', 462; Amy Mills, 'Becoming Blind to the Landscape: Turkification and the Precarious National Future in Occupied Istanbul', *Journal of the Ottoman and Turkish Studies Association* 5, no. 2 (2018): 100; and Esen Egemen Özbek, 'Commemorating the Armenian Genocide: The Politics of Memory and National Identity' (Ph.D. diss., Carleton University Ottawa, 2016), 278.
68. Tsolin Nalbantian, 'Going Beyond Overlooked Populations in Lebanese Historiography: The Armenian Case', *History Compass* 11:10 (2013): 821–32.
69. See for example, Robert Fisk, *Pity the Nation: The Abduction of Lebanon* (New York: Nation Books, 2002); Theodor Hanf, *Coexistence in Wartime Lebanon: Decline of a State and Rise of Nation* (New York: I. B. Tauris, 2015); Dilip Hiro, *Lebanon Fire and Embers: A History of the Lebanese Civil War* (London: Weidenfeld & Nicolson, 1993); David Hirst, *Beware of Small States: Lebanon, Battleground of the Middle East* (New York: Nation Books, 2011); Samir Khalaf, *Civil and Uncivil Violence in Lebanon: A History of the Internationalization of Communal Conflict* (New York: Columbia University Press, 2004); Elizabeth Picard, *Lebanon: A Shattered Country* (New York: Holmes & Meier, 2002); Kamal Salibi, *Crossroads to Civil War: Lebanon 1958–1976* (Delmar, NY: Caravan Books. 1976).
70. Max Weiss, *In the Shadow of Sectarianism: Law, Shi`ism, and the Making of Modern Lebanon* (Cambridge, MA: Harvard University Press, 2010); Linda Sayed, 'Sectarian Homes: The Making of Shi'i Families and Citizens under the French Mandate, 1918–1943' (Ph.D diss., Columbia University, 2013); Ussama Makdisi, *The Culture of Sectarianism: Community, History, and Violence in Nineteenth-Century Ottoman Lebanon* (Los Angeles: University of

California Press, 2000). There are of course, additional exceptions. See also Ziad Abu-Rish, 'Conflict and Institution Building in Lebanon, 1946–1955' (Ph.D diss., University of California, Los Angeles, 2014); Andrew Arsan and Cyrus Schayegh, eds, *The Routledge Handbook of the History of the Middle East Mandates* (New York: Routledge, 2015); Nadya Sbaiti, '"If the Devil Taught French": Strategies of Language and Learning in French Mandate Beirut', in *Trajectories of Education in the Arab World: Legacies and Challenges*, ed. Osama Abi-Mershed (New York: Routledge, 2010).

71. Lara Deeb, *An Enchanted Modern: Gender and Public Piety in Shi'i Lebanon* (Princeton: Princeton University Press, 2006) and Joanne Randa Nucho, *Everyday Sectarianism in Urban Lebanon: Infrastructures, Public Services and Power* (Princeton: Princeton University Press, 2016). See also Jared McCormick, 'Hairy Chest, Will Travel: Tourism, Identity, and Sexuality in the Levant', *Journal of Middle East Women's Studies* 7, no. 3 (November 2011): 71–97. In the field of political science, see, Melani Cammett, *Compassionate Communalism: Welfare and Sectarianism in Lebanon* (Cornell: Cornell University Press, 2014).

72. See for example, Nejla M. Abu Izzedin, *The Druzes: A New Study of Their History, Faith, and Society* (Leiden: Brill, 1993); Robert Brenton Betts, *The Druze* (New Haven: Yale University Press, 1990); and Kais Firro, *A History of the Druzes* (Leiden: Brill, 1992).

73. Kamal Salibi, *A House of Many Mansions: The History of Lebanon Reconsidered* (Los Angeles: University of California Press, 1990), 4, 46, 82, 138.

74. Ibid., 4.

75. Fawwaz Traboulsi, *A History of Modern Lebanon* (London: Pluto Press, 2012).

76. Ibid., vii–ix.

77. While an incredibly valuable and welcome addition, Christine Babikian Assaf, Carla Eddé, Lévon Nordiguian, Vahé Tachjian, eds, *Les Arméniens du Liban: Cent ans de presence* (Beirut: Presses de l'Université Saint-Joseph, 2017), aims to do just that. It focuses on the Armenian contribution *to* Lebanon and influence *in* Lebanon, and as such, considers Lebanon (and Armenians) as a separate, fixed construct.

78. See for example, Yezid Sayigh and Avi Shlaim, eds, *The Cold War and the Middle East* (Oxford: Oxford University Press, 2003) and Rashid Khalidi, *Sowing Crisis: The Cold War and American Dominance in the Middle East* (Boston: Beacon Press, 2009).

79. Still, these works that focus on the power of certain states and so-called 'key players' continue to be the majority. See for example Antonio Perra, *Kennedy*

and the Middle East: The Cold War, Israel and Saudi Arabia (London: I. B. Tauris, 2017) and Roby C. Barrett, *The Greater Middle East and the Cold War: US Foreign Policy Under Eisenhower and Kennedy* (London: I. B. Tauris, 2009). A related contention connects both American and Soviet Cold War policy in the region to the so-called growth of 'radical Islam'. See for example, Douglas Little, *American Orientalism: The United States and the Middle East since 1945* (Chapel Hill: University of North Carolina Press, 2008); Patrick Tyler, *A World of Trouble: The White House and the Middle East – from the Cold War to the War on Terror* (New York: Farrar, Straus and Giroux, 2009); Stephen Kinzer, *The Brothers: John Foster Dulles, Allen Dulles, and Their Secret World War* (New York: St Martin's Griffin, 2014); Yevgeny Primakov, *Russia and the Arabs: Behind the Scenes in the Middle East from the Cold War to the Present* (New York: Basic Books, 2009); and Galia Golan, *Soviet Policies in the Middle East: From World War Two to Gorbachev* (Cambridge: Cambridge University Press, 2009).

80. I. Zake, ed., *Anti-Communist Minorities in the U.S.: Political Activism of Ethnic Refugees* (New York: Palgrave, 2009) is an exception to this, but even this welcome work does not engage with communities in or from the Middle East. Ben Alexander's contribution in the work does profile the Armenians, but examines the community from the United States and their relationship with Soviet Armenia, and does not integrate works on the Middle East. Ben Alexander, 'The American Armenians' Cold War: The Divided Response to Soviet Armenia' in *Anti-Communist Minorities in the U.S.: Political Activism of Ethnic Refugees* (New York: Palgrave, 2009), 67–86.

81. Paul Thomas Chamberlin, *The Cold War's Killing Fields: Rethinking the Long Peace* (New York: HarperCollins, 2018).

82. See for example, Ien Ang, 'Together-in-difference: Beyond Diaspora, into Hybridity', *Asian Studies Review* 27, no. 2 (2003): 141–54; Anthony Gorman and Sossie Kasbarian, 'Introduction', eds Anthony Gorman and Sossie Kasbarian (Edinburgh: Edinburgh University Press, 2015), 1–30; Anthony Gorman, 'The Italians of Egypt: Return to a Diaspora', in *Diasporas of the Modern Middle East: Contextualising Community*, eds Anthony Gorman and Sossie Kasbarian (Edinburgh: Edinburgh University Press, 2015), 138–70; Kim D. Butler, 'Multi-layered Politics in the African Diaspora: The Metadiaspora Concept and Minidiaspora Realities' in *Opportunity Structures in Diaspora Relations: Comparisons in Contemporary Multilevel Politics of Diaspora and Transnational Identity*, ed. Gloria Totoricagüena (Reno, Nevada: Center for Basque Studies, University of Nevada, 2007), 19–51; May Farah, 'Palestinian Refugees in

Lebanon: Worthy Lives in Unworthy Conditions', in *Diasporas of the Modern Middle East*, 274–300; Anaheed al-Hardan, 'The Palestinian Refugee Community in Syria', in *Palestinians in Syria : Nakba Memories of Shattered Communities* (New York: Columbia University Press, 2016); M. H. Ilias, 'Malayalee Migrants and Translocal Kerala Politics in the Gulf: Re-conceptualising the 'Political'', in *Diasporas of the Modern Middle East*, 303–37; Finex Ndhlovu, 'A Decolonial Critique of Diaspora Identity Theories and the Notion of Superdiversity', *Diaspora Studies* 9, no. 1 (2016): 28–40; Dominic Pasura, 'Competing Meanings of the Diaspora: The Case of Zimbabweans in Britain', *Journal of Ethnic & Migration Studies* 36, no. 9 (2010): 1445–61; Khachig Tölölyan, 'The Contemporary Discourse of Diaspora Studies', *Comparative Studies of South Asia, Africa and the Middle East* 27, no. 3 (2007): 647–55.

83. For innovative works on Armenians see for example, Sylvia Alajaji, *Music and the Armenian Diaspora: Searching for Home in Exile* (Bloomington: Indiana University Press, 2015); Björklund, 'Armenians of Athens and Istanbul', 337–54; Der Matossian, 'The Armenians of Jerusalem in the Modern Period', 396–407; Sossie Kasbarian, 'The "Others" Within: The Armenian Community in Cyprus', eds Anthony Gorman and Sossie Kasbarian (Edinburgh: Edinburgh University Press, 2015), 241–73; Kasbarian, 'Between Nationalist Absorption and Subsumption', 177–97; Susan Paul Pattie, *Faith in History: Armenians Rebuilding Community* (Washington, DC: Smithsonian Institution Press, 1997); Susanne Schwalgin, 'Why Locality Matters: Diaspora Consciousness and Sedentariness in the Armenian Diaspora in Greece', in *Diaspora, Identity, and Religion: New Directions in Theory and Research*, eds Waltraud Kokot, Khachig Tölölyan and Carolin Alfonso (New York: Routledge, 2004), 72–92; Khachig Tölölyan, 'Elites and Institutions in the Armenian Transnation', *Diaspora: A Journal of Transnational Studies* 9, no. 1 (2000): 107–36; and Yaghoubian, *Ethnicity, Identity, and the Development of Nationalism in Iran*.

84. While perhaps 'merely' paying homage, most studies on diaspora, however inventive, continue to mention Armenians as a paradigmatic example. Waltraud Kokot, Khachig Tölölyan and Carolin Alfonso, 'Introduction', in *Diaspora, Identity, and Religion: New Directions in Theory and Research*, eds Waltraud Kokot, Khachig Tölölyan and Carolin Alfonso (New York: Routledge, 2004), 1–2; William Safran, 'Deconstructing and Comparing Diasporas', in *Diaspora, Identity, and Religion*, 9–30; and Khachig Tölölyan, 'The Nation-State and Its Others: In Lieu of a Preface', *Diaspora: A Journal of Transnational Studies* 1, no. 1 (1991): 4.

85. On the plurality of diasporas see for example, Donna R. Gabaccia, *Italy's Many Diasporas* (Seattle: University of Washington Press, 2000), 5; Anthony Gorman, 'The Italians of Egypt: Return to a Diaspora', in *Diasporas of the Modern Middle East: Contextualising Community*, eds Anthony Gorman and Sossie Kasbarian (Edinburgh: Edinburgh University Press, 2015), 139. Kim D. Butler calls for works on the diaspora to deal with 'metaconstructs and the millions of micro-level interations of which they are constituted', in Butler, 'Multilayered Politics in the African Diaspora', 25–7. While she is more concerned with a 'decentered diaspora' where the 'homeland is not the principal actor, but merely "the glue" that defines the community', *Armenians Beyond Diaspora* instead focuses on how Armenians in Lebanon used the concept of a homeland to (re)orient local and distant Armenians to power structures in Lebanon.
86. In this way, I veer slightly away from Tölölyan in 'Elites and Institutions in the Armenian Transnation', 107–36. His emphasis on the transnational, which he notably argues is not a synonym for diasporal, includes diasporic communities (importantly both new and old) and the homeland. *Armenians Beyond Diaspora* instead demonstrates how Lebanon became an Armenian centre, often at the expense and purposeful alienation of the Armenian Republic.
87. For more on the historic role of Constantinople/Istanbul for Armenians see Panossian, *The Armenians*, 83–6. For more on the centrality of Istanbul amongst revolutionaries and intelligentsia as well as the tension between these groups, the *amira* classes, and the Armenian Patriarchate see, Der Matossian, *Shattered Dreams of Revolution*.
88. Hakem al-Rustom, for example, divides works on Armenians into three group:1) history of the genocide, 2) diaspora communities, and 3) work on Armenians in Turkey, in 'Rethinking the 'Post-Ottoman', 452–79. And yet, while I certainly celebrate such interventions, these rubrics, however unintentionally, connect all works on Armenians to the Armenian Genocide. After all, they associate the formation of diaspora communities with the Genocide, and the labelling of the third category as Armenians *remaining* in Turkey links them with its destruction and trauma. In addition, these groupings encourage an anachronistic centring of Armenian power to Turkey, as they do not take into account the activity and agency in other locales.
89. There remains an overall frame around work on Armenians that seems to compel scholars to identify a community as a diaspora, and that homeland is contentious. This, even in scholarship that acknowledges the difficulty in defining diaspora, homeland, and return and their never-ending construction. See for example,

Pattie, *Faith in History*, on the Cypriot Armenian community. An exception to this reading is Kasbarian, 'Between Nationalist Absorption and Subsumption', 177–97, and the collection *Diasporas of the Modern Middle East*. Nevertheless, even while the contributors of this volume maintain that communities living and settling in diasporic and 'host' spaces are 'in practice, their homes', they likewise assume an overarching 'diasporic experience'. Gorman and Kasbarian, eds, *Diasporas of the Modern Middle East*, 2–3.

90. This, even in works that focus exclusively on Lebanese Armenians. Aida Boudjikanian, for instance, states that '. . . this community [Lebanon's Armenian community] has been considered for a long time as one of the most important of the Armenian Diaspora'. Aida Boudjikanian, 'Introduction', in *Armenians of Lebanon: From Past Princesses and Refugees to Present-Day Community*, ed. idem (Beirut: Haigazian University Press, 2009), xvii. See also Scout Tufankjian and Atom Egoyan, *There Is Only the Earth: Images from the Armenian Diaspora Project* (New York: Melcher Media Inc., 2015).

91. See for example Robin Cohen, *Global Diasporas: An Introduction* (New York: Routledge, 2008), where Armenians are constructed first as a category, and then slated under 'victim diasporas'.

92. While acknowledging the porous boundaries of the 'transnational moment' Khachig Tölölyan cautions against privileging this mobility, and stresses, along with Pnina Werbner, that contemporary diasporas require 'settled diasporic nodes in which a public sphere and civil society peculiar to them develop'. Tölölyan, 'The Contemporary Discourse of Diaspora Studies', 653–654; and Tölölyan, 'Elites and Institutions in the Armenian Transnation', 111–12. Rogers Brubaker is also sceptical of claims of 'unprecedented porosity'. Rogers Brubaker, 'The "Diaspora" Diaspora' *Ethnic and Racial Studies* 28, no. 1 (2005): 8–9. Ien Ang importantly notes that in forwarding the position that diasporas challenge the limitations of the nation-state, it must be noted that they 'have and assume their own boundedness and apartness'. Ang, 'Together-in-Difference: Beyond Diaspora, into Hybridity', 142–4. In 'Elites and Institutions in the Armenian Transnation' Tölölyan also profiles the importance of institutions, elites, and material resources in the Armenian Transnation (which he defines as the Armenian Diaspora and the homeland), and examines their impact not only in the case of Armenians, but also in the theory of diasporas. Tölölyan, 'Elites and Institutions in the Armenian Transnation', 107–36.

93. Perhaps the failure to consider Armenians outside of the diasporic model is due to the prominent place the Armenian case occupies in Diaspora Studies.

In this field, Armenians have been a 'classical' case, along with the Greeks and the Jews. William Safran, 'Diasporas in Modern Societies: Myths of Homeland and Return', in *Diaspora* 1, no. 1(1991): 83–99, was one of the first to ascribe this 'classical' status to Armenians, expanding from John Armstrong work on the Jewish Diaspora: *Nations Before Nationalism* (Chapel Hill: University of North Carolina Press, 1982). While these classical cases could be taken as starting points to look at non-normative cases, as Brubaker suggests, how does one go beyond them when the starting point is the very case they are considering? Brubaker, 'The "Diaspora" Diaspora', 1–19.
94. Safran, 'Deconstructing and Comparing Diasporas'', 12.
95. This goes beyond James Clifford, 'Diasporas', *Cultural Anthropology* 9, no. 3(1997): 302–38, and Paul Gilroy, *There Ain't no Black in the Union Jack: The Cultural Politics of Race and Nation* (Chicago: University of Chicago Press, 1991) which suggest that diaspora could be a way to express being part of the host country, rather than about longing. These works, while they expand the notions of diaspora and make significant contributions to the field, do not consider the daily construction of hierarchy within diasporas.
96. This counters William Safran's discussion in 'Deconstructing and Comparing Diasporas', in *Diaspora, Identity, and Religion*, 12.

1

REPOSITIONING ARMENIANS IN NEWLY POST-COLONIAL NATION-STATES: LEBANON AND SYRIA, 1945–1946

Introduction

This is the first of four chapters investigating how Armenians in Lebanon re-situated themselves and re-imagined their place in that Middle Eastern country and in the world more broadly during a sensitive, transitional time of change: the early post-colonial period. This chapter focuses on the mid-1940s. Existential political questions shaped those years. Lebanon was manoeuvering from de jure independence, in 1943, to its de facto independence, which it gained 'only' in 1946. This path was strewn with political and military mines; in fact, the ultimate shape of independence and hence of the Lebanese polity was not self-evident ahead of time, which is to say before 1946. External powers, principally France and Britain, maintained an interest and kept troops in Lebanon (and Syria) through 1946. In Lebanon and beyond, some intellectuals and politicians persistently advocated alternatives to Lebanese independence, including a union with Syria if not with other countries in the Arab East.

This chapter digs deep into the manifold triangulations and balancing acts constitutive of Lebanese Armenians' changing views of their place in and vis-à-vis the complex making of the Lebanese state and its wider Arab environment as well as vis-à-vis the Armenian Socialist Soviet Republic (ASSR).[1] It pursues this inquiry by closely analysing two ideologically opposed newspapers, the leftist, Hnchak *Ararad* and the firmly right-wing, Dashnak *Aztag*. These press outlets also became responsible for issuing political statements even though these political parties enjoyed civil representation, unlike other sites with an active Armenian press, such as Istanbul.[2] These papers reflected the issues of interest in this chapter implicitly, that is not in *what* they said, but *how*; I will open the chapter with a note on this dimension. More importantly, they explicitly reflected on these balancing acts. I will explore four themes. The first is Armenians' position in and vis-à-vis the Lebanese polity, as well as vis-à-vis Syria. A second concerns language, and specifically the multiple roles of Arabic. The next has to do with the ambiguities of spaces relevant for Armenians in and beyond Lebanon. And a last concerns the fascinating political positioning of the Armenian church that, although conservative, felt forced to support communist Armenia and the USSR as the ASSR's protector.

Newspapers' Implicit Reflection of Armenian Political Positioning vis-à-vis Lebanon

I will start this section by pointing out a simple and yet crucial point. The fact that these two ideologically different papers, *Ararad* and *Aztag*, time and again concerned themselves with Armenians' relationship vis-à-vis the Lebanese state and society throws into relief the centrality and impact of that relationship for the *entire* Armenian community. The need to not simply look inwards, to the community, but rather to ponder one's location in Lebanon was felt not only by some political groups, it occupied all Armenians.

This need showed also in the very format in which newspapers chose to cover Armenians' position in Lebanon. Specifically, newspapers habitually did not only write their own reports on Lebanese affairs but reproduced translated texts from the Lebanese press; they did not bury coverage of 'national' news in the back pages, but more often than not gave them pride of place in their front pages; and they treated important issues not punctually but oftentimes followed up on initial coverage for days on end. Of course, not only Lebanese but also other public addresses were often reproduced verbatim, partially and sometimes in their entirety, in those papers. For one thing, this concerned Armenian matters playing out in Lebanon. Thus, following the establishment of the ASSR, *Ararad* continuously covered the related anniversary celebrations in Lebanon, too. This included reprinting a laudatory address of Catholicos Karekin I, the highest figure of the Armenian church in Lebanon.[3] The paper seems to have wanted to keep up the conversation about Soviet Armenia's relationship to Armenians in Lebanon. *Ararad*, along with many figures in the community, continued to investigate the role of the Soviet Republic.

A last issue that implicitly demonstrates Lebanese Armenian newspapers' continued engagement with Lebanon were the recurrent textual translations from Arabic newspaper accounts. Often, newspapers used such texts to mark a political stance without having to do so themselves, directly and explicitly, thus avoiding attracting undue attention to the Armenian community in Lebanon's bifurcated, tense political scene. A case in point was *Aztag*'s use of Arabic texts to mark its opposition to Lebanon's merger with Syria, a political move proposed by some in the two countries in the mid-1940s (as well as before, and after). The Dashnak Party paper carried the latest Arabic news, translated into Armenian, reflecting one side of this debate: Lebanese nationalists' opposition to Lebanon's incorporation into Greater Syria. Under the headline 'Lebanon Rejects the Greater Syria Plan', it reported that Lebanon's Minister of Foreign Affairs, Hamid Franjieh, had stated in the Egyptian *al-Muqattam* newspaper that 'If the Greater Syria plan was not abandoned, he would pursue the matter on behalf of Lebanon in the Arab League'.[4] He went on to state, *Aztag* relayed to its readership, that 'Lebanon not only unequivocally rejects a union of Greater Syria, but also refuses to have such a change imposed upon the country. If such an amendment is made, Lebanon will exercise its right to consider all options'.[5] *Aztag* also relayed the editorial message of the nationalist and satirical Egyptian *al-Ithnayn* periodical, describing it as 'offering judgment on the Greater Syria project', and disclosed that King Abdallah of Transjordan supported the idea.[6] Directly after offering this last bit of information, presumably to draw attention to the project's support amongst non-Lebanese, thereby suggesting it did not serve the national interests of Lebanon, *Aztag* reiterated its own opinion – once again by quoting an Arabic newspaper. Referring to *al-Ithnayn*, it stated: 'Just as we do not want to live in Palestine, which would infringe upon the wishes of the populace, we cannot concede for an independent Lebanon under the tutelage state that the people do not support'.[7]

Aztag also used *al-Muqattam* and *al-Ithnayn* to reinforce the legitimacy of the Arab League.[8] Both papers mentioned that if the Greater Syria project continued, the only recourse left to Lebanese nationalist politicians was to seek the assistance of the Arab League. Effectively, Lebanese nationalists, *Aztag* and the Dashnak Party each sought to identify and preserve the authority of the Arab League as an effective arbitrator amongst newly emerging states in the region – although an imperialist power, Britain, had played a key role in creating the league. The last sentence that *Aztag* relayed from *al-Ithnayn* stated 'The paper also warned no one should attempt to interfere with the Arab League'.[9] One should note that *Aztag*'s engagement, in the form of translations, helped to involve the Armenian community in the political debates regarding Lebanon's present and immediate future, although it did so cautiously. The newspaper and the Dashnak Party leaders were invested in what the future Lebanese state should look like and how it would be associated with Syria. This interest was not academic. It reflected that the Dashnak Party was Lebanon's leading Armenian political organisation – and thus had much to lose should things go 'wrong'. Specifically, a union with Syria, or with Palestine for that matter, would have scrambled Lebanon's political map and increased the Armenian population; the Dashnaks may have lost some power. Besides, other populations categorised as 'official' communities by mandatory powers, including the Alawites and Druze, may have also increased their numbers, possibly also leading to lower representation rates for Armenians as a whole.

Armenian Newspapers' General Coverage of Lebanon: 'It' as well as 'Us'

This section uses a number of newspaper accounts to document the complexly changing relationship – and growing overlap – between Lebanon's Armenians and the Lebanese polity. On 17 March, 1944, the right-wing *Aztag Weekly* ran an editorial entitled 'The Arab Awakening'.[10] It supported the independence of Syria, Lebanon, Iraq, Egypt and Palestine, without addressing the Arab League or the Greater Syria project. At the same time, it accepted the French and British conventional imperialist claim that their presence in the region was aimed at aiding and guiding eventual independence (a claim it would show understanding for all the way up to 1946). While the article discussed the developments of Arab self-governance, it did so to explain how related changes would affect the region's Armenians. In this sense, *Aztag Weekly* considered the Armenians as a population separate from the Arabs, reassuring the former that they would continue to live in harmony and have a 'place' in the independent countries.[11] But there was another side to that coin. *Aztag Weekly* insisted that 'the 250,000 Armenians living in Lebanon, Syria, Iraq, Palestine and Egypt have integrated economically and socially into the political lives of these countries'. 'Most', it emphasised, 'are citizens and therefore subject to the benefits of their evolutionary developments'.[12]

The Armenians definitely had a role to play in these independent states, then. It is not merely that they would and should benefit from those states' new-found sovereignty. Rather, they should assume more active roles in the construction of these state's independence. The editorial continued, 'The fashioning of independence, which becomes more tangible by the day, and gains further legitimacy within the diplomatic domain, must be matched by our own physique and form'.[13] And yet, it was unclear whose physique and form the paper was referring to: Armenians? Lebanese? Both – and if yes, in which sort of integrated form? In the very next sentence, it seems it is the former. The sentence 'We saw how the Arab nationalist movement developed, overcame difficulties, and doggedly sought complete independence', is clearly spoken as an observer of Arab nationalism, rather than as an active participant.[14] And even when *Aztag Weekly* expresses awe at the resolve of the nationalist actors, it often remains an arms-length away. But to give the screw another turn, the editors then again followed up with sentences such as 'The Armenian masses, impregnated with national consciousness and love for the homeland, happily transferred these sentiments to Lebanon's and Syria's independence struggles and political ascent'.[15] In sum, *Aztag Weekly* seemed to suggest that such a transfer of nationalist identification was possible, but that it was fluid and not unidirectional. It certainly did not mean, simply, the dissolution of Armenian identity. Put differently, *Aztag Weekly* called on Lebanon's Armenians to view the coming independence of Lebanon and of its neighbours as a historical fact and fate that would lead to positive developments for the Armenian populations living there, as well. While it spoke in the past tense, it clearly referenced the present: 'Armenians made the plight of Arab independence and the establishment of the state their own. This happened because along with these independent governments came the security of the Armenian civilisation and its advancement'.[16] Given that the independence of Lebanon and Syria was inevitable, *Aztag Weekly* went to lengths to applaud the reality of independence while guiding the Armenian population to understand the coming reality in a specific way. Hence, the editorial concluded that '[T]he Arab World in the Near East has already begun the principal steps in the process of independence, and the wheel of history cannot be reversed. The Armenian nation will work and labour with the Arab nation in deep cognisance'.[17]

Just as *Aztag* negotiated conflicting constructions of belonging and illustrated struggles for power, it also celebrated milestones for the burgeoning Lebanese state. When, two years after Lebanon's de jure independence in November 1945, President Beshara al-Khoury visited the predominantly Armenian town of Anjar, in the Bikaa Valley about 60 kilometres to the east of Beirut, *Aztag* reported on this visit on its front page, along with the commemoration of Lebanon's independence.[18] In Beirut, Lebanon's Independence Day was celebrated with great splendour, in which *Aztag* also rejoiced.[19] It recounted the day's events that took place throughout the city, including a military parade, with crowds gathered to watch and pay their respects.[20] A large stage was erected upon which a number of guests sat along with cabinet ministers and President Khoury who proudly raised the flag and saluted the officers.[21] Emil Lahoud presided over the service, announcing that the 'public' had decided to bestow upon the president the national medal, because he sacrificed his own independence for that of the nation.[22] While *Aztag* did not offer any commentary, it avidly followed discussions of the early days of the Lebanese state. This formed part of a broader effort to transmit Lebanon's political developments and programmes to the Armenian population. This move naturally helped to incorporate the readership into the Lebanese nation, as the readership was informed and educated daily on the construction of the state.

The right-wing *Aztag* was not the only Armenian paper interested in Lebanese affairs and, in this case, in the Independence Day. On 23 November, 1945, the left-leaning *Ararad* also congratulated Lebanon for the freedom it had gained de jure two years ago. In an article entitled 'Lebanon's Big Day',

Figure 1.1 President Bechara Khoury in Anjar. From top: President of the Republic Bechara Khoury, Prime Minister Sami Solh, Minister of Health Jamil Talhouk at the back entrance of the tunnel; The president speaks eloquently; Ms Zaparian presents a bouquet of flowers to the president. *Aztag*, 24 November, 1945.

occupying much of the newspaper's front page that day, it reminded its readers of how 'much blood and tears had been spilt' in the name of that cause.[23] It also noted that Lebanese celebrated this day regardless of confession, community, or class.[24] At the same time, the *Ararad* editors deemed it necessary to embark on a campaign to demonstrate how and why Armenians should also partake in the celebration. At the article's start, *Ararad* spoke about Lebanon and the Lebanese as if the paper was speaking to one segment of a population about another. But in the second paragraph, the editors made a shift. Now they included Armenians within the 'Lebanese', using the pronoun 'our' when describing how Lebanon nurtured their physiques and filled their wells of despair with renewed hope.[25] But here, as well, a certain distance remained. *Ararad* asked its readers to show appreciation for Lebanon, reminding them of what that country had done for the Armenian people after the genocide.

The papers also covered international events related to Lebanon's path to full independence. When *Aztag Weekly* covered the establishment of the United Nations on 23 June 1944, it was as Lebanese citizens *and* as part of their Armenian populations that this newspaper celebrated the presence of Lebanon and Syria as founding members.[26] At the same time also here, the paper paid particular attention to Armenians as a group that also still saw itself as somehow separate. *Aztag* talked about how the establishment of the United Nations required Great Britain, France, the United States and the USSR to recognise the rights of Armenians living in member countries, most notably Lebanon, Syria and Iraq. The membership of these three countries, together with their 250,000 Armenians, *Aztag* explained, guaranteed the stability of civil and state life. This stability, in turn, would benefit both the Armenians and their 'Arab brethren'.[27]

The Knotty Question of Imperialism

This position revealed that even at the close of the French presence in the Middle East, Lebanon's Armenians continued to have feelings for that colonial power: of being in debt, having an affinity towards it, needing and/or depending on it. After all, France had not simply executed a few symbolic rescue missions of Armenians out of Turkey during the World War I genocide, but had also used Armenians' initially rather despondent, powerless state to try to recruit as many as possible of them for its colonial cause during the Mandate years.[28] Under French occupation, Armenians of Cilicia had allied with French.[29] This was the case even in the wake of weak responses by French forces against Turkish agitation in the area.[30] The encouragment, facilitation of and success of Armenian inhabitants returning to Cilicia along with an insufficient number of French forces present and a general political instability, ultimately proved untenable.[31] The French relinquished claims over Cilicia in favor of consolidating its power over Syria and Lebanon and its mandatory governments in Lebanon and Syria were simultaneously presented with the responsibilty for creating Armenian settlements in both countries.[32] And yet, to take distance from France, to imagine life without a French protective umbrella, was yet another piece in the larger puzzle of Lebanese Armenians' political recalibration in the mid-1940s: one that by necessity further complicated how Armenians reshaped their relationship in and vis-à-vis Lebanon and its independence in the making.[33]

Thus, *Aztag* avidly followed the slow French disengagement from Lebanon and Syria. On the front page of its issue of 15 December, 1945, the newspaper declared that 'England and France settle on Lebanon and Syria issues', announcing that these two European powers would begin to withdraw their forces before long.[34] This, the paper underlined, would eventually guarantee the independence of both Syria and Lebanon.[35] While certainly supportive of the French withdrawal and the self-determination of both countries – *Aztag* had already expressed its disproval of a Syria–Lebanon union through the reportage of the Arabic language newspapers, as noted above – the Dashnak paper thus also talked in an indebted tone to the French and English governments. 'It must be stressed that that the conversations amongst parties were very genuine and very amicable', it stated. 'Just as France aided and secured the blossoming of Lebanon and Syria, England did the same. This point demonstrates that Syria and Lebanon will favourably accept the British and French pledged agreement'.[36] In this manner *Aztag* hinted at its opinion on France's and Britain's future relationship with Lebanon and Syria. While it could not – and at this point perhaps did not – want to disapprove of the final departure of French troops from the region, it shared its vision of the relationship Lebanon should in the future have with its former occupying power. It is also interesting that *Aztag* included Great Britain when talking of the preparations invested into Lebanon and Syria: it played a very active role in those two countries 'only' from 1941, when it occupied them. In sum, *Aztag* wished for an independent Lebanon and Syria to maintain friendly relationships with both imperial powers. It did not share the more radical tones of other, Armenian and non-Armenian press outlets that despised European colonialism.[37] Still, and importantly, it did so tactfully, seeking to avoid confronting those with a more nationalist agenda.

Syria as 'It' as well as 'Us:' A Case Study

In April 1944, the annual athletic games for Armenians were organised in Aleppo between athletic chapters from Beirut and Zahle from Lebanon, and Damascus, Aleppo, Jarabulus and Der Zor in Syria.[38] Armenian newspapers dedicated enormous space to this event, imbuing it with tremendous symbolic importance. *Aztag Weekly* described the rumours and fears among Armenian participants that the weather would not be ideal; described the actual weather; detailed the exact running time and distance achieved of each and every individual match and competition; and named the teams it thought would win. Descriptions were incredibly lyrical. 'The struggle began at precisely four o'clock. And if we admit that the outcome would be surprising for many, the same level of astonishment can only be matched (or can perhaps only intensify) by the beginning of the truly beautiful Aleppo–Beirut competition'.[39] Covering the games in detail, *Aztag Weekly* reporters also drew attention to the fact that although it was the 18th annual Armenian General Athletic Union and Scouts] (HMEM) games, it was the first time that Armenian athletes had participated in tennis, basketball, volleyball and ping pong.[40] This demonstrated the development and progress of both the games and the Armenian athletes. They also noted with pride that athletes from Lebanon and Syria had travelled 400–600 kilometres to attend the games even during the holiday weekend of Easter. All regions of Syria and Lebanon were present, they added, including Arab Pounar, Damascus, Der Zor, Qamishli, Jarablous, Latakia, Aleppo, Zahle, Bourj Hamoud, Tripoli, Beirut and Nor Gyugh.[41]

To *Aztag Weekly*, then, this expansive assertion of athletic prowess mirrored and encapsulated the successful nation-building of both Armenian athletics and of Lebanon and Syria. In 'The Fountain of Strength', the Dashnak paper indeed lionised the games as a role model for the Armenian nation.

'The HMEM games of the Middle East chapters just concluded and a stirring wave continues to fill the Armenians hearts from Beirut to Damascus and Aleppo, Zahle to Jarablous, and wherever our people are found'.[42] The newspaper also specifically noted what athletic competitions accomplished for the Armenian inhabitants of the region. 'We are indebted to them. HMEM established these games at the beginning of the community. This celebration of resurrection is clearly full of youth and abundant life'. *Aztag Weekly* did not explain the confusing and conflicting conception and rebirth imageries. It did, however, link them to the extension of citizenship for the Armenians of Lebanon and Syria. It did so even though a community of Armenians had lived in Lebanon since the seventeenth century, although the largest, genocide-related, influx had begun in 1915 and HMEM had been active in Lebanon and elsewhere in the Middle East before 1926. For *Aztag Weekly*, in a sense, then, the Armenian nation could complete its rebirth only if granted full Lebanese citizenship and if given full recognition by the state.

In addition to linking the acquisition of Lebanese citizenship with athletic success and nation (re)building, *Aztag Weekly* posited Lebanon as *the* locus of and for the rebirth of the Armenian nation. It was through life and activities in Lebanon that the Armenian nation was reviving, rising from the ashes of the generation that had survived the trauma of the genocide. If Lebanon provided the space for this renaissance, it simultaneously constructed it. It was Lebanon that recreated the Armenian nation that *Aztag Weekly* was so proud of publicising. 'Nothing is as invigorating as seeing close to a thousand Armenian scouts parade upon this land of refuge, upon this foreign land. It is difficult for Armenians to watch that scene without feeling tears of joy fall from our once burning eyelids. Gathered from the desert, like a blossoming miracle, the traumatised generation marches: far from the homeland, yes, and yet also as a manifestation of our phoenix-like revival'.[43]

The marching of these young athletes also needs to be further expanded upon. While the athletic training and competition is consistent with other nation-building measures at the time, the Armenian press styled them as an army. This point was doubly crucial given that Armenians lacked their own independent state. '[The experience of watching] the army of our small boys march resurrects the Armenian soul with the warm breath of spirituality and self-awareness', *Aztar Weekly* asserted.[44] This army had a goal. *Aztag* was explicit: 'These games not only connect us to the past of our great civilisation, but they also secure us the respect and status in these foreign countries that we find ourselves'.[45] This demonstrated that the Armenian population – or at least the editors of *Aztag Weekly*, i.e. the Dashnak Party – felt that (continuing) to build (up) their nation was a necessity. Becoming Lebanese did not cancel out the need to train a new generation in athletic competition and perhaps in more vigorous types of combat. In this regard, then, Lebanon was a truly ambiguous place. It was a place of refuge and a foreign land but also the site of the Armenian nation's physical rebirth.

This ambiguity also showed itself at the athletes' parade. The *Aztag Weekly* reporter showed himself deeply impressed by the long parade, describing how 1,000 HMEM athletes 'marched with their heads and chests held high with pride'.[46] The procession was led by a HMEM member holding the Syrian flag, with individual HMEM chapters following in succession, each led by a member of their group holding their own flag. For *Aztag Weekly*, then, on the one side there was the perseverance of the Armenian nation manifested in the growth and spectacle of these athletic games, where different chapters competed in a plethora of sports. Yet on the other side, these Armenian games were inherently tied to and structured by their very location. It was within the national spaces of Syria and of Lebanon that Armenians vied for the nation's veneration.

Athletes did not compete only as individuals but as members of chapters, representing specific districts within Lebanon and Syria. These HMEM chapters did more than plainly indicate where its members resided. They were not just a place name. Rather, they instilled within its members an additional source of pride and an identity distinguishing one from the other. Thus, Lebanon and Syria interfaced with the very formulation of Armenian national pride not simply as generic nation-states; Syrian and Lebanese cities mattered for this process of identity reformulation, too. Armenians battled on the athletic field as members of different local chapters, and sports enthusiasts and supporters cheered on specific regional teams.

Not everything in the 1944 competition or in *Aztag Weekly*'s coverage of the event was fun and games, however. To the paper, the ongoing project to rebuild the Armenian nation was indelibly interlaced with memories of victimhood and of a tragic past. Describing the proud power of the prized athletes parading before the spectators, *Aztag Weekly* reminded its readers of another march that had occurred not so long ago: the Armenian victims of the Armenian Genocide who wandered through the Syrian Desert. *Aztag Weekly* likened those who had perished in the death marches to soldiers, invoking nationalist sentiments of heroes fallen in battle – and this although those killed were not military or paramilitary members but Ottoman Armenian civilians. Furthermore the Dashnak paper stated that '[A]t the same time, it was very emotional when those athletes and scouts stood at attention with their lowered flags, and the band played the song of mourning that reminded us all of the death marches and of all those who were martyred on the battlefield'.[47] Such statements enlisted the memory of those genocide marches. They at once relived these marches while also re-configuring their memory and their meaning through the very image of national physical strength. *Aztag Weekly* affirmed a continuity between the two times. Reversing regular birth–life–death cycles, the paper posited a movement from death march to life march, from national weakness to strength. And crucially, also in this regard the broader space within which this Armenian story of rebirth unfolded mattered greatly: it served as the necessary framework to both beautifully and terribly intimate and mirror World War I's Ottoman Syrian death marches. One single, symbolic generation later, Syria gave way to live athletic competitions.

Assertions of Armenian Contributions to the Arab Past

Aztag Weekly's effort to re-align its Armenian readership with the larger Arab population included interpretations of the past. Incidentally or not, the issue covering the HMEM games also featured an article entitled 'Arab and Armenian Friendship'.[48] It began by stating that '[T]his friendship that will begin is not new': for four centuries, an independent Arab state and Armenia had lived side by side.[49] Even when the Arab empires had swallowed Armenia, their mutual relationship had been so warm that Armenians had willingly fought with Arab armies against Arab enemies.[50] This was not all. The article's author, identified only by a pen name, Souren, then detailed how the Armenian state had in fact benefitted the Arab Empire – how that Empire's greatness was in actual fact owed to the benefits it drew from the Armenian state. The Euphrates and Tigris rivers keep 'running due to the melting of water from our mountains'.⁵¹ Baghdad was built with gold, copper and wood brought down from Armenia.⁵² Armenia's clement and fertile weather, its water, wind and clouds, brought rainwater – the very stuff of life! – to the empire.⁵³ Arab armies had also been powerful due to Armenian arms:⁵⁴ 'the relationship between Armenians and Arabs has been so firm and strong that Armenians fought in their armies against their enemies'. ⁵⁵ Moreover, Souren affirmed that Arabs and Armenians shared a moral compass: both are known for honouring their promises and for their generosity, bravery and patriotism.⁵⁶ In sum, the Arab nation's greatness was due not least to its association with, and closeness to, Armenia.⁵⁷ More to the point, this angle on Arab history and on Armenians' posited part in its accomplishments, effectively killed two birds with one stone. One could laud Arabs while lauding Armenians at the same time; or to be more precise, by lauding the Arabs' past one explicitly lauded Armenians as well.

Aztag Weekly, then, was clearly invested in representing Arabs' presence in the daily lives of Armenians in Lebanon and Syria as quasi-natural. It was the continuation of a many-centuries-old pattern that had, on top, always benefitted both sides. At the same time, *Aztag Weekly* also triangulated here. It educated Armenians on the historic Armenian presence and greatness outside of the region, *beyond* the world of the Arabs. It made sure to mention that the situation changed for both Armenians and Arabs – but in different ways – when Seljuk tribes arrived from the east. Armenians shared a deep history with their Arab neighbours – but this issue did not detract from, or undo, the specificities of Armenian history and trauma.

The afore-noted pattern – that Arabs' interests could also be to Armenians' benefit – also showed in how *Aztag Weekly* covered current matters. Besides cases mentioned above, another instance pertained to the international consecration of the states of Lebanon and Syria and to specific repercussions in the region itself. At the end of an editorial celebrating the benefits of the United Nations, *Aztag* insisted that the time was now ripe for Syria to press for its land claims in Sanjak against Turkey and in the border areas near Aleppo and the Jazira area. It then went on to explain how this would benefit that region's Armenians and the larger Armenian cause as well. Armenians benefitted from Syrian claims and positions against Turkey, which, *Aztag Weekly* argued, was therefore their shared enemy. This in effect reinforced and paralleled the paper's claim that Arabs had historically lived in peace with Armenians. Both had been harmed by the arrival of Seljuk and Ottoman tribes in the region. Both had also been victims of the injustices of the Ottoman Empire, and were seeking to gain compensation from modern Turkey.[58]

Lebanese and Syrian Politicians as both 'Ours' and 'Theirs'

Armenian newspapers presented Lebanese and Syrian politicians to their readers in a way that mirrored their complex reconfiguration of Lebanon and Syria: indelibly interlaced with Armenian life while also separate from it.

A case in point was the twenty-fifth anniversary of the establishment of the ASSR, on 2 December, 1945. This was 'an unprecedented day for the Armenians of Beirut' in the eyes of the leftist Hnchak *Ararad* – which then proceeded to use the rank and position of the non-Armenians in attendance to reinforce its viewpoint.[59] On the one hand, the paper continuously stressed the Lebanese-ness of Prime Minister Sami Bey Sulh and of other governmental dignitaries and parliamentarians, including the famous Sa'ib Salam, positing a difference between the Armenians present and their 'honoured guests'.[60] But on the other hand, to *Ararad*, those dignitaries sanctioned and justified celebrating the ASSR's birthday. More important still, the Armenian presence in Lebanon had added an important component to Lebanese politics, then: celebrating something Soviet, if only for merely a portion of the Lebanese population. Thus, *Ararad* took note not only of Armenian leaders like the catholicos, who gave a key speech that day, but also of the final person to speak that night: Prime Minister Sulh. It was a 'privilege to have him present, having left the comforts of the plush Lebanese forests to honour those gathered with his presence', *Ararad* gushed.[61] There was not sarcasm here, but rather real pride at his presence, proving that Armenians were full members of the Lebanese polity. There was an interesting linguistic twist and component to this emerging reality. As the prime minister had the last word – he articulated his 'unending satisfaction with the Armenian people and congratulated Soviet Armenia for its ascent to greatness' – he in effect sanctioned all that had been said before him, but did so without understanding any of it, for it had been in Armenian.[62]

Sulh's pronouncements illustrated something else. The statements of early post-colonial leaders like the Lebanese prime minister persuaded the Armenian community that its future and life was not in danger after France's departure, in the post-colonial situation. The Armenian press was extremely sensitive in this regard. It picked up signs and signals even from far away to help reassure its readers and the community at large, people for whom the traumatic memory of the genocide – of their (Ottoman) state turning against them and trying to eradicate them – was ever present.

It was not a fluke, then, that Beirut's Armenian papers covered a set of pronouncements that the Syrian Prime Minister Faris al-Khouri made during his visit to California in summer 1945. Armenians in this US state were invested in demonstrating that they, which is to say their co-nationals in Syria, would become loyal citizens of an independent, post-colonial Syria now that that country was emerging from under the French tutelage – and proceeded to invite the prime minister. Al-Khouri replied in the positive, and delivered a speech honouring Armenians deeply. 'We are unbelievably happy with the Armenians' in Syria, *Aztag* quoted him as telling his audience – 'for they teach Arabic in their schools, they are hardworking, and they have decided to participate in, and contribute to, Syria's national life and politics *beyond* the Armenian realm'.[63] The Prime Minister then proceeded to historicise the Armenian presence in Syria.[64] And crucially, he took care to connect the community to the establishment of Syrian citizenship. At the same time, he phrased his praise in a peculiar way, indicating that to him, that paragon of officialdom, Armenians' presence was as complex, as simultaneously 'in/side' and 'out/side', as it was to the Armenians themselves. While expressing Syrian contentment with the Armenians living in their midst and as one of them, his statement that 'Armenians have long lived on our lands' also posited a Syrian nativeness that did not include Armenians.[65] While many Armenians arrived in Syria during (the horrific circumstances of) World War I, *before* the foundation of a Syrian state and while they had an equal claim to Syrian citizenship, they still were not quite on par with other Syrians. Finally, what made al-Khouri's Armenian California visit even more interesting was how this news was circulated. This was a case not only of Syrian citizenship being (re)-articulated thousands of kilometres away from Syria itself – a case of the transnational articulations of nationalism. But also, the news was re-fed not so much directly to Syria, but via the Armenian newspapers of *Beirut*, the place whose Armenian press dominated the Arab East's Armenian political and journalistic landscape.

Back in Lebanon, leading politicians met with Armenians in the mid-1940s. And here, as well, the press paid much attention and delivered coverage that highlighted the complexities of Armenians' life as Lebanon, like Syria, transitioned from late colonialism to a post-colonial nation-state. A good example was the official meeting, in October 1945, between the Cilician catholicos and Lebanese President Beshara al-Khoury.[66] Dissecting that encounter in detail, *Aztag* started by noting that the catholicos visited the Lebanese president at his summer house in Aley and that they warmly greeted each other – and then immediately veered into a long note regarding a banquet that had been held at the catholicosate in Antelias in honour of President Khoury and Lebanese parliamentarians. This move proved and illustrated a de facto reciprocity between the two sides: this was an encounter between equals, *Aztag* seemed to be saying. In addition to the catholicos, Armenian bishops and archbishops as well as two Armenian members of parliament had been in attendance at that banquet. The banquet had been incredibly successful, *Aztag* assured its readers; the catholicos had taken care to thank the Lebanese people, government and president for offering their friendship to the Armenian people.[67] Filled with Armenian leaders and dignitaries as it was, this event consolidated the power of the catholicos as the highest representative of Lebanon's Armenians: *he* expressed, and hence represented, an entire population's gratitude. More important for our purpose, the catholicos' expression of gratitude in effect created two separate categories of people: here the Lebanese who had generously offered their friendship, there the Armenians who enthusiastically accepted that friendship. This representation of course reflected a hierarchical, bifurcated view of Lebanese citizenship. Armenians' own representatives showcased them as recent citizens. The Lebanese president reinforced the catholicos' words – but also gave them a twist, and in effect posited the existence of a unified Lebanese body politics. 'The president responded [to the catholicos]', *Aztag* continued, 'what the Armenians have felt in Lebanon is due to their rights as citizens'.[68] But then, in yet another turn, he posited a difference: 'Armenians, through their hard work and diligence became worthy of *our* full rights'.[69] Such declarations can be read as a veiled threat or at least a word of caution. Armenians are equal citizens *because* they are hardworking and advance Lebanon – which implicitly meant that things may have been different would Armenians not have been deemed industrious.

A similar case concerned President Khoury's afore-noted visit to the Armenian-majority town of Anjar.[70] *Aztag* printed the contents of his speech in full, after describing to the reader how he was met with prolonged applause when mounting the tribune. President Khoury began by addressing those present as his 'children'.[71] After accepting this post as the Armenian population's father, he then went on to declare, 'You must know that we do not make a distinction between Armenian citizens and other Lebanese. You are no longer a migrant or an immigrant, but authentic Lebanese, with the same rights and obligations as other Lebanese'.[72] This assertion, although – or perhaps exactly *because* – it asserted a lack of difference, in effect also posited a difference between the Armenian citizen and the 'other Lebanese', certainly regarding the past but as an echo also in the present. While this may have caused tensions, these were not relayed to *Aztag*'s readership. Perhaps that was due to President Khoury's respectful sentiment woven through his speech. 'We are thankful for the Lebanese Armenian people who serve this country in prosperity and forward its cause'.[73] Still, and again, the use of 'we' implied a difference between the audience members and another, majority population. In addition, it is the president who defines what constitutes success and prosperity for the country. Even when he thanked the two Armenian members of parliament 'who honestly and faithfully served and continue to serve Lebanon and its independence', President Khoury's very words – 'serving' – indicated there were subtle differences between those members of parliament.[74] And finally, President Khoury ended his speech by heading off any possible interpretation of his words as meaning disrespect: he raised his glass for a toast to the health of the Armenian people.[75]

The Multiple Roles of Arabic

Words and language indeed formed an important dimension in the complex renegotiation of Armenians' belonging in and to early post-colonial Lebanon and Syria. In the afore-noted twenty-fifth anniversary of the creation of the ASSR, for instance, language played a fascinating role. During this event's celebrations, in Beirut, some Armenians recited poems in Arabic.

This signalled accommodation with, respect for, and a linkage to the non-Armenian but Arabic-speaking Lebanese dignitaries attending this function. And more simply, fundamentally and crucially, it proved by example that Armenians – not long ago recent immigrants – had learned their new country's language, that they were able to communicate in it with non-Armenian speaking Lebanese; in short, that they were linguistically integrating into Lebanese society. At the same time, it implicitly also showed that Lebanese Armenians, unlike non-Armenian ones, were able to access both languages and national spaces.

Khoury's Anjar visit serves as a perhaps even more remarkable example of the importance of language.[76] Before his address, a series of other speakers had their turn. The first was the prelate of the Armenian Catholic patriarchate of Cilicia, Bedros Batanian. He spoke in Arabic.[77] The very fact that *Aztag* felt the need to offer this detail suggests that it was uncommon for an Armenian religious figure to communicate with an audience in Arabic. After all, it never mentioned the languages used by other speakers on other occasions, Armenian or non-Armenian. In addition, it suggests that the action of the prelate was for more than the benefit of the president. After all, the president had attended Armenian community functions before, and most if not all of these services were held in Armenian, with the exception of someone speaking from the Lebanese government in an official capacity. And because Arabic-speaking Lebanese would not be able to read *Aztag*, the added detail of mentioning the use of Arabic was directed at the paper's Armenian readers. The paper, using the Armenian Catholic church as its intermediary, was letting the Armenian readers know that knowing Arabic was a necessity – certainly now that the French were departing and Lebanon was becoming a fully-independent country.

But the use of Arabic as the form of communication to both the Lebanese president and to those Armenians in the audience in Anjar was not a one-dimensional message. While Archbishop Batanian, other Armenian church authorities and *Aztag* told Armenians that knowing Arabic had become a necessity, they also affirmed differences from non-Armenian compatriots. *Aztag* reported that the Archbishop thanked the president for his gracious visit to this 'Armenian village' and officiated the opening of a turbine.[78] Claiming Anjar as Armenian simultaneously differentiated Armenians from non-Armenians and did so from within the national space of Lebanon. While couched in an Arabic speech thanking the president, this gratitude was concurrently a type of offensive, as it claimed a village within Lebanon as Armenian, and did so directly to the president of the country. One could not claim that the archbishop had done so to gain favor within Armenian circles alone, because it was not uttered in the language Armenians would have understood. In fact, most in attendance may not have understood what the archbishop was saying at all, suggesting that the claim was done for the audience of non-Armenians in attendance, most notably the Lebanese president. While not a Maronite, it is interesting that it was a fellow Catholic who made this claim to the president.[79] That it was then repeated, this time in Armenian, for the Armenian readership affirmed how both *Aztag* and the Armenian Catholic church constructed the village: as a specifically Armenian space.

The complexity of the archbishop's use of Arabic – in his case, to call Anjar 'Armenian' – was also manifest in the subsequent speakers' words. The representative of the people of Anjar, Ms Arshalouys Chaparian, read a poem in Arabic with the very aim of expressing how Armenians feel grateful, faithful and thankful to the Lebanese.[80] By talking in *Arabic* about *appreciation*, she also somewhat paradoxically reiterated a difference between two populations: one, the Armenian, thanking another, the Lebanese. But the reading of a poem in *Arabic* also at the very same time demonstrated a respect for – and a willingness to learn if not master – that language and evinced the desire to communicate directly with the non-Armenian population.

Another bridge – one other than, but expressed in, language – concerned religious imagery. The representative of the catholicos, Archbishop Artavasd employed religious imagery to symbolise the primacy of the Lebanese president over the Armenian people.[81] Using religion mitigated any affront that a non-Armenian audience, including the Lebanese president, could have felt when the archbishop called Anjar 'Armenian'. Through the retelling of the biblical story of Jesus raising the daughter of Jairus from the dead, Archbishop Artavasd compared her resurrection with the revival of the Armenian community.[82] And, just as the Armenian community replaced Jairus' daughter in the story, President Khoury in a sense functioned like the son of God: he facilitated resurrection. Of course, the president could not have received a greater honour. The archbishop's nationalist–religious retelling of a biblical story did not simply flatter the president, then, by describing him as a modern-day Jesus. It also in effect placed the Armenian community under the president's wings and mercy, reinforcing the president's own projected image as the father of Armenians. The archbishop ended his speech by talking about how hardworking the Armenian people were in this 'peaceful and happy country [of Lebanon]' 'thanks to the goodness and care that emanated from the country's [Lebanon's] government and people'.[83] This served a dual purpose. It praised the Armenian community while situating their success by being among Lebanese, indeed almost making it dependent on living with them and as part of them. Both mattered; they were intertwined; and (only?) together they could be successful – a similarity, here, to the afore-noted views of Armenians' role in the past Arab empire.

Finally, we should note that not only Armenians but also Arabic-speakers thought language mattered. A good example here is the afore-noted meeting between Syrian Prime Minister Faris al-Khouri and Armenians in California. When specifying what made Armenians such upright citizens, remember, he did not only call Armenians 'a hardworking people'. He also – and this clearly mattered to this Syrian Arab nationalist and his broad constituency at home, in Syria – commended Armenians for the fact that 'at their [Armenian] schools they give special attention to the Arabic language, and hence the mutually beneficial relationship only becomes tighter'.[84] Prime Minister Khouri identified Arabic language proficiency as an important hallmark of being a real, honourable Syrian citizen. Related and as a consequence thereof, he emphasised that non-Arab Syrian citizens like the Armenians had to connect to Arab Syrian issues, whatever they may be. 'The presence of Armenian members of parliament [in the Syrian parliament] not only serves as an expression of Armenian national life. It also demonstrates the Armenian people's concern for their adopted country [of Syria], for its success'.[85] According to Prime Minister Khouri, then, Armenian parliamentarians experienced a dual national responsibility: speaking Arabic, they were able to promote Armenian national life and at the same time aid in Syrian national issues.

Spatial Ambiguities

Unsurprisingly, the complexities of Armenians' position in Lebanon had a spatial dimension. We have come across a first example already: that of Anjar, called an Armenian town in an Arabic address to Lebanon's president. This section focuses on another, more crucial issue: the question of the place of the ASSR in the collective imaginary of Lebanon's Armenians.

Leftist Armenian papers played a major role in relaying and highlighting the role of the Soviet Union in promoting Armenian nationalist claims.[86] In an article entitled 'The Armenian People Have Appealed Again to Stalin', *Ararad* related how a member of the Communist Party of the ASSR, one Sahag Garabedian, took to write to the 'Great Leader' Joseph Stalin.[87] The letter, *Ararad* explained, began by thanking the Soviet regime for Armenia's past 25 years of success and happiness. It then moved to matters that were 'heavier in content'.[88] Garabedian recalled how much blood had been spilt in World War II, and reminded Stalin that Armenians from both the ASSR and from the diaspora has engaged in battles with the enemy; 42,500 had been awarded medals in combat, and 100 martyrs had been posthumously awarded the Hero of the USSR medal.[89] Garabedian ended by expressing the Armenian people's endless gratitude to Stalin and, according to *Ararad*, 'eloquently' asked the Soviet government to end the imperialist governments' injustice and dishonour towards the Armenians.[90]

By publishing this article – and on its front page at that – *Ararad* demonstrated the importance of the USSR and its role in ensuring the survival of the Armenian nation. It also made clear that the ASSR was to be considered the Armenian homeland. It was here that the USSR would 'correct' years of injustice – an injustice that, while centred on Turkey and its Ottoman predecessor state, was now, for leftist Armenians, perpetuated and aided and abetted by the imperialist powers of Great Britain, France and the United States. In this sense, the USSR was much more than simply the ultimate sovereign and protector of the ASSR. Rather, it was the ally of all Armenians, everywhere – including Lebanon and Syria, of course. But if the USSR, and Stalin as its father figure, functioned as the linkage between the ASSR and the Armenian community worldwide, this relationship was not, so *Ararad* stipulated, unidirectional. Garabedian, it related, had insisted that the USSR also depended on ASSR. Armenia and its determined men and women were 'the impenetrable fortress at the southern border' of the Soviet Union.[91] Not quite unlike the afore-mentioned Souren, who had lionised Armenia's contribution to the Arab Empire in days past, so Garabedian insisted that Armenia played a critical strategic role for the Soviet Union as a whole. Moscow depended on Yerevan; a super power relied on the impregnability of its southern republic.

Two days after it covered Garabedian's letter to Stalin, *Ararad* dedicated the entirety of its front page to the anniversary of the establishment of the Soviet Republic of Armenia.[92] As an ode to the republic, it placed four photos on its front page: on the upper left hand side, a picture of the 'immortal' Vladimir Lenin, on the upper right, a picture of Stalin, in the bottom left, A. Miasnikyan, the 'Builder' of the Transcaucasian Socialist Federative Soviet Republic (TSFSR) and in the bottom right, Matsak Papyan, the current president of the ASSR.[93] The middle of the page was adorned by the insignia of the Soviet Republic: Mount Ararad basking under rays emanating from the communist hammer and sickle (see Figure 1.2).[94]

Under Lenin's and Stalin's photos, *Ararad* reproduced quotations by them about Armenians, issued in the first days of the establishment of the Soviet Republic in 1920.[95] Lenin's words were taken from his *Proletariat Issues in Our Federation*; Stalin's were excerpts from a speech on 18 December, 1920. Translated into Armenian (neither Lenin nor Stalin spoke the language), *Ararad* reproduced Lenin's words in the Eastern dialect of that language, and did not paraphrase it into Western Armenian, the dialect of its readership.[96] This is peculiar as the paper contextualised Sahag Garabedian's letter to Stalin for its readership in Western Armenian. Printing and therefore bringing Eastern Armenian to a Lebanese Armenian paper was a peculiar decision to make as most if not all its readers could not easily understand that dialect. *Ararad* here may therefore have been writing with the opinion of Soviet Armenian authorities in the back of their mind.

Ararad's quotations also affirmed the Soviet Union's commitment to the Armenian people more generally, not merely to those in the then newly established Soviet Republic. Lenin was quoted as stating that the 'Russian government defended Armenian self-determination in Turkish-Armenia and is committed to the return of the migrated Armenians to Turkish-Armenia.

Figure 1.2 Front page of *Ararad* commemorating the ASSR. 'Oghjoyn Khorhrdayin Hayastani Kʻsanēhing Ameay Hobelyanin' [Long Live Soviet Armenia on its 25th Anniversary], *Ararad*, 30 November, 1945, 1.

The People's Committee will explicitly demand this of the Turkish government'.[97] While *Ararad* may have reprinted these words in Eastern Armenian to demonstrate its dedication to the Soviet Republic, it also worked to demonstrate to those Armenians in Lebanon and Syria that the founders of the USSR were committed not simply to its own Armenian Soviet Republic but also to larger Armenian issues relevant to the Armenian diaspora as a whole. The invocation of the Soviet Union's support of Armenians' territorial claims against Turkey played a particularly crucial role here.

In relating the Soviet leaders' words against Turkey and against Lebanon's Western allies, *Ararad* suggested that Lebanon was not really a home for Armenians. Indeed for political as much as historical–territorial reasons, it could not be, and it certainly was not *the* home. It could not be more than a temporary resting-spot. Only the ASSR could be, indeed *was*, that home – again for historical–territorial as well as political reasons, i.e. Soviet support. Related in the Western Armenian dialect of the readership, Stalin's words were clear. 'The Armenian nation had been relegated to starvation and pending annihilation. Everyone had tricked Armenia and it preserved itself through the Soviet Union. It is only the Soviet Union that gave Armenia peace. Let all know that the "Armenian Question", which led to slaughter for no reason was solved only through its Sovietisation'.[98] Stalin's words were principally directed against Moscow's key Cold War political rivals, the United States and Britain, and also France. But they could be read as being directed also at Lebanon, which continued to enjoy a warm relationship with its wartime occupier, Great Britain, and with the United States.

Interestingly, *Ararad* did not provide excerpts from the two Armenian figures it placed on the front page, Miasnikyan and Papyan. It was as if their words did not matter, or that they did not need to establish these figures as advocating for Armenian interests. But *Ararad* did, as a matter of course, advertise the celebration of the establishment of Soviet Armenia in Beirut on 2 December, 1945.[99] The ad boasted that both Syrian and Lebanese government representatives would be present. So would Catholicos Karekin, the highest figure of the Armenian Orthodox church in those two countries. And there would be coinciding commemorations in Damascus, Aleppo, Zahle and elsewhere. Lebanon and Syria, as well as the Armenian church were not pro-Soviet, *Ararad* knew and seemed to say – but the reality of a (however

Soviet) republic just for Armenians was so powerful that they had to doff their hats to it, still.

Leftist Armenians, including *Ararad*, were not the only ones who broached the broad question of Armenia in the Middle East's Armenian press centred in Lebanon. The anti-Communist, nationalist Dashnak Party and its affiliated newspaper *Aztag* did so as well. From late 1945, it covered the movement of repatriation to the ASSR, which will be at the centre of the next chapter. On the same date, it announced that the Echmiadzin See had requested the return of Armenian lands from Turkey.[100] The latter seemed more crucial for *Aztag*, and in that issue, it was indeed physically placed above the announcement of the repatriation movement.[101] The greater importance given to the Echmiadzin See's territorial demands could have been a result of the Dashnak Party's concern towards the Soviet Union's good relations with its rival political parties. For example, the Armenian National Council of the Americas (ANCA) had sent a memorandum to the San Francisco Conference as the representatives of 'all the Armenians civic, social, cultural and religious institutions in the United States, except a small fascist faction known as the Tashnags [Dashnaks]' strongly supporting Soviet and Soviet Armenian claims over 'Armenian Provinces of Turkey'.[102] In addition, the Armenian General Benevolent Union (AGBU), an organisation with a primarily North American and European membership base ideologically aligned with the Ramgavar Party, contributed financial aid to Soviet Armenia.[103] With the Echmiadzin See calling for the annexation of Kars and Ardahan to Soviet Armenia, that See, along with the USSR and Soviet Armenia, nurtured claims of legitimacy, authority and national loyalty over Armenians outside of its jurisdiction, challenging the self-image of the Dashnak Party in Lebanon and its imaginations of defending the Armenian nation.[104] With the abrogation of the Soviet–Turkish Treaty of Neutrality and Friendship in May 1945, the Dashnak Party's Armenian politcal rivals in Lebanon seemed poised to flaunt the triumph of their ideological partner, the USSR.

And yet even at this juncture, *Aztag* did not identify the repatriation destination as 'Armenia'.[105] While it used the word 'repatriate' to describe the movement of Armenians worldwide, it also used the word 'immigrate', rather than 'return' and went on to explicitly state that those concerned would do so to the *USSR*, failing to mention Armenia at all.[106] By failing to name the repatriation destination as Armenia, *Aztag* communicated its deep ambivalence about the project's politics and relationship to its own nationalist goals. What seemed to be more paramount was the Dashnaks' demand of Turkey to return Armenian lands. A worldwide move to the USSR was clearly much less important, if not ideologically problematic. Last but not least, while *Aztag* used the word 'repatriation', it referred to the move of Armenians as an 'issue'. It never imagined or described it as the righting of a historical wrong.[107]

Moreover, in the week following its 'soft' coverage of the onset of the repatriation movement, *Aztag* dropped the issue altogether while continuing to cover the territorial requests and protests levelled at Turkey. Under the headline 'The People of Armenia Demand the Historical Rights of the Armenian People', the Dashnak paper reported demonstrations in cities in Armenia and other parts of the Caucasus.[108] *Aztag* quoted the press release of TASS, the Soviet press agency: 'The Soviet Armenian syndicates along with the cultural and *kolkhoz* organisations held mass demonstrations in major Armenian cities demanding the unification of the Armenian states currently under Turkish occupation with Soviet Armenia'. It printed the entirety of 'th[is] urgent important news'.[109]

Aztag's decision to cover these demonstrations was not all that surprising. Mass demonstrations in the Soviet Union were rare, especially in Soviet Armenia. While surely encouraged by the Soviet Union in a claim against the Turkish Republic for its own political gains, the topic also united diasporic Armenians with those in the Soviet Union. Accordingly, the Soviet Union was keen on supporting these demonstrations as they would elevate its status amongst diasporic Armenians as the protector of the Armenian nation. This was especially necessary in the context of repatriation, as its success was dependent upon large numbers of Armenians willing to move to the Soviet Union regardless of whether they were living in non-communist countries and were active nationalists and capitalists alike. The official press release reflected these potential concerns: 'The people of Armenia connect their voices with those Armenians living in the Diaspora, just as they do with the Armenian National Council of the Americas (ANCA), whose demands are the same'.[110]

The decision of *Aztag* to publicise these demonstrations and the Soviet

Union's support of their demands is surprising and unsurprising alike. The Dashnak Party and its media outlet, *Aztag*, fashioned themselves as strident nationalists, consistently reminding their followers and readers of the Armenians' tragic history and of the Dashnaks' own unwavering commitment to seeking justice and retribution for the Armenian nation. In this way, *Aztag* had no choice but to cover these demonstrations. If they were so dedicated to retribution, how could they not support another power – especially one as mighty as the USSR – that mirrored their own claim? *Aztag* de facto and implicitly conceded here that it did not have a monopoly over the 'Armenian cause'. In this instance, it chose to not compete with the USSR for the title of the most legitimate defender of the Armenian cause. At the same time, this coverage also made it easier for it to not do so here, at the very onset of the repatriation movement, choosing instead to demonstrate another shared cause with the USSR.

By offering a complete translation of the TASS announcement, *Aztag* also in effect related the Soviet Union's self-identification as a super power protector of the oppressed and as the creator and protector of a homeland for the Armenian people. *Aztag* furthermore advertised Soviet military might when it included, in its TASS translation, how the Soviet Armenian military paraded in the streets of Yerevan and how the celebrated *Taman* division participated in the parade, as well.[111] Last but not least, *Aztag* mentioned that the demonstrations occurred in 'Tiflis, Baku, and other cities in the Caucasus, where large numbers of Armenians live' – all under Soviet control.[112]

Aztag may have published the TASS announcement because Beirut's Dashnaks may have felt that they could not ignore the goings on in the ASSR and the USSR and decided it best to publicise and support them. In fact, the Dashnak Party could claim to be the real pioneer of these claims for the 'return' of these lands – albeit not to Soviet Armenia, but to the Armenian nation – years before the related demonstrations in the USSR. And it could also be said that the Dashnak Party was aware that it could not match the might and power of the Soviet Union and accordingly supported the Soviets when its actions aligned with the party. In this way, the Dashnaks could even make the claim that they defended the rights of the Armenian nation regardless of political affiliation or persuasion, presenting itself as a truly inclusive Armenian party in Lebanon.

Nevertheless, it was of course the leftists among Lebanon's Armenians, and the Hnchak daily, *Ararad*, that truly stood on the Soviet side. This showed also in that newspaper's coverage of the Beirut commemoration of the ASSR's 25th birthday. All speakers at the event, *Ararad* took care to note, evoked not simply that date but also the continued progress of Armenia – always referred to as 'the homeland' – and the ongoing development in all aspects of its life for the past 25 years.[113] The USSR, the speakers maintained, was behind all of this, guiding it all.[114] They also likened Soviet efforts in the Armenian homeland to the rebuilding of war-torn Germany.[115] Finally, all of the speakers wished Soviet Armenia a shining future, and expressed their hope that it would succeed in expanding to cover all of historical Armenia and in seeing the return of all Armenians from their diasporic places.[116]

The Conservative Cilician See's Support of the Communist ASSR

Aztag's de facto, though situational, contingent embrace of specific events in the Soviet Union knew a fascinating parallel: the conservative Armenian church in Lebanon, the Cilician See. At the 25th anniversary of the ASSR's foundation, Catholicos Karekin, of that See, gave a laudatory speech in which he closed by articulating his supreme hope: 'when the entirety of the Armenian people are finally gathered on the homeland's soil, Armenians will have an even greater opportunity to showcase their talents and to serve both mankind and its civilisation'.[117] Before returning to his seat, *Ararad* reported, he offered his respects to 'Lenin the Great', the Russian people and the people of the sister Soviet Republics.[118] He was met by unending applause.[119] While other speakers expressed similar wishes that evening, the embrace by the catholicos greatly enhanced their validity and expanded their purchase. The catholicos was the highest Armenian religious figure not only in Lebanon, but also, for a majority of Armenians living in the Middle East. Historically, his authority was parallel to the highest religious body in Armenia. When the catholicos in Lebanon expressed his admiration for Lenin, thanked the USSR for its support, or identified Soviet Armenia as the homeland, he thus automatically set an example for his followers anywhere around the world. And he inspired others to follow in his footsteps: similar odes were made by Armenians living in Greece, Iran, Lebanon and Syria, among other countries. Citizens of a myriad of countries were told they could, and even should, respect the Soviet Union, if this was needed to ensure the Armenian nation's future.

That the conservative Catholicos Karekin furnished the headline at an event that de facto celebrated the Sovietisation of the Armenian Republic signalled that the leadership of the Armenian Orthodox church approved of that event.[120] Perhaps as importantly, certainly from the institutional perspective of the Cilician See, it also signalled a basic acceptance of the structure of the religious establishment in the USSR generally and in the ASSR specifically. The year 1945 saw the start of a slight reprieve in Stalin's attacks against religious institutions in the USSR. Among other measures, Stalin allowed Kevork VI to become the catholicos of the Echmiadzin See in Armenia, after that position had been left vacant for seven years. This appointment was a doubly serious change given preceding confiscations of Armenian church properties and the death of Kevork VI's predecessor, Catholicos Khoren (Muradpekyan) during Stalin's Great Purge.[121] Catholicos Karekin's presence in the Beiruti celebration thus in a sense also reflected a recognition of a change in Soviet policy towards Armenian churches, even if the church in question was the Echmiadzin rather than the Cilician See.

At this event, the speakers, organisers, and covering newspaper all focused on a message aimed specifically towards Armenians. The Arabic-speaking Lebanese governmental officials who were present did not understand the language of the ceremony, Armenian. They were a captive audience. They did not understand when the catholicos of Lebanon declared that 'Armenians can only grow by supporting the foundations of Soviet Armenia'.[122] He also went on to stress the longevity of the Armenian people and their contribution to 'world civilisation'.[123] He placed Armenia, the Armenian people and their history and legacy far beyond the contemporary political organisation of the nation-state. Put differently, the catholicos in effect placed a segment of the Lebanese citizenship beyond the limits of the republic – and this in front of senior members of its government. Armenia's contribution to civilisation was ageless and classic, Karekin insisted – that is, it went far beyond the modern history of Lebanon (and of course of the Soviet Union, whose support for Armenia he had just praised). Yes, it was small in population and size. But, the catholicos reminded the audience, it had always produced the world's highest skilled and most sought-after artisans. Armenian architects and architecture were renowned not only in the present day, but also during the apex of Western Civilisation in Greece and Rome.[124] He also reasserted the secondary stature of Lebanon, emphasising Soviet Armenia as the homeland.[125]

The content of the catholicos' address also demonstrated how he (felt compelled to) reconfigure(d) the relationship between his congregations and the ASSR. After all, the Soviet Union had just announced that repatriation would go ahead, effectively calling on, and laying a claim to, members of Karekin's congregation, encouraging them to move permanently to the USSR. With this move, the population under the care of the catholicos in Lebanon would automatically decrease, and his power would accordingly decline. This was a problem, of course – but it emanated from the fulfillment of an ideological trope so central to Armenians that the catholicos, like the anti-communist Dashnak *Aztag*, could hardly voice open opposition. In a sense, then, the catholicos' support was inevitable, void of any real alternative. It is interesting and telling, then, that the beginning of Catholicos Karekin's address struck a defensive tone. As if replying to somebody hypothetically accusing him of showering the ASSR with too much attention, he stated right at the beginning that '[O]ur parental love and gratitude for our supreme motherland is not excessive'.[126] But he also insisted that the motherland was not only for those living there: members of his congregation also played a role in its maintenance, then – not only and simply the Soviet Union. Here, in a sense, his speech came full circle: from giving in to the inevitable and lauding the Soviet support for the ASSR, to a claim that he and his community and others beyond the USSR and ASSR had also played a role in its continued success.

Conclusion

Rather than being seen as evidence of the formation of an enclave 'within' (read: separate) from Lebanon, the Armenian establishment of civil organisations and vibrant press demonstrate additional articulations and manoeuverings of Lebanese citizenship in the early years of independence. At the same time, the often-contentious debates in the press reveal the intra-Armenian struggles for power. These arguments situated Armenian belonging in Lebanon, even as the subjects and ideological questions of conflict were both transnational and/or foreign. As these discussions in the Armenian press both continue and adapt to new issues facing Armenian inhabitants, Lebanon begins to be Armenianised, just as Armenians become ensconced as locals.

Notes

1. It is not only in Lebanon that one can discern the changing views of place and their relationship with the state amongst its Armenian inhabitants. Ekmekçioğlu analyses the refashioning of belonging in Istanbul (and to a lesser extent the Ottoman provinces) during and immediately after the Armenian Genocide. She likewise examines how self-identification was then recalibrated with the victory of Kemalist forces and the establishment of the Turkish Republic. Ekmekçioğlu, *Recovering Armenia*, 2. Suciyan likewise focuses on how Armenians responded, internalised, and countered the 'denialist habitus of Turkey', Suciyan, *The Armenians in Modern Turkey*, 30. In so doing, both authors offer additional examples of studies that demonstrate how inhabitants change, engage, perform identity in changing political, economic and social environments. Nevertheless, there is an added tension in these works, related to Armenian Genocide historiography and the Turkish state's policy of denial: the ongoing debate about whether Armenians in Istanbul can be regarded as a diaspora; or whether the 'homeland' remained a homeland in the wake of Genocide; the response to either of which positions one within an additional discourse of the 'institutionalization of denial'. Suciyan, *The Armenians in Modern Turkey*, 26–31. See also Melissa Bilal, 'Longing for Home at Home: The Armenians of Istanbul', in *Diaspora and Memory: Figures of Displacement in Contemporary Literature, Arts and Politics*, eds Marie-Aude Baronian, Stephan Besser and Yolande Jansen (Amsterdam: Brill | Rodopi, 2007), 62, and Ekmekçioğlu, *Recovering Armenia*, 18.
2. Suciyan, *The Armenians in Modern Turkey*, 127.
3. 'Libanani, Surioy ew Kibrosi Hawatats'eal Hay Zhoghovurdin' [To Lebanon's, Syria's and Cyprus' Faithful Armenian People], *Ararad* (Beirut, Lebanon), 29 December, 1945, 1.
4. 'Libanan Kĕ Merzhĕ Metsn Surioy Tsragirĕ' [Lebanon Rejects the Greater Syria Plan], *Aztag* (Beirut, Lebanon), 28 November 1945, 1. For more on the history of the *al-Muqattam* newspaper and its pro-British stance, see Abbas Kelidar, 'The Political Press in Egypt 1888–1914', in *Contemporary Egypt: Through Egyptian Eyes: Essays in Honour of P. J. Vatikiotis*, ed. Charles Tripp (New York: Routledge, 1993), 5–18.

5. 'Libanan Kĕ Merzhē Metsn Surioy Tsragirĕ' [Lebanon Rejects the Greater Syria Plan], *Aztag*, 28 November, 1945, 1.
6. Ibid. For more on the periodical *al-Ithnayan*, see Walter Ambrust, 'History in Arab Media Studies, A Speculative Cultural History', in *Arab Cultural Studies: Mapping the Field*, ed. Tarik Sabry (New York: I. B. Tauris, 2012), 44 and Roberta L. Dougherty, 'Badi'a Masabni, Artiste and Modernist: The Egyptian Print Media's Carnival of National Identity', in *Mass Mediations: New Approaches to Popular Culture in the Middle East and Beyond*, ed. Walter Ambrust (Berkeley: University of California Press, 2000), 243–68.
7. 'Libanan Kĕ Merzhē', 1.
8. This is particularly interesting as both press outlets represented opposing political platforms, *al-Muqattam* decidedly being pro-British, and *al-Ithnayn* often accusing the British of meddling. Kelidar, 'The Political Press in Egypt', 5; and Dougherty, 'Badi'a Masabni', 262.
9. 'Libanan Kĕ Merzhē', 1.
10. 'Arabakan Zart'onk'ĕ' [The Arab Awakening], *Aztag Weekly* (Beirut, Lebanon), 17 March, 1944, 1.
11. Ibid.
12. Ibid.
13. Ibid.
14. Ibid.
15. Ibid.
16. Ibid.
17. Ibid.
18. 'Libanani Ankakhut'ean Tonĕ' [Lebanon's Independence Holiday], *Aztag*, 24 November, 1945, 1.
19. Ibid.
20. Ibid.
21. Ibid.
22. Ibid.
23. 'Libanani Mets Ōrĕ' [Lebanon's Big Day], *Ararad*, 23 November, 1945, 1.
24. Ibid.
25. Ibid.
26. *Aztag Weekly*, 23 June, 1944, 1; and 'Libanani Chanach'umĕ Khorhdain Miut'ean Koghmē' [The United Nations' Recognition of Lebanon], *Aztag Weekly*, 11 August, 1944, 1.

27. 'Libanani Chanach'umĕ Khorhdain Miut'ean Koghmē' [The United Nations' Recognition of Lebanon], *Aztag Weekly*, 11 August, 1944, 1.
28. For more on the short-lived French rule in Cilicia, see Garabet K. Moumdjian, 'Cilicia Under French Administration: Armenian Aspirations, Turkish Resistance, and French Strategems', in *Armenian Cilicia*, ed. Richard Hovannisian and Simon Payaslian (Costa Mesa: Mazda, 2008), 457–89. On the Légion d'Orient, or Armenian Legion, the roughly 6,000 Armenian troops fighting in the Levant and later Cilicia on behalf of the French, see Richard G. Hovannisian, 'The Postwar Contest for Cilicia and the "Marash Affair"', in *Armenian Cilicia*, 495–518 and Vahé Tachjian, 'The Cilician Armenians and French Polity, 1919–1921', in *Armenian Cilicia*, eds Richard Hovannisian and Simon Payaslian (Costa Mesa: Mazda, 2008), 539–55.
29. Vahé Tachjian, 'The Cilician Armenians and French Polity', 541.
30. Moumdjian, 'Cilicia Under French Administration', 463.
31. Tachjian, 'The Cilician Armenians and French Polity', 542–43.
32. Ibid., 547.
33. On the hasty withdrawal of the French and its consequences for the repatriated Cilician Armenians, see Hovannisian, 'The Postwar Contest', 495–518. On the strategies and failings of French and British policies in repatriating Armenians to Cilicia see Tachjian, 'The Cilician Armenians and French Polity', 539–55; Vahé Tachjian, 'L'établissement définitif des réfugiés arméniens au Liban dans les années 1920 et 1930', in *Armenians of Lebanon: From Past Princesses and Refugees to Present-Day Community*, ed. Aïda Boudjikanian (Beirut: Haigazian University Press, 2009), 59–94; and Vahé Tachjian, 'Des camps de réfugiés aux quartiers urbains: processus et enjeux', in *Les Arméniens 1917–1939: La quête d'un refuge*, eds Raymond Kévorkian, Levon Nordiguian, and Vahé Tachjian (Paris: Réunion des musées nationaux, 2007), 113–45. On the ceding of the Sanjak Province to Turkey and the resettlement of most of its Armenian inhabitants in Lebanon see Keith David Wattenpaugh, 'Armenians, Alawites, and the Alexandretta Crisis (1937–1939)', in *Armenian Communities of the Northeastern Mediterranean: Musa Dagh–Dört-Yol–Kessab*, ed. Richard G. Hovannisian, (Costa Mesa: Mazda, 2016), 193–206; and Vahram Shemmassian, 'The Settlement of Musa Dagh Armenians in Anjar, Lebanon 1939–1940', in *Armenians of Lebanon (II) Proceedings of the Conference (14–16 May 2014)*, ed. Antranik Dakessian (Beirut: Haigazian University Press, 2017), 129–54.
34. 'Anglia ew Fransa Hamadzainets'an Surioy ew Libanani Harts'erun Shurj'

[England and France settle on Lebanon and Syria Issues], *Aztag*, 15 December, 1945, 1.
35. Ibid.
36. Ibid.
37. Ibid. *Ararad* and *Zartonk* would have definitely taken on a more anti-imperialist tone.
38. 'HMĚM Halēpi Mēj 18rd Mijmasnachiwghats'in Mrts'umnerě' [HMEM in Aleppo: 18th Interregional Games], *Aztag Weekly*, 21 April, 1944, 1, 3. Armenian university students of middle and upper classes first established sports teams and athletic tournaments in the late nineteenth century in Istanbul. In 1918, the alumni of these clubs, trumpeting the European-style sports training that they had received in Europe, launched the Armenian General Union of Body Culture (known by the Armenian acronym HMEM). In Mandate Syria and Lebanon, Armenians correspondingly established HMEM chapters. In addition to athletic games and tournaments, HMEM was also a popular scouting organisation. Since its inception, the organisation touted the athletic Armenian body, tagging it to rebirth and modernity. It should be noted that HMEM had stressed these principles already during the genocide and maintained them afterwards, pointing to a continuity that demonstrated that the notion of resurgence was not predicated on loss or trauma. For example, on the occasion of the first football championship matches between the various Armenian clubs in Istanbul in 1911, the editors of the athletic journal *Marmnamarz* stated: 'We have begun the road to rebirth, and we must not stop. These athletic competitions are the first victories of the rebirth of our youth's power'. 'Nawasardean Khagherě' [The Navasardyan Games], *Marmnamarz* (Istanbul), 8 April, 1911, 1. In Beirut almost 35 years later, the editor of *Aztag* similarly wrote of 'our beautiful victory, our new rebirth', when referencing 'our athletic and cultural programmes – our scouts and our athletes'. 'HMĚMi Metz Ěntanik'ě' [HMEM's Large Family], *Aztag Weekly*, 4 April, 1947, 1. For more on the history of the HMEM and its importance in the region see Nerses Apeghia Pakhdigian, *Hratarakut'iwn HMĚM-i Surwoy, Libanani, ew Hordanani Shrjanayin Varch'ut'ean Hushamatean 1918–1958* [A Publication of the HMEM Regional Governing Board of Syria, Lebanon, and Jordan: A Registry 1918–1958] (Beirut: n.p., 1958).
39. 'HMĚM Halēpi Mēj', 1, 3.
40. Ibid.
41. Ibid.

42. Ibid.
43. Ibid.
44. Ibid.
45. Ibid.
46. Ibid.
47. Ibid., 8.
48. 'Hay ew Arab Barekamut'iwnĕ' [Arab and Armenian Friendship], *Aztag Weekly*, 21 April, 1944, 2.
49. Ibid.
50. Ibid.
51. Ibid.
52. Ibid.
53. Ibid.
54. Ibid.
55. Ibid.
56. Ibid.
57. This is in marked contrast to past perceptions of Arabs by Armenian elites, suggesting an interesting 're-write' of the past. Vahé Tachjian discusses how most Armenian depictions of Arabs by the Ottoman (Turkish and non-Turkish) elite were rife with Orientalist notions, and described Arabs as backwards and uncivilized. In addition, he profiles two accounts of Armenian survivors of the Genocide who expressed their gratitude towards Arab inhabitants in the region (though they do not comment on their status of civilisation). Tachjian, *Daily Life in the Abyss: Genocide Diaries, 1915–1918* (New York: Berghahn Books, 2017), 58–66.
58. 'Libanani Chanach'umĕ Khorhdain Miut'ean Koghmē' [The United Nations' Recognition of Lebanon], *Aztag Weekly*, 11 August, 1944, 1.
59. 'Soviēt' Hayastani 25 Ameaki Tōnakatarut'iwnĕ Pēyrut'i Mēj' [The 25th Anniversary Celebration of Soviet Armenia in Beirut], *Ararad*, 5 December, 1945, 1.
60. Ibid.
61. Ibid.
62. Ibid.
63. 'Ch'ap'azants' Goh Enk' Hayerēn K'ĕsē Suriow Varch'apetĕ' [We Are Extremely Content with Armenians Says the Prime Minister of Syria], *Aztag*, 4 August, 1945, 1.
64. Ibid.

65. Ibid.
66. 'Kat'oghikosarani Chashkeroyt'ĕ' [The Catholicosate's Banquet], *Aztag*, 14 October, 1945, 1.
67. Ibid.
68. Ibid.
69. Ibid. (Emphasis added.)
70. 'Hanrayin Nakhagahĕ Aynchari Mēj' [The People's President in Anjar], *Aztag*, 17 November, 1945, 1, 2.
71. 'My children, I offer my warm thanks for this heartfelt, sincere, and enthusiastic welcome', in Ibid.
72. Ibid.
73. Ibid.
74. Ibid.
75. Ibid.
76. Ibid.
77. Ibid. Armenians of Apostolic, Evangelical, and Catholic denominations lived in Anjar. Each denomination had their own church, which in turn, ran their own school. For more on the history of Anjar and its establishment as an 'Armenian town' see Herant Katchadourian, 'Culture and Personality: The Case of Anjar', in *Armenian Communities of the Northeastern Mediterranean*, 237–51; Shemmassian, 'The Settlement of Musa Dagh', 129–54; and Salih Zahr al-Din, *Min Jabal Musa ila Hawsh Musa – ʿAnjar: malhama armaniyya bayna al-mawt wa-l-hayat* (Beirut: Dar Hamaska'in li-l-nashr wa-l-tawziʿ, 2015).
78. 'Hanrayin Nakhagahĕ', 1, 2.
79. It is possible that Archbishop Batanian spoke in Arabic because he was better able to do so, rather than his Apostolic counterparts who were also in attendance. (It is not clear if Evangelical Armenian officials were present.) The pre-Genocide Armenian community in Lebanon was largely Catholic (Pope Benedict XIV recognised the Armenian Catholic community as a separate Patriarchate in 1742), and well-versed in Arabic. Nevertheless, Archbishop Batanian had arrived more recently from Turkey and while he clearly had mastered Arabic, he was not a member of a historic Armenian community in the country. Thus it is more likely he was also speaking to President Khuri as a fellow Catholic, a fact that would not have been lost amongst the Armenians of attendance, the readers of *Aztag*, or possibly even the president himself. For more on the Armenian Catholic community in Lebanon see Irina Papkova, 'The

Three Religions of Armenians in Lebanon', in *Armenian Christianity Today: Identity Politics and Popular Practice*, ed. Alexander Agadjanian (Burlington, VT: Ashgate, 2014), 171–96 and 'The Lebanese Armenian Church and Its Milieu', in *Armenians of Lebanon (II) Proceedings of the Conference (14–16 May 2014)*, ed. Antranik Dakessian (Beirut: Haigazian University Press, 2017), 51–62.
80. 'Hanrayin Nakhagahě Aynchari Mēj' [The People's President in Anjar], *Aztag*, 17 November, 1945, 1, 2.
81. Ibid.
82. Ibid. The story of Jairus is told in Mark 5:22–41 and Luke 8:41–56.
83. 'Hanrayin Nakhagahě Aynchari Mēj' [The People's President in Anjar], *Aztag*, 17 November, 1945, 1, 2.
84. 'Ch'ap'azants' Goh Enk' Hayerēn K'ěsē Suriow Varch'apetě' [We Are Extremely Content with Armenians Says the Prime Minister of Syria], *Aztag*, 4 August, 1945, 1.
85. Ibid.
86. Such articles coincided with Soviet territorial demands for Kars and Ardahan that were made upon Turkey at the founding conference of the United Nations in San Francisco in 1945. For more on these territorial demands, the Soviet use of Armenian nationalist sentiment to legitimise their claims over the area, how Armenians lobbied for these territories to be unified with Soviet Armenia, along with Turkish and American responses to these claims see Jamil Hasanli, *Stalin and the Turkish Crisis of the Cold War, 1945–1953* (Lanham: Rowman & Littlefield, 2011), 123–220. For more on the competition amongst Armenians amidst the San Francisco Conference see Suciyan, *The Armenians in Modern Turkey*, 143–49.
87. 'Hay Zhoghovurdě Norēn Dimets' St'alini' [The Armenian People Once Again Appealed to Stalin], *Ararad*, 28 November, 1945, 1.
88. Ibid.
89. Ibid.
90. Ibid.
91. Ibid.
92. 'Oghjoyn Khorhrdayin Hayastani K'sanēhing Ameay Hobelyanin' [Long Live Soviet Armenia on its 25th Anniversary], *Ararad*, 30 November, 1945, 1.
93. Ibid.
94. Ibid.
95. Ibid.

96. Ibid.
97. Ibid.
98. Ibid.
99. 'Hamazgayin Mets Tonagatarutʻiwn' [Pan-National Big Celebrations], *Ararad*, 30 November, 1945, 1. *Ararad* also reported on the banquet in its 5 December, 1945 issue. 'Soviēt' Hayastani 25 Ameaki Tonakatarutʻiwnĕ Pērutʻi Mēj' [Soviet Armenia's 25th Anniversary Celebrations in Beirut], *Ararad*, 5 December, 1945, 1.
100. 'Ējmiatsni Hayrapetĕ Kĕ Pahanjē Haykakan Hogheru Ktsʻumĕ' [The Catholicos of Echmiadzin Calls for the Annexation of Armenian Lands], *Aztag*, 5 December, 1945, 1.
101. 'Hayeru Pʻokhadrutʻyan Khndirĕ' [The Issue of the Armenians' Move] appears directly under 'Ējmiatsni Hayrapetĕ Kĕ Pahanjē Haykakan Hogheru Ktsʻumĕ', *Aztag*, 5 December, 1945, 1.
102. Suciyan, *The Armenians in Modern Turkey*, 143.
103. Ibid., 148. For more on the history of the relationship of the AGBU and the USSR see Vahé Tachjian, '"Repatriation": A New Chapter Studded with New Obstacles, in the History of AGBU's Cooperation in Soviet Armenia', in *The Armenian General Benevolent Union: A Hundred Years of History, 1906–2006, Volume 2*, eds Raymond H. Kévorkian and Vahé Tachjian (Cairo: AGBU Central Board, 2006), 291–309.
104. Michael Bobelian and Talin Suciyan detail how it is this dynamic that may have also prompted Turkey to pursue a closer alliance with the United States in the aftermath of World War II. Suciyan, *The Armenians in Modern Turkey*, 148–53 and Michael Bobelian, *Children of Armenia: A Forgotten Genocide and the Century-Long Struggle for Justice* (New York: Simon and Schuster, 2009), 86–106.
105. 'Hayeru Pʻokhadrutʻyan Khndirĕ' [The Issue of the Armenians' Move], *Aztag*, 5 December, 1945, 1.
106. Ibid. Emphasis mine.
107. Ibid.
108. 'Hayastani Zhoghovurdĕ Kĕ Pahanjē Hay Zhoghovurdi Patmakan Irawunkʻnerĕ' [The People of Armenia Demand the Historical Rights of the Armenian People], *Aztag*, 11 December, 1945, 1.
109. Ibid.
110. Ibid.
111. Ibid.

112. Ibid.
113. 'Soviēt' Hayastani 25 Ameaki Tonakatarut'iwně Pēyrut'i Mēj' [Soviet Armenia's 25th Anniversary Celebrations in Beirut], *Ararad*, 5 December, 1945, 1.
114. Ibid.
115. Ibid.
116. Ibid.
117. Ibid.
118. Ibid.
119. Ibid.
120. Ibid.
121. Felix Corley, 'The Armenian Orthodox Church', in *Eastern Christianity and the Cold War, 1945–91*, ed, Lucian Leuştean (London: Routledge, 2010), 190–3.
122. 'Soviēt' Hayastani 25 Ameaki Tonakatarut'iwně', 1.
123. Ibid.
124. Ibid.
125. Ibid.
126. 'Libanani, Surioy ew Kiprosi Hawatats'yal Hay Zhoghovurdin' [To Lebanon's, Syria's, and Cyprus' Faithful Armenian People], *Ararad*, 29 December, 1945, 1. The catholicos' address at the celebration in November was printed in its entirety in the 29 December, 1945 issue.

2

THE HOMELAND DEBATE, REDUX: THE POLITICAL–CULTURAL IMPACT OF THE 1946–1949 REPATRIATION TO SOVIET ARMENIA

Introduction

On 5 December, 1945, the Soviet news agency TASS announced the establishment of the Repatriation Commission, the organised drive to collect all worldwide Armenians and 'return' them to the Armenian Soviet Socialist Republic (ASSR).[1] A little less than a month later, in mid-January 1946, Soviet authorities started to circulate information that the repatriation authorities required from each potential repatriate. That circulation happened partly through leftist and communist Armenian newspapers like *Joghovourti Tzain*, printed in Beirut, which, as seen in Chapter 1, was the foremost centre of Armenian community, political and intellectual life in the Middle East. Besides data like name, date of birth, occupation and education, the Soviet authorities were also interested in more personal information: whether the repatriate had friends or acquaintances in the USSR; if yes, where; and what they did. They also asked for a detailed account of the goods that the repatriate would bring to the USSR and the work that s/he would hope to perform in the USSR.[2] In short, the ASSR, the destination of those repatriates, was already before their arrival starting to order and categorise them as citizens. The speed with which the initiative had been made reality continued apace.

The Soviet repatriation registration drive began on 1 February, 1946.[3] In Greater Beirut alone, there were ten locations, some in community centres like the one in Beirut's Zareh-Noubar centre, others in people's private homes, such as in Achrafieh or in the Nor Yozghad neighbourhood.[4] While there were other prominent repatriation centres in the Middle East, including Aleppo, Damascus and Tehran, over one-third of the more than 100,000 Armenians worldwide who repatriated to the ASSR travelled via Beirut or came from it, which made Lebanon's capital the most central origin and staging point for the repatriation initiative.[5] The repatriation ship, the *Russia*, one of the two transportation ships (the other was the *Transylvania*), arrived at the port of Beirut.[6] Repatriates from both Syria and Lebanon were housed near the area, in the Karantina quarter.[7] They remained there for two days before the departure.[8] The first caravan departed on 22 June, 1946: an event covered with great pomp and fanfare in the following days.[9] Leftist Armenian newspapers like the *Joghovourti Tzain* dedicated their entire front page to describing how the *Transylvania* sailed into the Mediterranean from port Beirut, destination: 'home'. The *Russia* and the *Transylvania* alternated transporting Armenians from Karantina to the Soviet Georgian port of Batumi, whence they boarded trains to their final destination, the capital of the ASSR, Yerevan.[10]

The story of the repatriation drive itself has been told before, by historians and in memoirs.[11] Rather than rehashing the details of the story, then, this chapter focuses on the Lebanese Armenian political–cultural understandings of repatriation. Put differently, it does not so much focus on the Lebanese and Syrian Armenian response, 'on the ground' as it were, to the Soviet initiative. Rather, it is principally interested in exploring how that initiative formed a chapter of Lebanese (and other Middle Eastern) Armenians' review, revision and renegotiation of national belonging in early post-colonial times. Thus, although, as noted, about a third of all Armenian repatriates travelled via Beirut, I also look at those who remained in Lebanon and in other countries in the Middle East.

The emerging Cold War was more than simply a backdrop to the repatriation story. Moscow's initiative made repatriation possible in the first place. It was the USSR that, on 5 December, 1945, announced the initiative to unite Armenians from around the world in the ASSR; that organised the transport of tens of thousands of Armenians to the USSR and that allowed

Figure 2.1 The first caravan departure from Beirut. The *Russia*, one of the repatriation boats. Photo courtesy of Verjine Svazlian; taken by her father, Karnik Svazlian.

them to enter the country; and that housed them in the ASSR, making them Soviet citizens. Also, the Soviet initiative was a victory vis-à-vis the USSR's rivals: at a time of peace, citizens of some countries voluntarily sold their belongings and moved to become part of the motherland of state socialism. But most importantly for this chapter, the heating-up Cold War – and the very divergent readings of, and responses to, the repatriation initiative among Lebanese Armenians – reinforced tensions between Armenian rightists and leftists. The Lebanese example shows that Armenians' response to repatriation did not simply reflect their extant political–cultural positions. Rather, repatriation sharpened those positions.

In thinking through these issues, this chapter specifically broaches three themes. First, I show how responses to repatriation echo the issues raised in Chapter 1 by helping to shed light on the changing Lebanese/Syrian/Armenian identity complex at the dawn of the post-colonial nation-state. Second, I examine how responses to repatriation included a retelling and a reconstitution of the history of the tragedy of the genocide. Three decades after the genocide, the initiative automatically triggered questions about the location and nature of the Armenian homeland. And finally, I demonstrate how repatriation added fuel to the division between Dashnaks and Armenian leftists. Before broaching these three themes, however, I outline and contextualise the Soviet initiative and sketch out the initiative's execution in Syria and Lebanon.

The Soviet Initiative

As noted above, TASS announced the establishment of an Armenian Repatriation Commission in December 1945. The respective decree, authorised by the Council of People's Commissars, one of the main executive bodies of the USSR, pledged that the USSR would take the lead in organising such a move, facilitating sea and land transport for all Armenians requesting repatriation. On the one hand, this was primarily a Soviet–Armenian initiative; and the support of the initiative by the Armenian church in the ASSR (and demands, by the church, for a return of Armenian lands now under Turkish rule to the USSR) was quasi-automatic and clearly served the Soviet state: after all, Stalin had appointed Kevork VI as new catholicos after the See had remained vacant from 1939 to 1945. But on the other hand, the initiative affected and accordingly involved a number of countries with a large concentration of Armenian residents or citizens, including the newly-established states that had formerly been part of the Ottoman Empire such as Lebanon, Syria and Egypt, and the British-administered Palestinian Mandate.[12]

And yet, of the locations in which TASS directly broadcast the repatriation announcement, only Beirut enjoyed a sizeable Armenian population. As a matter of fact, the other three, Paris, London and Ankara were at first sight curious choices. The Armenian population of London was not very substantial. That of Paris, while significantly larger, was still small compared to the large number of Armenians in Eastern Europe, in particular Romania and Bulgaria and in Greece. Even stranger, the Armenian population in Ankara was minuscule.[13] Significant Armenian populations lived, rather, in Istanbul and in the south near the Syrian border in the Hatay province.

The solution to the above puzzle has to do with the fact that the repatriation initiative, including the very act of its announcement by TASS, entailed multiple messages. The USSR was not simply pronouncing itself able and willing to organise the 'return' to the ASSR of Armenians from around the world. If that were the case, TASS would surely have issued direct announcements in cities in Greece, Romania and Bulgaria, in addition to Aleppo, Cairo, Tehran and other Middle Eastern Armenian centres. By announcing the repatriation initiative in Paris and London, Moscow also sought to assert a certain hold over some – Armenian – citizens of France and Britain. Coming less than half a year after the end of World War II and at the time when the Cold War was slowly crystallising, this step, then, was nothing less than an assertion of political power. While Washington could have also been a target for the TASS announcement, the number of Armenians living in the US capital was small. Plus, it perhaps didn't wish to speak directly to its main competitor. Instead, the USSR gunned for the United States' main European allies.

The inclusion of Ankara as one of the four broadcast centres also demonstrated the versatility of the repatriation movement: few Armenians lived there, and Armenians in Turkey and their Armenian organisations (such as they existed) did not dare to openly discuss what and where a 'homeland' other than Turkey might be.[14] And yet, the repercussions of this announcement were felt in Istanbul, Ankara and Adana almost immediately.[15] Turkish newspapers launched a campaign against Armenians, including the raid of the *Tan* publishing house in Istanbul and the use of racist and hostile language in various Turkish newspapers, including *Yeni Sabah*, *Vatan* and *Cumhuriyet*, amongst others.[16] Talin Suciyan details how the head of the Patriarchate of Istanbul paid a visit to the governor of Istanbul affirming Armenian loyalty to the state and that *Marmara*, the Armenian language daily, published an editorial in *Turkish* 'There is No Armenian in Turkey to be Instrumentalised by Foreigners'.[17] This is not surprising given that they lived in Turkey, the successor state of the very empire that had committed a genocide in World War I, and given the continued power of strong-state Turkish Republicanism. TASS included Ankara as one of its four locations from which it broadcast the repatriation initiative to indirectly send a message to the Turkish government and to Armenians living outside Turkey. As noted in the preceding chapter, just a few months prior to this the USSR had abrogated the Soviet–Turkish Treaty of Neutrality and Friendship and pressed for the regions of Kars and Ardahan at the San Francisco Conference.

Armenians worldwide, as well as those in Lebanon, had been pressing for another 'return' – not to the ASSR but to lands in Turkey that had been inhabited by Armenians before World War I. Broadcasting the ASSR repatriation initiative in Ankara also reinforced an additional Soviet message, to intimidate Turkey, while maintaining for Armenians worldwide that their home was the ASSR.

The broadcast in Beirut seemed to also have a particular goal. The USSR called the Armenians home *from* Beirut – a step imperative as Beirut was the largest Armenian population concentration outside the ASSR. (While Aleppo was also home to a sizeable Armenian population, it did not boast the same community infrastructure.) In addition, the level of formal power, including guaranteed ministerial positions and parliamentary seats, that Armenians enjoyed under the Lebanese confessional political system was unparalleled anywhere else in the world; and Armenian factions could also seek to influence larger platform by strategically allying themselves with other sects, which they often did. On top of this, Lebanon, and Beirut in particular, was a worldwide leading Armenian press and print centre. This included the fact that Armenian newspapers printed in Beirut also served the Armenians of Syria. Accordingly, Lebanon's Armenian press considered 'local' Armenian news to take place in both Syria and Lebanon; while those papers covered Syria, their priority and ideological backers were firmly part of the Lebanese, rather than Syrian, political scene; and Syrian Armenians had little power to help set the political debates occurring in the Armenian press. By having TASS make the repatriation initiative announcement in Beirut, but not in Aleppo or Damascus, Moscow effectively laid a claim to this dynamic. The USSR tackled Beirut's (and its Armenians') power head-on, trying to shift the gravitation point of Armenian life in the Middle East from Beirut to the ASSR.

Repatriation as an Element and Chapter in Lebanese/Syrian/Armenian Linkages

As other Armenian newspapers worldwide began to publicise the repatriation movement, *Joghovourti Tzain* positioned itself as a global source of news for repatriation efforts. In so doing they also identified Lebanon as a figurative centre for Armenian affairs. In the 10 January, 1946, issue, it ran an article on its front page originally printed in Tehran's *Veratsnund* (Rebirth)

Armenian daily.[18] The act of reprinting simultaneously oriented attention of its readership to Tehran and simultaneously 'back' to both *Joghovourti Tzain* and to Lebanon. Reprinting articles from various Armenian press outlets transformed *Joghovourti Tzain* as a vehicle of information about Armenian communities outside of Lebanon, and directed attention of their activities to their readership in Lebanon. As it supported and covered the global movement of Armenians to the Soviet Union, it reinforced Lebanon as a gathering source of information for Armenians.

Joghovourti Tzain followed repatriation procedures in Europe as well. On the same day it re-ran an article from Iran, it ran a short article on its front page on the arrival of French–Armenian repatriates to Yerevan. As if to both impress and comfort the Armenian readership in Lebanon, the paper detailed how Mélinée Manouchian, the widow of Misak Manouchian, who now worked for an organisation to strengthen cultural ties between the Armenian diaspora and Armenia, was also among the repatriates.[19] It even mentioned that she studies at the Yerevan university.[20] Both Manouchians would have been known to the readership, and Mélinée's decision to repatriate would have surely impressed those who still had not signed up and reinforced those who awaited the first caravan. While *Joghovourti Tzain*'s coverage of repatriation might not have been surprising, given its avid support for the movement, the gathering of information on its pages also presented both the paper and Lebanon as a centre for Armenian information. It was as if it elected itself and the party it was associated with – the Armenian Communist Party – as the spokesperson for global Armenian affairs. It tracked the movement of Armenians. That they were heading to the USSR almost was secondary. Its communication held the paper and Lebanon paramount.

On 6 March, 1946, *Joghovourti Tzain* ran a translated copy of an article from the 18 February edition of the Aleppo Arabic daily *al-Hawadith*, which covered the repatriation registrations in the city.[21] It described how orderly the registrations had been, and how repatriation officials would soon head to the Jazira region and east towards the region of the Euphrates to continue repatriation efforts there.[22] It then went on to 'take the opportunity to speak on behalf of the Syrian nation' to express their gratitude and offer respect to those registering to repatriate.[23] In particular, the article explained, it was grateful and impressed with the behaviour of those who wished to repatriate considering that their remaining time in Syria was limited.[24] According to *al-Hawadith* 'they [the repatriating Armenians] proved that they were authentic citizens to this country [of Syria] that had sincerely welcomed them and provided them with a place to live'.[25] The deployment of the discourse of citizenship demonstrated its importance to the Syrian daily. It simultaneously claimed the population while supporting their impending departure. 'We cannot stand against their first homeland, or oppose their desire to unify with their Armenian brothers'.[26]

And yet, the paper also lamented their exodus. 'After they [the repatriates] leave we will feel the absence of their excellent talents, which have played such a role in the rebirth and progress of our nation'.[27] The article was rife with a duality of messages: it celebrated their departure and their contributions to Syrian society and to the larger achievements of the Syrian nation. It wished them happiness in the first homeland and claimed friendship between the two peoples, mentioning the Armenian struggle for progress, freedom and independence.[28] While acknowledging the Syrian citizenship of the Armenian people, the newspaper also differentiated between the Armenians and the larger Syrian population. In addition, while it referenced Soviet Armenia as the 'first' or 'authentic' homeland for the Armenian population, it did not do so explicitly. It never mentioned 'Soviet Armenia' but rather consistently used 'first/authentic homeland' to represent the location. This was opposed to the treatment of Soviet Armenia within *Joghovourti Tzain* itself, which went to great lengths to stress the Soviet character of the homeland, even in an effort to undermine the memory of other locations of the Armenian home.

Joghovourti Tzain here used *al-Hawadith* to reinforce its position on repatriation. It employed the correspondent in Aleppo who had overheard encounters between registration officials and potential repatriates to delegitimise locations in the Ottoman Empire as potential loci of the Armenian homeland, and the coverage of a local Arabic newspaper to disassociate the present location of Syria and its legal link of citizenship from the potential repatriates. In so doing it also reinforced itself as the vehicle of communication and even in this case translation for the Armenian inhabitants, and transported these messages to the readership located in Lebanon. This transnational movement of information through the newspapers both reinforced its prowess as an authority to Armenian inhabitants and also directed attention to yet another international location: the homeland of the Soviet Republic of Armenia.

Covering the departure of repatriates from Damascus, *Joghovourti Tzain* mentioned the dignitaries who were present at the station to see the repatriates off: Soviet members of the repatriation committee, representatives of the Soviet Armenian government, numerous priests, the prelate of the Armenian church of Damascus and members of the local Damascus committee for repatriation.[29] The article then also noted that before the train departed the station, all those gathered, together and in unison, sang first the Syrian national anthem, followed by the anthem of the Soviet Republic, and that the excitement and applause was unparalleled.[30] Harutyun Madeian, the chairman of Damascus' repatriation committee, also thanked not only 'the Soviet Union, Great Stalin, and the Great Russian people' but also the Syrian people, 'who looked upon us like brothers', and expressed gratitude to the Syrian government and president.[31] It is indeed interesting that while Armenians were Syrian citizens, and had been so since the days of the French mandate, Madeian categorised them 'like' brothers, as opposed to brothers themselves.[32] This distinction echoed *Joghovourti Tzain*'s positioning of Syria (and Lebanon for that matter) as a temporary shelter, rather than a permanent home. This was doubly peculiar given that Syria's Armenian communists were an integral part of the country's communist party, and that in the Middle East as elsewhere, ethnic divisions were supposed to not count (too much) in communist parlance and practice.

The farewell in Damascus also echoes an issue first raised in Chapter 1: that of language. Damascus Armenians made sure to express portions of that fateful day in Arabic. Not only were both the Syrian *and* Soviet anthem sung, but also, thereafter, Boghos Bashirian spoke in Arabic about the virtue of the Syrian people, offering his sincere gratitude to them and to the Syrian government on behalf of the Armenian people.[33] To be sure, he may have made his speech in Arabic simply to ensure that his appreciation was noticed, and could be conveyed, in the local Arabic-language press. Still, the very fact that *Joghovourti Tzain* mentioned Bashirian's speech indicates that it thought coverage of this point to be necessary. But again, in doing so, it at the very same time implicitly maintained that Armenians and Syrians were two differ-

Figure 2.2 Armenians aboard the first repatriation ship holding placards in Arabic and Armenian. The Armenian sign states: 'Thank you Father Stalin / We, your children, are coming, to the homeland'. Photo courtesy of Verjine Svazlian; photo taken by her father, Karnik Svazlian.

ent groups. Armenians should be thankful for the benevolent actions of the Syrian people.

Still, even though *Joghovourti Tzain* worked to reinforce a separation between Armenians and, in this case, Syrians, its description of the emotional scene also demonstrated that the parting was not straightforward or natural. 'The departure was very emotional – for both the repatriates and for those who had gathered'.[34] While these moving expressions could be seen as testimony to the painful separation of the Armenian community in Syria, with a part repatriating, and a part remaining, it is likewise an expression of the movement of Armenians from one place to another. All those gathered had not signed up to leave. The emotion was also a manifestation of loss of belonging and being *of* Syria. Still, there were competing imageries occurring at the same moment. *Joghovourti Tzain* also described the 'long-standing applause', along with 'the waving handkerchiefs that could be seen for miles'.[35] It took about fifteen hours or so to reach Beirut, *Joghovourti Tzain* reporting that the train arrived at 6:30 am and that its passengers and belongings were transferred to the Karantina port under the guidance of Beirut's repatriation committee.[36]

Finally, departure scenes in port Beirut also reflected the intertwinement of Armenian and Lebanese identities. Once all the repatriates of the first caravan to the USSR had boarded the ship, they began to sing the Lebanese national anthem, *Joghovourti Tzain* reported.[37]

The role played by the catholicos of the Cilician See, headquartered in Antelias, near Beirut, also underlined – and added yet another layer to – the continually complex relationship between Armenians and Lebanon, even as and when some were departing. The catholicos was present during the ship's departure from port Beirut, indeed boarded it and toured it, blessing those aboard.[38] This quintessentially religious act demonstrated an intimate bond with those who were about to leave his congregations. Indeed, it suggested an approval of their act although that act was removing them from his circle – and, worse, to a country whose very ideology was non-religious if not decidedly anti-religious. But while the catholicos blessed those aboard, and while he identified the destination of the ship as 'our' homeland, he referred to its citizens as 'their' brothers, thereby differentiating Armenians in both spaces.[39] He also did not mention the ASSR or the leader of the USSR, Stalin.[40] He articulated his own understandings of Armenian attributes, presumable as the political and religious head of the Armenian community in Lebanon, and as the spiritual leader of Armenians throughout the Middle East. 'I want you to be worthy citizens in the new country in which you will live. Be hardworking and reliable, because these are the ways to show your love for your country and be ideal citizens'.[41] These words neither mentioned a final homecoming, nor were they particularly instructive for this apparent historic moment. In fact, the catholicos reclaimed those very repatriates moments before they left Lebanon for good. 'Dear ones, I do not want to hear that within the *Lebanese* repatriates there are bastards, thieves, scoundrels and wicked travellers. Just as you are model citizens here, I want you to be the same with your brothers there.[42] The catholicos continued to claim his congregants, transnationally, beyond all borders, even as he blessed their very departure. While such a transnational claim was hardly new for the Armenian church – its centres had never adhered to imperial or nation-state boundaries – catholicoi had not claimed authority over congregations within another See's jurisdiction, which is exactly what he symbolically did do here. For this catholicos, those Armenian repatriates remained symbols of, and tied to, Lebanon. As he put it, addressing the repatriates on the ship: 'continue to be grateful to this homeland that you are leaving. Remember that it was these people [the Lebanese] who welcomed you in your time of need, and soothed your suffering. Remember this homeland with gratitude'.[43]

This quest to preserve (or claim) power by both the catholicos and *Joghovourti Tzain* continued immediately following the ship's departure. *Joghovourti Tzain* published the catholicos's announcements in its entirety.[44] He acknowledged how popular repatriation was. At the same time, he also highlighted the challenge faced by Soviet Armenia in taking in hundreds of thousands of people. And he addressed many repatriate-hopefuls' difficulty to pay for the journey, stating that it was 'the familial responsibility to offer a hand'.[45] The authority such a declaration wielded was unparalleled within the Armenian community. The catholicos then said he supported the efforts of the Ramgavar Party in Lebanon and Syria to collect money. And not to be eclipsed, he offered – indeed called on – individual church congregations throughout the region to assist in fundraising.[46] While acknowledging that this was only a small gesture, his ability to recruit parishes in this way demonstrated his authority to congregations and readership alike – even to communist Armenians. Likewise, the fundraising spearheaded by the catholicos, and *Joghovourti Tzain*'s front-page coverage thereof, highlighted his role in repatriation and, more broadly, his power within the Armenian communities of the Middle East. His very encouragement to leave for a *communist* country in fact – and only seemingly contradictorily – demonstrated his *religiously-derived* power among Armenians in Lebanon and beyond in the Middle East.[47]

Repatriation and the Reconstitution of Armenian Time and Space

Repatriation organisers considered the movement to Soviet Armenia as 'a long time in the making' and connected it to a historical need and desire to 'gather the nation'.[48] They also connected the population transfer to both a correction and due process of history.[49] Newspapers, most notably the communist *Joghovourti Tzain*, consistently evoked Armenian suffering and loss and Armenian bravery. Specifically, they referenced the catastrophe of 1915 – but also highlighted that Armenian brigades had participated in the liberation of Berlin and the defeat of Hitler in 1945. The editors of *Joghovourti*

Tzain worked to link loss in World War I to their participation and therefore victory of Soviet troops in World War II. This, as if the deaths during the Ottoman massacres could be avenged and could then be connected to Armenian brigades fighting alongside their Soviet compatriots. *Joghovourti Tzain* then used these experiences to demonstrate the compulsion of the repatriation project. (Armenian) victory was connected to joining the USSR. In doing so, they also assumed that history operated linearly, connecting tragedy and the plight of one population in one location, to the participation of another, much smaller brigade in a different place. They joined them to call for yet another population – a worldwide Armenian one – to travel permanently to the Soviet Union.

The question of how repatriation fit into the larger arc of Armenian history, and most importantly into the only-too-recent chapter of the genocide, was not only broached by newspapers. Accounts from repatriation registration centres suggest that repatriates themselves were also thinking in such broad categories – and forcefully so, though in a personalised manner. *Joghovourti Tzain* covered the repatriation registration not only in Beirut but also in Aleppo, Syria. The unnamed correspondent reported that there were 21 registration centres packed with people and that sign-ups took place within a general state of euphoria. They also detailed a few overheard conversations. A woman yelled in front of the registration centre located at the Cilician school 'For 40 years I have been waiting for this day – let me be the first to register'.[50] In another office, a repatriation official, while filling out the form of a potential repatriate, and noting that they were from Kilis, asked, 'If they [Turkey] give us Kilis, would you go there, or to Soviet Armenia?'[51] The repatriate immediately answered: 'No, I have lost many people there, I will go to Armenia, that land allows for us to forget everything'.[52]

The two incidents communicate a variety of emotions and messages to the reader. The woman shouting demonstrates the high level of excitement present at these centres, but also the deep, almost visceral, desire to 'return'. She was actually fighting with her countrymen to be the first to register, as if being recorded as the 'first' to leave ensured the realisation of her dream, one that she purportedly had for the duration of her entire life. While potentially a figure of speech that should not be taken literally, her declaration of 'waiting for this day for forty years' implied this desire existed first, even while she lived in her ancestral home in the Ottoman Empire; and two, before the establishment of the USSR and by extension, the Soviet Republic of Armenia. It is meant to stress the Soviet destiny of the Armenian homeland and its location within the boundaries of the Soviet Republic at the time. These representations are dually enforced by the description of the conversation that transpired in the office inside as well. In noting that the potential repatriate hails from Kilis, the official acknowledged that the destination of the repatriates was not where they were 'from'. And instead of creating a type of tension that a return was not a literal return, the repatriate's answer severs a link to the past while reinforcing the contemporary construction of the homeland in Soviet Armenia. This conversation engaged with the past hometowns of these repatriates and the Armenian Genocide and its associated loss to explicitly emphasise that Soviet Armenia did not share that history. The inability of Soviet Armenia to compete as this type of home however was precisely the point–as it ensured that it did not mirror these places as sites of death, thus buttressing the newspaper's and the repatriation movement's imagination of the Soviet Republic exemplifying progress/life.

The correspondent also described a scene in another office of an exasperated repatriation official asking a potential repatriate, 'Brother, does a man forget the names of his children?' recounting how the man stood there for five minutes dumbfounded until his wife reminded him that his youngest daughter was called Loucine.[53] Aside from the interesting gendered roles that can be observed in this incident, in that it is, not surprisingly, the mother who remembers the names of the family members as the nurturing caretaker and it is the man who is actively registering the family, the correspondent uses this incident to convey the degree of excitement present at the centre. A father can even forget the name of their child.

One can assume that the Nor Kyugh registration centre in Aleppo catered to the lower classes of Armenians. The correspondent did not explicitly state this, but the inclusion of the local priest and method in which the woman attempted to hide the fact that she was a mother to ten children suggests that the woman hailed from a traditional and simple background.[54] And still, her presence at the centre was necessary. She conveyed that the homeland (she used the term *hayrenik* to describe Soviet Armenia) not only accepted her, but also, celebrated her.[55] This traditional woman, from an incredibly modest background, would be leaving such ignorant structures, such as the church that looked down upon her family, behind. Through this story, the correspondent thus represented the homeland as not only an accepting place, but one where traditional power structures were insignificant. The words that the woman used to describe the different locations were also telling. When she described the anger of the local priest, she did not label the place where she had been bullied as the homeland.[56] Instead she used an alternative word, *erkir*, which, while could insinuate a homeland, did not in this case. After all, she used the word, *hayrenik* or 'homeland' for Soviet Armenia, where her numerous children would be accepted and where traditional power was apparently dislocated.

In addition to accepting those who traditional power authorities would denigrate such as a woman from a modest background, the homeland welcomed older generations as well. The correspondent also described a man of 60, from Zeytun in the Ottoman Empire who was overheard telling the repatriation official: 'Register me, my son, I can still become soldier in Armenia'.[57] The detailing of this man's birthplace, similar to the repatriate from Kilis, worked to dislodge the locations of the Ottoman Empire from an imagination of the Armenian homeland. Kilis was a place of loss. Zeytun, on the other hand, was renowned for being one of the only locations in the Ottoman Empire where Armenians took to arms in an attempt to defend themselves against massacre and deportation orders. The communal memory of Zeytun was used in such a way that it simultaneously worked to disassociate Zeytun from that very communal memory of resistance. Instead, a native of Zeytun was used to convey that if a location presently needed to be defended it was the homeland, Soviet Armenia.

Addressing repatriates departing from Damascus, that city's repatriation committee chairman, Comrade Harutyun Madeian, spoke to all those Armenians gathered in the train station on the two needs that Armenians had. 'The first, was independence, the second was the end of exile',[58] he said. The first, he explained, 'had been achieved 25 years ago [with the establishment of the Armenian Soviet Republic] and the second, repatriation, had just begun'.[59] In this fashion, Madeian, like others, inscribed the ASSR's repatriation into the broader historical sweep of the Armenian people's (modern) history, turning that initiative into the reference and solution-end-point of that history. In this rendering, the ASSR had become Armenia *tout court*; and by consequence, return to the ASSR became the quasi meta-historical solution to Armenian suffering and to the Armenian question. As Madeian expressed it so pointedly when thanking 'the Soviet Union, Great Stalin, and the Great Russian people': their repatriation drive had 'ended Armenian exile'.[60] In his view of things, an entirely new chapter in the history of the Armenian people had begun.

The very process of repatriation was also represented as changing the very nature and logic of Armenian history. A *Joghovourti Tzain* correspondent in Beirut quoted a crying Lebanese Armenian woman's sentiment at seeing the hundreds of Damascus repatriates de-board the train in Lebanon's capital. 'Again, we migrate. And look at our condition. Nothing has changed in 25 years [the number of years since the establishment of the Soviet Armenian republic]. We migrate every quarter century'.[61] But this woman's lamentation was merely the counterpoint to the *Joghovourti Tzain*'s own, very different, historical interpretation. The correspondent quoted another spectator's presumed response to that woman. 'This is not a migration, sister. This is a return to the homeland. This is the end of migration. This is salvation. Clap! Clap! Clap like the others. We too will follow them soon'.[62] The correspondent then noted that his reaction was applauded by his surrounding friends, that is, that a (weak) female interpretation of repatriation had been firmly rebuffed by the overwhelming majority of those present, represented by a (strong) male voice.[63] Like that man, the newspaper was ordering the readership to clap, as it were, and told them to soon follow those repatriates. Cheer accompanied the repatriates and escorted them all the way to the port of Karantina. The correspondent stressed that 'the Armenians are a people of song and dance, contrary to their tragic experiences that have befallen them', and described the entrance to the port as a scene filled with joy.[64] Repatriation was the Armenian people's final, highest song, so to speak – and a happy one. 'This time, instead of past hopeless and tearful songs, the atmosphere reverberated happy and joyful ones of a people who claim their future'.[65] Further, these dancing and singing Armenians were met, in the port of Karantina, by Soviet Armenian representative Zaven Zarchyan who 'mixed with the people, asking how their travels thus far had been, making sure they were all comfortable'.[66] While *Joghovourti Tzain* acknowledged the difficulty of the travels, it did so only to stress that this was the Armenian people's final journey: a 'truth' evidenced by tunes of not being sad and defeated any more, but being joyful and victorious.

In this changing atmosphere, Armenians were also said to turn from victims and objects of history to moulders and subjects of their own history. A *Joghovourti Tzain* writer used the imagined presence of non-Armenian Lebanese to make this point when covering the Armenians' departure from port Beirut. The writer imagined what a non-Armenian, using the word foreigner in Armenian (*odar*), would think of the scenes of Karantina. 'After a few minutes of watching, they would confidently declare: "An ordinary scene: the parting of Armenians"'.[67] Not so, the author insisted. This was not yet another departure, but a final departure – and one that resulted in a homecoming. The writer used the imaginary *odar* to maintain an epistemological break with this departure. And he reaffirmed Armenians' agency in this departure, and the lack of agency in other seemingly similar moves. In fact, for him and for *Joghovourti Tzain* more broadly, this departure was like no other. 'Yes, Armenians separate from one another. Armenians have separated a lot from one another. But the more correct formulation is that others have separated Armenians'.[68] The writer also juxtaposed this departure caravan with those of the past, and how historically massacres of Armenians preceded the forced exodus of Armenians to the deserts 'where they were buried in the sand'.[69]

A note by *Joghovourti Tzain* about the final scenes of the first caravan's departure, by ship, from port Beirut confirms the above point. Having sung the Lebanese national anthem when the ship pulled away from the port, the song that the repatriates intoned *after* the ship had moved away from the dock was the anthem of the ASSR. *Joghovourti Tzain* spent some lines detailing exactly how the song sounded – and then described how the song affected the ship itself: as if guiding it rhythmically through the waters.[70] 'As if moving the ship, those squeezed along the railings of the deck and through the portholes of the ship opened their mouths and began to sing, slowly at first, but then steadily louder, until it became loud enough to drown out the tragic past of our history, and instead, shone the brightness of our future. That song was the anthem of the Soviet Armenian Republic'.[71] Lest the move, separation of families, or the singing of the Lebanese national anthem be seen as a lament, the author associated the singing of the Soviet Armenian national anthem to the change in the otherwise tragic course of national Armenian history.

In *Joghovourti Tzain* reporting, Soviet Armenian officials also participated in this reconstitution of history. 'From this moment onwards, you stand in your homeland, and you no longer have to fear the Ottoman tyranny',[72] they were reported to have declared – in an address broadcast by Radio Yerevan – when welcoming repatriates arriving in the ASSR. They thereby elided, deleted and repressed the thirty-odd years of life in Lebanon that repatriate adults (let alone children born after the genocide) had led, effacing the efforts by both Arabs and European powers to save their 'fellow' Armenians in the decades following World War I. In this interpretation of Armenian History with a capital H, repatriates' post-genocide life in Lebanon and Syria had been nothing more than a long pause, a break unworthy of a mention and at best a bridge between the trauma of 1915 and the redemption of 1946–1949.

Repatriation shifted thinking not only about Armenian Time, but also Space, as it were. As a matter of fact, it was even before the repatriation initiative was launched that *Joghovourti Tzain* claimed that the ASSR was the prime locus and representative for the Armenian Cause. In early 1945, for instance, it printed the transcript of a speech given by nobody other than the highest ecclesiastic figure of the Cilician See, Catholicos Karekin I in Antelias, at the occasion of the celebration of the 25th anniversary of the ASSR's establishment.[73] Having congratulated the ASSR for its achievements over the past quarter century, Catholicos Karekin proceeded to call it 'our small but precious homeland'.[74] He then gave the floor to Archbishop Rouben, who had arrived from the Soviet Republic to take part in the celebrations. The archbishop went on to speak briefly before reading a short message from Catholicos Kevork, the highest ecclesiastic figure of the Echmiadzin see, in the Soviet Republic of Armenia. The public joint appearance of the two catholicoi (albeit one present through a representative) was a new form of connecting Armenians in Lebanon, Syria and Cyprus to the ASSR and the USSR more broadly. It brought a leading Soviet Armenian figure to Lebanon, and offered him a public platform. It also placed him as equal to or at least in competition with the catholicos in Lebanon. After all, who would be the supreme ecclesiastic leader of Armenians worldwide? If Armenians moved to the Soviet Union, this question would be quickly and definitely answered. And even if they did not, his presence in Antelias, the seat of the Cilician See, challenged Catholicos Karekin's authority. Karekin indeed seemed to take the power of the ASSR into account when stating that the 'diasporic Armenian community is prepared to do its share in maintaining peace and stability in Soviet Armenia'.[75]

On 17 January, 1946, *Joghovourti Tzain* announced that the ASSR had declared the start of the repatriation.[76] It represented the initiative and organisation of the repatriation movement as a solely Armenian affair. It did not discuss the involvement of non-Armenian Soviet forces. It is unclear if the newspaper purposely represented these activities as insular, that is, as between the Soviet Armenian government and the Soviet Armenian repatriation committee. What *is* clear, however, is that by representing the movement as such, the communist newspaper depicted the ASSR as the power to have the ability to, and responsibility for, uniting Armenians from around the world. In this reading, the ASSR was – by the sheer weight of its political power as part of a sovereign state – the centre for Armenians worldwide. Armenians elsewhere, including in Lebanon, could not compete with the ASSR's abilities, that is, were a periphery relative to the ASSR, and Armenian communists abroad were the bridge between the two.

At the same time, however, *Joghovourti Tzain* also described what would occur to the homeland, to the ASSR, if repatriation were to succeed. It linked the future of the Armenian nation and homeland with that of the repatriation initiative and of the ASSR. The ASSR, it held, was like a flower ready to blossom; it would do so only, however, when the world's Armenians would migrate to it. Country and people depended on one another. To make this point, *Joghovourti Tzain* referenced 'the Armenian writer Derenik Demirchyan', who, it related, 'state that it is time for Armenia to blossom in its Armenianness'.[77]

Joghovourti Tzain also addressed other needs of the ASSR. A thought piece by the Soviet Armenian writer Avetik Isahakyan, for instance, connected the ASSR's needs to the success of repatriation.[78] 'The Armenian People', he stated, 'have always demanded the return of historical Armenia, but were only able to save and assemble Soviet Armenia . . .'[79] With repatriation, he went on to explain, Soviet Armenia was too small for the Armenians of the Diaspora. 'For this reason, and in accordance with their inalienable rights, the Armenian people demand the return of their lands from Turkey, those lands where they have lived and worked, and from which point their ancient culture proliferated'.[80] While Isahakyan did mention the Armenian's entitlement to the land, he used the repatriation movement to demonstrate the actual need for the land transfer. Indeed, as the population transfer was being engineered by Soviet authorities, Armenian intellectuals and newspaper outlets such as *Joghovourti Tzain* used their movement to demand land from Turkey to increase the size of Soviet Armenia. The movement of citizens from a variety of countries was used to justify a Soviet Armenian claim for land that would expand the size of the USSR.

On a different note, *Joghovourti Tzain* also strove to represent the USSR in general and the ASSR in particular as modern. Thus, in the selfsame issue that included the reference to Demirchyan and that talked at length about repatriation, *Joghovourti Tzain* reprinted a photo (see Figure 2.3) of a group of male and female university students from the ASSR: ten smiling individuals, five men and five women, dressed neatly and holding books and objects associated with education such as scrolls and papers.[81] Interestingly, only a simple caption without additional text accompanied the photograph.[82] It spoke for itself, *Joghovourti Tzain* seemed to be saying. One may argue that the newspaper inserted this presumably un-staged still into the newspaper as a performance of sorts for its readers. The photo exuded happiness and intelligence, camaraderie and equality. There were an equal number of men and women here, suggesting that the Soviet republic was just and modern. The books indicated erudition. Faces were beaming, and clothes and hair were in fashion, denoting modernity, success and even elegance. These, the newspaper seemed to say without having to say it, were the ASSR country-men and -women who were awaiting the repatriates. They did not seem traumatised and marked by the genocide and its memories, but happy and prosperous – something aspiring repatriates could and should be looking forward to.

A similar story was told by a two-week exhibition on the ASSR organised by the Lebanese chapter of the Friends of Soviet Armenia Association. Opened during, and clearly in support of and in preparation for, the repatriation initiative, it showcased over 600 photos of the achievements of the last 25 years of the 'supreme homeland' in the fields of 'prosperity, industry, manufacturing, science, literature, fine arts, military arts and physical activity'.[83] *Joghovourti*

Figure 2.3 'Sovet Hayastani Petakan Hamalsarani Usanoghnerēn Khumb Mě' [A Group of Soviet Armenian National University Students], *Joghovourti Tzain*, 20 January, 1946, 1.

Tzain literally ordered its readers to visit this show of the very place that they were encouraged to move to and become part of. The achievements that exhibition visitors were to witness had only been accomplished during the past 25 years, since the ASSR's establishment. Before, *Joghovourti Tzain* seemed to suggest, Armenians did not have such a life. This narrowed form of Armenian achievement and success identified the Soviet style of governance and the communist ideology as being indispensable for modernity, development and progress – a view that also subverted Lebanon as an Armenian home, asserting the ASSR as the sole homeland for Armenians worldwide.

Praise of Soviet life was easily transposed to the question of the broader advantages, beyond gaining a homeland, of repatriating to a place that formed part of the USSR. 'The diasporic Armenians are living in a momentous time', *Joghovourti Tzain* insisted. 'For Soviet citizens, that's old news. For us, however, this most hardworking–and persecuted–people, is there a greater fortune to be granted than to be protected by the Red Army? To bask in the bliss of Stalin's fatherly concern, to advance through his thoughtful leadership?'[84] *Joghovourti Tzain*'s celebration of Stalin's leadership and Armenians' forthcoming transformation into Soviet citizens was plain here. In a sense indeed, it saw becoming a Soviet citizen as the most fateful outcome of Armenians' repatriation – beside and beyond the very fact of a return home. Becoming Soviet was a monumental gift bestowed upon an industrious people and would heal past injustices. At the same time, by reminding the reader that the gift was already enjoyed by millions of Soviet citizens, *Joghovourti Tzain* in effect provided a counterpoint to its own discourse of Armenian distinction.

This fascinating, tension-filled combination of readings – return as an ethnic cause versus a (communist) universal cause; Armenians as Armenians versus Armenians as citizens of the world's purportedly most modern, most progressive country, the USSR – showed also in *Joghovourti Tzain*'s coverage of the repatriates' arrival in the USSR, and specifically in Batumi, Soviet Georgia. In early July, the newspaper reproduced an article written by the left-leaning pro-ASSR Egyptian Armenian newspaper, *Araks* (named after a river in Armenia), published in Alexandria, which recounted that scene.[85] Batumi was the first location where Georgians inserted themselves (or were inserted) into the repatriation story. Until that moment, Armenian newspapers spoke about the voyage as if Armenians were directly taken from Lebanon to Soviet Armenia. The reprinted *Araks* article noted how smoothly the trip had passed, and how once the repatriates arrived in Batumi, they were met with 'thousands of Armenians that had gathered along the dock, along with Georgians, both young and old, with many schoolchildren'.[86] The throngs of Georgians gathered at the dock were not the only Soviet ethnic group used to welcome Armenians to their new home. Along large signs draped aboard the ship's decks bearing the mottos 'Long live Soviet Armenia', 'Long live the Soviet People' and 'Long Live Father Stalin',[87] *Araks* also noted another slogan: 'Long live our Georgian and Azerbaijani brothers'.[88] And it mentioned that upon disembarkation, the Armenian repatriates were surrounded not only by Armenians but also by Georgians and Azerbaijanis, who helped them carry their belongings. Laughter, shouts, kisses and salutes filled the air.[89] This note served to allay potential fears of how interested repatriates would be greeted and treated by other Soviet citizens. The repatriates would be Soviet citizens first – although or rather precisely *because* they had returned home.

Araks also reported that the repatriates would spend a few days in Batumi before heading via railway to Yerevan.[90] Those who brought placards that showed Stalin's face led the convoy to the city and the parade of the repatriates through the centre. This spectacle played a role in the Georgian imaginary as well. This linked Georgians to the realisation of the Armenian dream and involved them in the process of constructing a national home for worldwide Armenians in Soviet Armenia. This, along with the slogan 'Long live the Georgian and Azerbaijani People' recast the historical experiences of the Armenian nation to support one imagined by the Soviet Union and Soviet Armenia. Aside from Armenians from the region of the Middle East not having an everyday familiarity with Georgians and Azerbaijanis, they may have accessed them only through national histories learned in Armenian schools in Lebanon and Syria. These stories would have surely given an alternative, and negative, experience of both peoples, as conquerors and occupiers of the very homeland they were heading towards.

While in transit in Lebanon and Syria, repatriates functioned as a virtual extension and embodiment of the homeland. Being close to them was equal to being as close as possible to the homeland. Thus, when on the morning of the arrival of the train carrying Damascus' repatriates to Beirut's port, *Joghovourti Tzain*'s correspondent arrived at Beirut's train station at 5am, an entire hour before the train was scheduled to arrive from the Syrian capital, dozens of Armenians were already there, eagerly awaiting the repatriates.[91] The correspondent wrote that he asked these spectators to wait outside the station to make it easier for the repatriation committee to process the arrivals and their belongings.[92] His entreaties were to no avail. This made him ponder: 'how can one ban the people from watching their brothers go to the homeland?'[93] And as if to answer his own question, he quoted one of those gathered: 'there is no power present in this world that can prevent our people from this eruption. They have been here for hours in an effort to satisfy their visceral longing for the homeland'.[94] Being close to the repatriates was a (temporary) relief of the desire to reunite with the homeland. In addition to supporting the repatriation initiative, and to 'wholeheartedly cheering and clapping as the train pulled into the station', those gathered at the station helped the repatriates.[95] They immediately began carrying their belongings, and headed towards Karantina.[96] 'The caravan towards Karantina's caravan [to the ship that was to transport the repatriates] was also a caravan towards the homeland–with even the children and the elderly moving at the same pace',[97] *Joghovourti Tzain*'s correspondent noted. This reading infused the description, also, of scenes in Beirut's Karantina port itself. The meaning of the homeland was apparent to any person there that day. 'For a moment', he stated, 'just being with the repatriates made one feel that they were with the homeland'.[98] The intention of this statement was to describe the realisation that this first caravan was, in fact, going home. But of course, in a sense, it also subverted its own intention: for at the same time, it suggested that Armenians did not necessarily need to be in the ASSR to feel as part of, and presumably belong to, the Armenian nation.

On a related note, repatriates were also the pioneers, as it were, of an expected wave of return to the homeland. Thus, *Joghovourti Tzain*, congratulating the Armenian nation on repatriation, stated that 'just as the first caravan moves towards the homeland, the entirety of Beirut's Armenian community moves along with it'.[99] The correspondent coupled exchanges overheard at the port with his own message to those members of the Armenian community that were staying put in Beirut and to potential non-Armenian witnesses present at the port. He confessed how both the departing and the remaining did not want to part from each other. 'They couldn't stop holding hands, couldn't stop embracing one another', and more significantly for the author, 'couldn't stop giving one another advice'.[100] But then he proceeded to recount the instructions given by a repatriate to a loved one who was remaining behind: 'Garbis, don't forget to come quickly – we're waiting for you', to which Garbis replied 'We won't be late, just keep creating homes for us – and we'll be there!'[101] This point was also reflected in the pages of *Joghovourti Tzain*, in its description of the atmosphere as the ship moved away from the dock. It juxtaposed the celebratory atmosphere aboard the ship with the feelings of those who witnessed their happiness along the dock. Aside from the lone cry that went up 'Send our greetings to the homeland!' as the caravan moved away, the masses were silent.[102] No one spoke, tears continued to fall, *Joghovourti Tzain* wrote.[103] People longingly looked at the ship that moved towards the horizon. The description of those who stayed back, sad and forlorn, reinforced the message to leave.

By the end of July 1946, as the first caravans were starting to arrive in the ASSR, *Joghovourti Tzain* started to directly compare the life of (especially poor) Armenians in Lebanon with those now residing in Soviet Armenia.[104] A

Figure 2.4 Well-wishers gathered at the port of Karantina. Photo courtesy of Verjine Svazlian; taken by her father, Karnik Svazlian.

series of pictures (Figure 2.5), all without a title, of a dense Armenian neighbourhood in Nahr, just north of Beirut, depicted the squalor and difficulty encountered by its inhabitants.[105] It showed how for 25 years, residents there had been living in shacks made of decaying pieces of wood.[106] A photo of youngsters from the neighbourhood bore the caption 'a group of downtrodden and unlucky children'.[107] Of the five photographs, the final two shared *Joghovourti Tzain*'s sense of hope and reflected its understandings of where these Armenians belonged.[108] One was entitled a 'repatriating family preparing their goods' for departure', and the final shot showed a newly constructed modern apartment building that was awaiting repatriates.[109] There were also trees in the photograph, promising air and space for recreation and fun. Soviet Armenia was the future that awaited them when they left Lebanon and Syria. It was new and clean, away from the filth they had been living in for a quarter of a century.

Figure 2.5 Comparing Lebanon to ASSR: *Joghovourti Tzain*, 28 July, 1946, 1.

Repatriation, the USSR's Greatness and the Reinforced Division Between Armenian Leftists and the Dashnaktstyun

The context of the repatriation initiative also allowed – and required – *Joghovourti Tzain* to glorify the USSR. This was both doubly important and doubly 'easy', as it were, as the USSR had just defeated, in history's most brutal and costly war ever, Nazi Germany. *Joghovourti Tzain* glorified that accomplishment both through its own and through other writers. A thought piece by Soviet Armenian writer Avetik Isahakyan in 1946 glorified the greatness of the Soviet Union and lionised how it fought Hitler's armies and defeated fascism.[110] *Joghovourti Tzain* also drove home to its readers the related fact that the ASSR's accomplishments included participation in World War II. The newspaper highlighted controversial meetings that officials from the Dashnak Party had met with Nazi officials; and juxtaposed these with the Soviet Armenian legion that, in spring 1945, had helped conquer Berlin.[111]

Celebrating the opening of the registration centres in early 1946, *Joghovourti Tzain* editor Hovhannes Aghbashian expressed his hope 'that each Armenian will work to make sure they are not left out of the repatriation caravans and will run immediately to the sign-up centres to register'.[112] Here, repatriation was a communal moral and practical duty. More than that: failure to 'join' the caravan questioned one's belonging to the 'tribe'.[113] Then he shifted gears, returning to an issue that was brought up by repatriation time and time again. He reasserted that 'evil-minded' people were working to confuse people's minds and spreading lies and rumours about repatriation, identifying members of the Dashnak Party as responsible.[114] 'Because of their years of conducting anti-Armenian activities in the diaspora', he added, they 'were barred from returning to the homeland'.[115] He added that these Dashnaks engaged in such divisive activities, trying to keep Armenians from repatriating and to infect others with their very own tragic fate: their inability to return home.[116] His description was reminiscent of the dire fate of the biblical Garden of Eden: the Dashnak Party luring Armenians away from paradise, from the ASSR, was Eve tempting Adam.

Joghovourti Tzain indeed very consistently disavowed the Armenian Dashnak Party and warned its leadership of its lies. 'All Armenians must ignore any prospective deviation—*especially those fictitious ploys of the Dashnak leadership* – whether they come from the right or the left – and must sign up to repatriate'.[117] Specifically, the communist newspaper derided *Aztag* and *Aztarar*, two newspapers adhering to the ideology of the Dashnak political party, for 'condemning' the public's excitement for repatriation.[118] Moreover, the editor of *Joghovourti Tzain* accused its rivals of acting at the behest the Turkish press.[119] In a long introduction, the editor detailed how the Turkish press had just convened a meeting that ended a few days ago. There, the editor explained, members of the Turkish press syndicate awarded certain worldwide press outlets in recognition of their contribution to promoting 'Turkish perspectives' in the press. While *Joghovourti Tzain* did not mention the specific outlets, it sarcastically stated that while it did not know if *Aztag* and *Aztarar* were present at such event (they weren't) they might as well have been.[120]

It followed such a wrathful line, it was later revealed, because it took issue with *Aztag*'s previous day's issue. *Joghovourti Tzain* explained that under the section, 'Life in the Armenian Neighbourhoods', *Aztag* had attacked the repatriation movement. Nevertheless, its purported stance did not infuriate *Joghovourti Tzain* as much as its reasoning. *Aztag* claimed repatriation to be a cover for a larger takeover of 'Armenian lands' and had stated: 'be they the Bolsheviks of Moscow or their slaves who live in Yerevan – it doesn't matter – we will not forfeit our lands'.[121] *Joghovourti Tzain* attacked *Aztag*'s position on repatriation to reinforce its own position as the source of news to its readership. It dismissed *Aztag*'s view of the USSR as a usurper of Armenian lands. And it accused *Aztag* of playing the role of a Turkish newspaper to detach the paper, its associated Dashnak ideology and its readership from a larger Armenian struggle in which it situated itself as its spokesperson.

And yet *Joghovourti Tzain* not only engaged in shaving members of the larger Armenian community in Lebanon from a whole that it itself delineated, it also took the opportunity to attack another Dashnak leaning paper as well: *Aztarar*. What's interesting about this attack is its slight geographical shift. *Joghovourti Tzain* attacked *Aztarar* for how it covered an event in Aleppo, Syria. It described *Aztarar*'s coverage of a HMEM (the acronym for the Armenian General Athletic Union and Scouts, the athletic organisation of the Dashnak Party) event, and that organiser M. Chololyan reportedly characterised the people of Soviet Armenia as slaves.¹²² For *Joghovourti Tzain*, *Aztarar*'s coverage of Choloyan's remarks was tantamount to them both acting as mouthpieces of the Turks.¹²³ It funnelled an event that reportedly took place in Syria, broadcast in a rival Armenian newspaper in Lebanon, to consolidate its position amongst Armenians in Lebanon. *Joghovourti Tzain* appropriated its own symbolism and fashioned itself into a mouthpiece for Armenians in Lebanon, but also of those beyond its borders. Through speaking against those who labelled Armenians slaves, it also articulated the agency of Armenians in Soviet Armenia. And it used the distorted images of the USSR and its relationship with its republics to attack a rival in Lebanon and claim that it bore the 'truth' for its Armenian inhabitants.

Joghovourti Tzain did not construct itself as *the* mouthpiece for the Armenian inhabitants in Lebanon and Syria solely through the coverage of repatriation or even to affairs that took place in Lebanon, where it was published. On 1 May it reported on how members of the Armenian Scholars' Organisation in Aleppo defended themselves against the 'anti-Armenian' activities of the Dashnak Party, thereby forcing this 'explicitly non-partisan organisation' to distance itself from the Armenian community centre where meetings took place.¹²⁴ It employed a moralistic tone, split between concern for the Armenian Scholars' Organisation, and firm opposition to the actions of the Dashnak Party. *Joghovourti Tzain* reported that the Armenian Scholars' Organisation had been prevented from using the local Armenian community centre as a meeting space due to the pressure exerted by 'certain members of the Dashnak Party'.¹²⁵ Without offering details of the incident, the newspaper defended the actions of the members of the scholarly organisation, who 'weren't even anti-Dashnak individuals, but rather', it contended, 'had become weary of the anti-Armenian activities of the Dashnaks, and therefore had wanted to distance themselves from the community centre'.¹²⁶ The decision of the scholarly organisation to discontinue using the community centre as a base for its meetings, *Joghovourti Tzain* explained, was a loss to the community as whole, and solely, it maintained, the fault of the anti-Armenian troublemakers.¹²⁷

The ability of the newspaper to take an incident in Aleppo and transfer it to Beirut through its coverage resulted in two additional actions: it reclassified the incident as a political confrontation between the two groups based on ideological differences, and morphed this confrontation in Aleppo into a local, and Lebanese Armenian affair. Even if the reader did not quickly identify the ideological differentiation that the newspaper implied, the way *Joghovourti Tzain* (re)constructed the affair was sufficient in transferring meaning and value to the two sides: the Armenian Scholarly organisation was merely trying to meet in the community centre and carry on its 'neutral, non-political activities' but was confronted by the anti-Armenian actions of the Dashnak Party.[128]

The reader could connect the presence of these articles to the newspaper's platform that supported repatriation and was able to identify and speak out against the anti-Armenian actions of the Dashnak Party, and thereby uphold itself as the defender of the Armenian people. Given that editorials critical of the Dashnak Party became more and more commonplace and developed into anti-Dashnak rants, perhaps it did not surprise the reader that this particular article went on to attack the Dashnak Party for completely different actions at yet another location. Speaking to 'those people' without identifying precisely who, the article then went on to attack both the spectators and the athletes for their purported 'inaction' towards the anti-Armenian activities during the HMEM athletic games.[129] After the singing of the Syrian national anthem, *Joghovourti Tzain* explained, in lieu of the anthem of the ASSR, *Harach Nahadag*, 'that pathetic song', was played instead.[130] While not explicitly expressed, the Armenian national anthem was not played at the HMEM athletic game because of its ode to the Soviet status of the state and its heralding of Lenin and Stalin as its saviours. HMEM, being the athletic wing of the Dashnak Party would not have supported the playing of the anthem at any of its events. What would have been far more common and acceptable was either the song that was played, *Harach Nahadag*, a revolutionary song celebrating the Armenian tri-colour flag, which was not in use in the Soviet Republic, or possibly *Mshag Panvor*, the official anthem of the Dashnak Party. For *Joghovourti Tzain*, it registered the absence of the Armenian national anthem as a snub against the Soviet Republic and its own moral register.

Adopting the same moralistic tone it deployed when speaking of the confrontation at the community centre, *Joghovourti Tzain* went on to state 'We're sure that just as the Armenian Scholars refused to become pawns for those opportunists, the HMEM athletes will speak against such anti-Armenian actions that are done in their names'.[131] This moralistic tone doubled as a both a threat and an appeasement for the reader. The newspaper then went on to state that due to such exposure, these types of activities would lessen until there was only 'a handful of those who were serving foreign powers, whose days were numbered anyway, and would be banished to either Madagascar or New Guinea as they so desire'.[132] While it did not oppose the singing of the Syrian anthem or label such an activity as serving a foreign power, *Joghovourti Tzain* was concerned with an element of foreignness of some sort, otherwise it would not have accused its Armenian rivals of supporting or being supported by a foreign power.

About a month before repatriation, *Joghovourti Tzain* began to address 'rumours' printed in the rival newspapers of *Aztarar* and *Aztag* that claimed that the first repatriation caravans would be postponed.[133] It angrily attacked *Aztarar* for disseminating false information, accusing it of spreading malevolent gossip aimed at criticising repatriation preparations and their organisers. It read *Aztarar*'s 'report' of the possible postponement of repatriation as an indirect claim that the movement would be cancelled. 'To say that it will be postponed is just a cover to really say that it's [repatriation] not going to happen'.[134] This alleged concealment, however, also served *Joghovourti Tzain*. After all, it explained, *Aztarar*'s indirect language demonstrated its cowardice. Not only did it engage in baseless accusations, but it did not possess the bravery to even make a direct attack.[135] *Joghovourti Tzain*'s used *Aztarar*'s questioning of the feasibility of the repatriation caravans to make a larger claim against their rival's moral character, all the while maintaining its own sense of superiority. At the same time, it also prided itself for the dual ability of being able to detect such cowardice while providing the 'genuine' information regarding repatriation and its ongoing preparations. In this way, it also upheld itself as the guardian of the Armenian inhabitants of Lebanon and Syria.

In the same editorial, *Joghovourti Tzain* also delicately addressed the different living conditions for Armenian inhabitants of different locations and compared them to the everyday experiences of Armenians in Lebanon and Syria. Once again, it used *Aztarar*'s coverage of repatriation to simultaneously attack its rival and communicate to its readership a particular message. *Aztarar* had written 'Given the life or death situation, it is imperative that the

Balkan Armenians move [to SSR] first'.¹³⁶ *Joghovourti Tzain* took issue with this assessment. It wanted all Armenians, regardless of location to repatriate. And it understood *Aztarar*'s statement as an attempt to discourage Armenian inhabitants of Lebanon and Syria from repatriating. But it had to construct a delicate argument: living conditions indeed varied from place to place, and Armenians in Lebanon and Syria certainly enjoyed a position of privilege vis-à-vis state and civil rights compared to say, Turkey. And yet, repatriation was the solution for all Armenians – not just those living in more precarious situations. Plus, it did not want to insinuate that Armenians in Lebanon and Syria did not appreciate both countries. After all, both states were invested in facilitating their move, and it would have been folly to rupture an otherwise amiable relationship. Nevertheless, if it did not agree with *Aztarar* on some level, it consequentially likened the living conditions and experiences of Armenians in Turkey with those in Syria and Lebanon, thereby insinuating to all parties – Armenian and non-Armenian – that the present conditions in Lebanon and Syria were unacceptable and the reason for repatriation. This had the potential to delegitimise the project of repatriation itself – after all for *Joghovourti Tzain*, the project was one of fate – and not connected to present conditions of living. If conditions suddenly improved in Turkey, for example, repatriation would still have been necessary for *Joghovourti Tzain*, as it was deemed a permanent solution to the perennial problem of the Armenian diaspora. And yet disregarding the circumstances in Turkey posed problems as well: it had the potential of delegitimising the newspaper as a vehicle of information and one of accurate representation.

Joghovourti Tzain therefore mitigated its opposition to *Aztarar*'s call to move the Balkan Armenians 'first'.¹³⁷ It did so by reiterating that while it was indeed correct that Balkan Armenians lived in more trying conditions, so did Greek Armenians, and 'especially our Turkish Armenian brothers'.¹³⁸ 'Plus', it added, 'that doesn't mean that Syrian and Lebanese Armenians do not want to repatriate', and referenced 'the high numbers who had signed up to leave as evidence to the contrary'.¹³⁹ It then attacked *Aztarar* for its dissemination of false news. 'The first caravan will sail – without a doubt. It is not the USSR that tricks, but rather, *Aztarar* and its allies who deceive. And even then, they only deceive themselves – as they are only speaking and listening to themselves at this point'.¹⁴⁰ *Joghovourti Tzain* used *Aztarar* to reiterate its call for universal Armenian repatriation and to elevate itself as both the most trustworthy disseminator of news and its bravest source.

Joghovourti Tzain had particular contempt in store for the Dashnak-leaning daily *Aravelk*. Adopting a mocking tone, it railed against the Dashnak papers for claiming to be supportive of repatriation. 'Not only do they [the Dashnak newspapers] claim that the Dashnak Party is the ultimate supporter of repatriation, but they actually claim that it is thanks to the Party that repatriation is happening!'[141] In order to discount this claim – *Joghovourti Tzain* said it felt compelled to do so 'given the Dashnak Party's attempt to cover up the damage it has inflicted on the Armenian people' – the communist newspaper reminded its readers that it had taken years to organise the repatriation project.[142] 'It didn't take a day, a month, or even a year for repatriation to become a reality. It was a decision that was not taken lightly. Repatriation became a reality due to years of toil and sacrifice'.[143] It then doubled down by linking the execution of the repatriation scheme to the USSR's victory over Nazism – 'At our core, we are indebted to the Soviet people's victory over Hitler's Germany'[144] – and by asking: 'what role did the Dashnak Party play in that victory, if from the beginning of the battle it wished defeat upon the Soviet Union and Soviet Armenia, and served Hitler's Germany . . . spreading its propaganda through people like [General] Dro?'[145] Without the Soviet victory, there would have been no repatriation for *Joghovourti Tzain* – and Dashnak General Dro's action, in World War II had equalled nothing less than a treasonous attempt to effectively thwart the reunification of Armenians with their homeland.[146]

Joghovourti Tzain also attacked the Dashnaks by publishing resignation letters to their party by ex-members who had decided to repatriate. To *Joghovourti Tzain*, these defections showed up the Dashnak Party's suspicious behaviour. Its treacherous nature was not a thing of the past. It was very much present. Although officially in favor of repatriation, the Dashnak Party was nothing but. Why else would dozens of party members have to resign before, during and even after the first caravan had sailed? 'It was *despite* the work of the Dashnak Party', *Joghovourti Tzain* concluded, 'that its members continued to sign up and leave'.[147] For the newspaper, their registration to repatriate was a supreme demonstration of the enduring faith of the Armenians people in repatriation – a faith highlighting the very failure of the nation-building efforts of their former party.

One resignation letter, reprinted together with two similar letters under the headline 'They Resign from the Dashnak Party and Stand with the Homeland', was by Antranik Barsegh Yaylakhanian, the head secretary of the Aleppo chapter of the Dashnak Party and a Sahakian School teacher.[148] It read like a confession. Yaylakhanian described – admitted! – how he had squandered his energy working against the repatriation; it would never turn real, he had believed. And yet, here he was, now registering to sail on the *Russia*, aboard the third caravan. 'Let's be honest', he concluded. 'I probably caused more disorder than most, but today I regret all the energy I wasted that could have been used for the greater good. I sincerely implore you: be brave and stop that group that hurts Armenianness'.[149]

Resignations were not only common in Aleppo, but also elsewhere. Thus, *Joghovourti Tzain* reprinted multiple resignation letters originating from Tehran's Armenian *Veratsnuntd* newspaper. In one, signed by 32 former Dashnak members, the signatories requested that their notice be printed in the newspaper, clearly demonstrating a desire to go on the record. They declared 'The Dashnak Party no longer has any meaning and it is only the Soviet Armenian Republic that commands us'.[150] Such letters were strikingly similar, even though the resignations occurred at a distance. Thus, tens of former Dashnak Party members wrote the lines: 'I must resign from the Dashnak Party due to the party's transformation into an Anti-Armenian party, and given the reality of repatriation, I consider its existence superfluous. I pledge my allegiance to my homeland and its authentic government'.[151] And to take another example, on the same page that it printed the resignations from Tehran, *Joghovourti Tzain* printed resignation letters from members of the Beirut HMEM, the Dashnak athletic organisation. Similar to their Tehrani counterparts, they maintained that there was no longer a need for Dashnak organisations and parties, 'now that the doors of the homeland have opened for all Armenians'.[152]

What also began to appear in the reprints of the resignation letters was the village or town the resigning Armenians hailed from, presently in Turkey. Perhaps this was *Joghovourti Tzain*'s inclusion, though given the number of letters it was running, it was probably already included in the letters themselves. This helped to forward an idea of the authenticity of repatriation. If repatriates originating from Ainteb, living in Damascus or Beirut, maintained that Soviet Armenia was their homeland, they reinforced the uniformity of the republic as the singular Armenian homeland for all Armenians.[153] This also challenged the Dashnak Party's public concerns over what they called 'the continued Turkish occupied lands of Armenia', that is, it weakened the Dashnak Party's demand that all historic Armenian lands should be regained before repatriation could become serious. If people from Ainteb signed up to repatriate, those Turkish occupied lands, *Joghovourti Tzain* implied, could be returned at a later date.

Conclusion

Repatriation intended to unify worldwide Armenians and organise them within one national space, the ASSR. Armenians used the concepts surrounding repatriation, including the question of the location of a homeland, and the actions of repatriating to challenge one another's political ideology in a bid over power. That these battles occurred in Lebanon, meant that a nation-building project become located there that simultaneously had transnational consequences. In fact, Lebanon became the confluence of various 'Armenian' issues, including the 'return' of formerly Armenian populated areas of Anatolia. As the departure point for Syrian and Lebanese repatriates, it likewise became the site of imagination for the idealised Armenian who would go on to serve the Armenian nation – be it in the ASSR or not.

Notes

1. This was following the decree made on 21 November, 1945 by the Soviet of the People's Deputies of the USSR. Ronald Suny, *Looking Towards Ararad* (Indianapolis: Indiana University Press, 1993), 168. 'Haykakan Nergaghtʻē Artōnuetsʻaw' [The Armenian Repatriation Was Granted Permission], *Ararad*, 5 December, 1945, 1.
2. 'Nergaghtʻoghneru Ardzanagrutʻyan Hartsʻaran' [The Questionnaire for those Registered for Repatriation], *Joghovourti Tzain*, 17 January, 1946, 2.
3. 'Nergaghtʻi Ardzanagrutʻiwnnerě Ksksin Urbatʻ Ōr Pʻetrvar Mēkin' [Registration for Repatriation Begins on Friday, February 1], *Joghovourti Tzain*, 29 January, 1946, 1.

4. Ibid. In Achrafieh, hopeful repatriates gathered at Alexsious Nalbandian's residence, in Nor Yozghad at Dikran Kekyah's residence.
5. Razmik Panossian, *Armenia: From Kings and Priests to Merchants and Commissars* (New York: Columbia University Press, 2006), 360.
6. 'Aṛajin Karawanĕ Hayrenik' Gĕ Mekni Erkushabt'i' [The First Caravan Is Off to the Homeland on Monday], *Joghovourti Tzain*, 15 June, 1946, 1.
7. 'Aṛajin Karawanĕ', 1.
8. Ibid.
9. *Joghovourti Tzain*, 23 June, 1946, 1–3; 25 June, 1946, 1–3; 25 June, 1946, 1, 4; 27 June, 1946, 1–2; and 28 June, 1946, 1, 3;
10. 'Bari Chanaparh Hayrenik' Meknoghnerun' [Bon Voyage to the Departing], *Joghovourti Tzain*, 23 June, 1946, 1.
11. See for example, Joanne Laycock, 'The Repatriation of Armenians to Soviet Armenia, 1945–49', in *Warlands Population Resettlement and State Reconstruction in the Soviet-East European Borderlands, 1945–50*, eds Peter Gatrell and Nick Baron, (London: Palgrave Macmillan, 2009), 140–62; Joanne Laycock, Armenian Homelands and Homecomings, 1945–9, *Cultural and Social History* 9, 1 (2012): 103–23; Panossian, *The Armenians*, 358–65; Susan Pattie, 'From the Centers to the Periphery: "Repatriation" to an Armenian Homeland in the 20th Century', in *Homecomings: Unsettling Paths of Return*, eds Fran Markowitz and Anders H. Stefansson (Oxford: Lexington Books, 2004), 109–24; Ronald Suny, *Looking Towards Ararad*, 163–9; and Sevan Nathaniel Yousefian, 'The Postwar Repatriation Movement of Armenians to Soviet Armenia, 1945–1948' (Ph.D. diss., University of California, Los Angeles, 2011). For an example of a memoir by a leading Lebanese repatriation proponent see Hagop Touryantz, *Search for a Homeland* (New York: issued privately, 1987).
12. British troops remained in Egypt until 1952, French and British troops in Syria and Lebanon until 1946.
13. Most Armenians in Central Anatolia had been forcibly deported or killed during the planned extermination of the Armenian population during World War I under the reactionary wing of the Committee of Union and Progress. Some children who escaped deportation were either raised by Muslim families in the area or placed in missionary-led orphanages in the cities. For more, see Nazan Maksudyan, *Orphans and Destitute Children in the Late Ottoman Empire* (Syracuse: Syracuse University Press, 2014). On how the Armenian community 'survived' living in Turkey, see Lerna Ekmekcioglu, *Recovering*

Armenia: The Limits of Belonging in Post-Genocide Turkey (Stanford: Stanford University Press, 2016) and Talin Suciyan, *The Armenians in Modern Turkey: Post-Genocide Society, Politics, and History* (New York: I. B. Tauris, 2016). Others converted to Islam and 'Turkified' themselves, an interesting case of changing identifications. Even until this day, within the political realm it is still taboo to speak of the responsibility of these massacres. The topic has, however, been broached in Turkish literature.

14. Suciyan notes that such pressure to emphasise Armenians' loyalty to Turkey was not restricted to the period of repatriation alone. Suciyan, *The Armenians in Modern Turkey*, 151.
15. Ibid., 150. For more on the impact of repatriation on Armenians in Turkey see ibid., 142–68.
16. Ibid., 150.
17. Ibid., 151. Emphasis added.
18. 'Hayastani Ashkhataworut'iwně Urakhut'eamb Kspasē Artasahmani Ir Eghbayrnerun Hayrenik' Veradardzin' [Armenia's Workers Joyously Await the Return of Their Diaspora Brothers], *Joghovourti Tzain*, 10 January, 1946, 1.
19. 'Fransahay Nergaght'oghneru Khumb Mě Erewan Gě Hasni' [A Group of French Repatriates Arrives in Yerevan], *Joghovourti Tzain*, 10 January, 1946, 1. Missak Manouchian was executed for his involvement in resistant activities in Nazi occupied France in 1944. For more on the Manouchians see Anouche Kunth, Claire Mouradian, *Les Arméniens en France* (Toulouse: Attribut, 2010), 48.
20. Ibid.
21. 'Nergaght'i Masin' [About Repatriation], *Joghovourti Tzain*, 6 March, 1946, 2.
22. Ibid.
23. Ibid.
24. Ibid.
25. Ibid.
26. Ibid.
27. Ibid.
28. Ibid.
29. 'Damaskosahay Nergaght'oghnerě Pēyrut' Hasan' [The Damascus-Armenian Repatriates Have Arrived in Beirut], *Joghovourti Tzain*, 21 June, 1946, 1.
30. Ibid.

31. Ibid.
32. Ibid.
33. Ibid.
34. Ibid.
35. Ibid.
36. Ibid.
37. Grigor K'ēshishyan, 'Ew Karawanĕ Meknets'aw' [And the Caravan Was Off], *Joghovourti Tzain*, 25 June, 1946, 2.
38. 'Aṛajin Karawanĕ Nawun Vray' [The First Caravan Aboard the Ship], *Joghovourti Tzain*, 25 June, 1946, 3.
39. Ibid.
40. Ibid.
41. Ibid.
42. Ibid. Emphasis added.
43. Ibid.
44. 'Vehap'aṛ Hayrapetin Kondakĕ' [The Catholicos' Declaration], *Joghovourti Tzain*, 26 June, 1946, 1.
45. Ibid.
46. Ibid.
47. Ibid.
48. Hovhannēs Aghpashyan, 'Dardz Dēpi Erkir' [Return Towards the Homeland], *Joghovourti Tzain*, 1 February, 1946, 1.
49. Ibid.
50. 'Nergaght'i Ardzanagrut'iwnnerĕ Halēpi Mēj' [Repatriation Registration in Aleppo], *Joghovourti Tzain*, 28 February, 1946, 2.
51. Ibid.
52. Ibid.
53. Ibid.
54. Ibid.
55. Ibid.
56. Ibid.
57. Ibid.
58. 'Damaskosahay Nergaght'oghnerĕ', 1.
59. Ibid.
60. Ibid.
61. 'Nergaght'oghnerun Het' [With the Repatriates], *Joghovourti Tzain*, 23 June, 1946, 3.

62. Ibid.
63. Ibid.
64. Ibid.
65. Ibid.
66. Ibid.
67. 'Bari Chanaparh Hayrenikʻ Meknoghnerun' [Bon Voyage to Those Departing for the Homeland], *Joghovourti Tzain*, 23 June, 1946, 1.
68. Ibid.
69. Ibid.
70. 'Grigor Kʻēshishyan, 'Ew Karawanĕ Meknetsʻaw' [And the Caravan Was Off], *Joghovourti Tzain*, 25 June, 1946, 2.
71. Ibid.
72. 'A. Karawani Pet Tokʻtʻor G. Manushakyan Kĕ Khōsi Erewani R̄atioyēn' [The Head of the 1st Caravan, Dr. G. Manushakyan, Speaks on Yerevan Radio], *Joghovourti Tzain*, 3 July, 1946, 1.
73. 'Sovet Hayastani 25 Amyaki Ar̄itʻov Libananahayutʻyan Nuiratuutʻyan Handisawor Batsʻumĕ Antʻiliasi Mēj' [The Lebanese Armenians' Impressive Opening of Donations in Antelias on the Occasion of the 25th Anniversary of Soviet Armenia], *Joghovourti Tzain*, 1 January, 1946, 2.
74. Ibid.
75. Ibid.
76. 'Sovetakan Hayastani Gar̄avarutʻiwnĕ Gĕ Hrahangē Sksil Nergaghtʻe Artsanagrutʻeantsʻʻ [The Government of Soviet Armenia Begins Repatriation Registration], *Joghovourti Tzain*, 17 January, 1946, 1.
77. Derenik Demirchyan, 'Hayun Nergaghtʻe' [The Repatriation of the Armenian], *Joghovourti Tzain*, 20 January, 1946, 1.
78. Awetikʻ Isahakyan, 'Hay Zhoghovrdi Dzgtumnerĕ' [The Aspirations of the Armenian People], *Joghovourti Tzain*, 19 June, 1946, 1, 2.
79. Ibid.
80. Ibid.
81. 'Sovet Hayastani Petakan Hamalsarani Usanoghnerēn Khumb Mĕ' [A Group of Soviet Armenian National University Students], *Joghovourti Tzain*, 20 January, 1946, 1.
82. The caption read: 'Sovet Hayastani Petakan Hamalsarani Usanoghnerēn Khumb Mĕ' [A Group of Soviet Armenian National University Students], *Joghovourti Tzain*, 20 January, 1946, 1.
83. 'Aytsʻeletsʻēkʻ Sovet Hayastani Patkerawor Tsʻutsʻahandēsĕ' [Visit Soviet

Armenia's Photograph Exhibition!], *Joghovourti Tzain*, 1 February, 1946, 1.

84. Hovhannēs Aghpashyan, 'Shnorhakalutiwn Stalinin' [Thank you Stalin], *Joghovourti Tzain*, 23 June, 1946, 1, 4. Stalin was praised, and his feature was ubiquitous, also at the arrival of repatriates in the USSR: see for example 'Erevani Mēj Nergaght'oghnerě Tsaghiknerov ew Drōshnerov Zardaruats Ink'nasharzhnerov Gě Taruin Irents' Tunerě' [In Yerevan the Repatriates Are Taken to Their Houses in Decorated Cars with Flowers and Flags], *Joghovourti Tzain*, 5 July, 1946, 1.
85. 'Nor Manramasnut'iwnner A. Karawanin Pat'um Zhamanelun Masin' [New Details on the 1st Caravan's Arrival in Batumi], *Joghovourti Tzain*, 3 July, 1946, 2.
86. Ibid.
87. Ibid.
88. Ibid.
89. Ibid.
90. Ibid.
91. 'Nergaght'oghnerun Het', 3.
92. Ibid.
93. Ibid.
94. Ibid.
95. Ibid.
96. Ibid.
97. Ibid.
98. Ibid.
99. 'Bari Chanaparh', 1.
100. Ibid.
101. Ibid.
102. Grigor K'ēshishyan, 'Ew Karavaně Meknetz'aw ...' [And the Caravan Departed . . .], *Joghovourti Tzain*, 25 June, 1946, 2.
103. Ibid.
104. *Joghovourti Tzain*, 28 July, 1946, 1.
105. Ibid.
106. Ibid.
107. Ibid.
108. Ibid.
109. Ibid.

110. Isahakyan, 'Hay Zhoghovrdi Dzgtumnerĕ', 1, 2.
111. 'Ew Hantsʻawor, Ew Zrpartogh' [Culpable and Accusatory], *Joghovourti Tzain*, 7 July, 1946, 1.
112. 'Dardz Dēpi Erkir' [Return to the Homeland], *Joghovourti Tzain*, 1 February, 1946, 1.
113. Ibid.
114. Ibid.
115. Ibid.
116. Ibid.
117. 'Tʻurkʻ Mamuli Hay Tʻmbakaharnerĕ' [The Armenian Drummers of the Turkish Press], *Joghovourti Tzain*, 13 January, 1946, 1.
118. Ibid. However, the Dashnak Party officially started to speak out against repatriation only in late 1947: see the (pro-Dashnak) *Aztag*, 4 October, 1947, 1. This happened just after the Catholic Armenian Patriarchate had started to speak out against repatriation. Word had reached people outside the ASSR about the dire conditions there. See also Panossian, *The Armenians*, 361.
119. 'Tʻurkʻ Mamuli Hay Tʻmbakaharnerĕ', 1.
120. Ibid.
121. Ibid.
122. Ibid.
123. Ibid.
124. 'Halēpi Hay Usanoghneru Boghokʻĕ Dashnaktsʻutʻyan Hakahayastanyan Gortsunēutʻyan Dēm' [Aleppo's Armenian Students' Rally Against the Dashnak Party's Anti-Armenian Activities], *Joghovourti Tzain*, 1 May, 1946, 2.
125. Ibid.
126. Ibid.
127. Ibid.
128. Ibid.
129. Ibid.
130. Ibid.
131. Ibid.
132. The reference to Madagascar and New Guinea is unexplained. Ibid.
133. Hōvahannes Aghpashyan, 'Azdarar' Inchʻ Khntrē' [What does *Aztarar* Request], *Joghovourti Tzain*, 26 May, 1946, 1.
134. Ibid.
135. Ibid.
136. Ibid.

137. Ibid.
138. Ibid.
139. Ibid.
140. Ibid.
141. Paroyr Erēts'yan, 'Ew Hants'awor, Ew Zrpartogh' [Culpable and Accusatory], *Joghovourti Tzain*, 7 July, 1946, 1.
142. Ibid.
143. Ibid.
144. Ibid.
145. Ibid. General Dro, or Drastamat Kanayan was the former Minister of Defense of the independent republic of Armenia, which lasted until 1921 when it became a Soviet republic. He was also a member of the Dashnak Party, and in World War II became in charge of Armenian Legion, made up of Armenian Soviet prisoners of war who fought on behalf of Nazi Germany against the USSR, who pledged to free the republic from Soviet rule.
146. For more on Armenians who fought on behalf of Nazi Germany against Stalin see Thomas de Waal, *Great Catastrophe: Armenians and Turks in the Shadow of Genocide* (Oxford: Oxford Unversity Press, 2015), 112.
147. Hōvahannes Aghpashyan, 'Dits'atip Kusakts'ut'iwnĕ Araspel Gĕ Patmē' [The 'Righteous' Party Tells Myths], *Joghovourti Tzain*, 21 July, 1946, 1.
148. 'Kĕ Hrazharin Dashnakts'ut'enēn ew Kĕ Kangnin Hayrenik'i Koghk'in' [They Resign from the Dashnak Party and Stand With the Homeland], *Joghovourti Tzain*, 19 July, 1946, 3.
149. Ibid.
150. 'Kĕ Hrazharin Dashnakts'ut'enēn' [They Resign from the Dashnak Party], *Joghovourti Tzain*, 21 July, 1946, 3.
151. Ibid.
152. Ibid. For another specific letter, by HMEM athlete George Manougian who had won third prize in a body building competition in Paris in 1939, see 'Kĕ Hrazharin Dashnakts'ut'enēn' [They Resign from the Dashnak Party], *Joghovourti Tzain*, 23 July, 1946, 3.
153. Ibid.

3

COLD WAR, BOTTOM-UP: THE 1956 CATHOLICOS ELECTION

Introduction

In 1952, Catholicos Karekin I (Hovsepian) passed away. As the highest figure in the Armenian Apostolic Church of the Cilician See, headquartered in Antelias, near Beirut, he headed one of the most powerful, and independent, ecclesiastic units in the Orthodox Armenian world. For four years, Karekin's seat remained vacant. The Cilician See repeatedly postponed electing the next catholicos. Internal disagreements irked it, and it did not wish to aggravate relations with the Echmiadzin See. Headquartered in the Armenian Soviet Socialist Republic (ASSR), that capital see was independent from and equal to the Cilician See, which saw it as Moscow's long arm. Finally, in early 1956, Antelias decided to go through with the catholicos election.[1] The run-up to that event was dramatic. On 3 February, Vasken I (born Levon Garabed Baljian, 1908–1994), the catholicos of the Echmiadzin See, visited Lebanon in a rather undisguised attempt to influence the election outcome. To no avail: On 20 February, the Cilician See's bishops chose as new catholicos an outspoken critic of communism and the USSR, Zareh I (born Simon Payaslian).[2] He did not lose time to condemn what he considered 'organised attempts by Soviet authorities to use the Echmiadzin See as an instrument to control the Armenian communities of the Diaspora'. In effect, his election officially positioned the Cilician See against the Echmiadzin See, the ASSR and the USSR.³ Chaos ensued. In Beirut, supporters and opponents of Zareh clashed. Pro-Western Lebanese President Camille Chamoun (1900–1987; r. 1952–1958), who had taken a vivid interest in the election and met with all parties concerned, ordered government troops to secure Armenian neighbourhoods in Beirut.⁴ A month later, the *ach*, a solid gold mould of the right arm of St Gregory who is credited with converting the pagan Armenians to Christianity in 301, along with a few other relics were stolen from the Cilician See's monastery complex in Antelias: an act universally seen as an attempt to embarrass the Cilician See and to torpedo Zareh's ordination. In September, Zareh was ordained anyway. And the following year, the relic was 'found' in Jordanian-ruled East Jerusalem and returned in triumph to Beirut.⁵

The present chapter tells the story of the 1956 catholicos election as a site of contestation by Cold War powers and their state and non-state allies and proxies in the Middle East. Lebanon, staunchly pro-Western and pro-American under Chamoun, was not the only state directly involved in that election, indeed. So were Egypt and Jordan, among other Middle Eastern states and the Soviet Union, principally through Catholicos Vasken. The United States and key European states like France and Britain also made appearances in the story. Even so, it was the Armenians who were this story's main protagonists – that is, Armenians of different, if not diametrically opposed political convictions. As the last chapter showed, during the 1946–1949 ASSR repatriation initiative, leftists wielded considerable power in the Armenian community of Beirut and beyond; and the repatriation initiative further boosted their influence at that juncture. But a decade later, in 1956, things had changed. Ironically, the very success of the leftist repatriation drive, i.e. the emigration to the ASSR, depleted the leftist presence in the repatriation 'donor' countries. As a consequence, from the late 1940s the rightist Dashnak Party became more preponderant, certainly in Beirut.⁶ What is more, the Cold War was much more heated by the mid-1950s than it had been in the mid-1940s, when it just about began.

In sum, then, the 1956 election allows us to look at the Cold War in the Middle East not from the top down, through the eyes of Washington or Moscow (or Lebanon's or Egypt's state authorities, for that matter) during flashpoints like the 1958 US intervention in Lebanon or the US and Soviet reactions to the Tripartite Aggression against Egypt in 1956. Rather, in this election, Armenians made use of Cold War tensions to designate a leader of the Armenian church who was seen to suit the community's interests.[7] That story also expands historians' understanding of Lebanon's Armenians: from refugees and outsiders in national politics to true participants, whose own internal politics, moreover, were also of interest to Lebanon's authorities, and who by now felt free to invade and use public spaces beyond their own neighbourhoods to make political statements.

In what follows, I tell that story while keeping an eye on three analytical aspects. One is the overlap between the global Cold War and regional Middle Eastern inter-state competition. Another is the mutual use, if not exploitation, of state actors and Armenian actors. And a third is the fascinating duality of states' approaches to the Armenian issue: both nation-state-bound and transnational. States sought to assert their sovereignty vis-à-vis ecclesiastical Armenian matters that happened on their territory; thus, the Lebanese state, and in particular Chamoun, was involved politically and symbolically in the 1956 catholicos election. But states also tried to use Armenian issues and religious Armenian bodies, whose authority was non-secular and whose reach was not quite bound by nation-state borders (to say the least), to affect third countries' politics; the foremost example in the present case was the Soviet attempt to meddle in the 1956 election in the person of Vasken, the catholicos of the Echmiadzin See, which was headquartered in the ASSR.

In taking this approach to the 1956 election, this chapter, as with the other chapters of this book, addresses lacunae in the secondary literature on Armenians in the Middle East and especially Lebanon, and reflects on the light their case can shine on larger topics. Power struggles, political differences and alignments among Armenians have long been ignored in the historiography of modern Lebanon, which has described the Armenian population as a coherent community. The Cold-War-related nature of inner-Armenian events and their place within the broader history of Lebanon and the Middle East has been accordingly ignored.[8] The 1956 catholicos election is absent not only from overview accounts such as Kamal Salibi's *A House of Many Mansions* and Fawwaz Traboulsi's *History of Modern Lebanon*, but also from monographs like Caroline Attié's *Struggle in the Levant: Lebanon* *in the 1950s.*⁹ As for Armenian historiography, texts like Simon Payaslian's 'The Institutionalisation of the Catholicos of the Great House of Cilicia in Antelias', by identifying the election of 1956 as the 'most significant event in modern Armenian Church history', describes the event simply as an internal Armenian issue, disregarding the Cold War context and the involvement of multiple states.[10]

Antelias' Announcement of the Catholicos Election and the Echmiadzin See's Response

On 7 February, *Aztag* announced that the Cilician See's next catholicos would be elected on 14 February.[11] It likewise reported that Catholicos Vasken of the Echmiadzin See would take part in the election, a move welcomed by an, albeit-surprised, acting head of the Cilician See, Archbishop Khoren Paroyan.[12] This was the first time that the Soviet government had allowed the catholicos of the Echmiadzin See to leave the USSR; indeed, his visit to Lebanon as a whole was sponsored by Moscow and occurred as part of the USSR's broader Cold War policies. As Vasken's jurisdiction did not extend to the Armenian populations of Lebanon, or to many Armenians in the Middle East for that matter, his visit to Beirut was seen by many in Beirut as directly connected to, and triggered by, the election at the Cilician See – and therefore as a political issue.[13] More generally, Vasken was part of the Soviet Union's political infrastructure. His movements were monitored; his very election and his sermons were sanctioned by the USSR; and in 1956, he flew from Yerevan to Beirut not directly but via extended stops in Moscow and Paris, where he met with Soviet government officials.[14]

At the same time, Vasken's visit, even though at Moscow's behest, can also be seen as an attempt to extend his power to areas outside the USSR. (He had himself barely arrived in the Soviet Union by the time he visited Beirut. Elected catholicos in 1955, he had lived before, and been born in, Romania, where he had risen through the ranks of the ecclesiastical hierarchy loyal to the Echmiadzin See.) The overlapping dual motivation for Vasken's visit – both his own ecclesiastical motivations, as well as his own *and* Moscow's political ones – showed up in his address to the Armenian Lebanese press and, through the Soviet news agency TASS, to the ASSR's population. 'To the acting-Catholicos Archbishop Khoren: because of our love of our church and because we have the foresight to protect and affirm its unity, we have decided to participate personally in the election and anointment of the Catholicos of the Cilician See'.[15] This statement violated the principle that Armenian sees operate independently from each other, and that one is not supposed to directly interfere in the internal affairs of the other.[16]

A Look Back in Time

At this point, a quick look back to the more distant past is in order, to provide a bit of background to the above story. Under the Ottoman and Russian empires, there were more than the twentieth century's two sees, or catholicosates, though already then each had its own jurisdiction and hierarchy.[17] The Echmiadzin See was, and still is, located in Echmiadzin, at the time Russian-ruled Armenia. On Ottoman territory were the Aghtamar See, near Van, and the Cilician See.[18] Located in Sis (presently Kozan), the latter had been established alongside the Kingdom of Cilicia after the fall of the Kingdom of Ani at the end of the eleventh century.[19] Like the other sees, it had its own parishes and its own catholicos, archbishops, bishops and priests. At the same time, it stood in permanent contact with the other sees. These relationships crisscrossed imperial, and later nation-state, borders.[20] While the sees were recognised as Armenian community representatives by imperial (and later nation-state) powers, none directly and systematically sought the approval of the Ottoman or Russian state in their everyday relationships with one another. In this sense, they were supra-state structures.[21]

These Armenian sees also stood in contact with two patriarchates, one in Istanbul, the other in Jerusalem.[22] Although doctrinally subject to the sees' authority, the two patriarchates enjoyed organisational autonomy. In additon, due to their locations and size of congregations and because of the political status assigned to them by the Ottoman authorities as official representatives of the Armenian community to the Ottoman state, they played powerful intermediary roles between their community and the state. The Patriarchate of Istanbul represented the Armenian *millet* to the Ottoman government;[23] and the Patriarchate of Jerusalem represented its city's Armenians throughout Palestine and was the guardian of the Armenian niches in the Church of the Holy Sepulchre in Jerusalem and in the Church of the Nativity in Bethlehem.[24] Moreover, states' influence on Armenian religious bodies showed when Istanbul made the capital patriarchate its key interlocutor. It also showed in the fates of the Aghtamar, Cilician and the Echmiadzin Sees.[25] And in 1924, the newly founded Soviet Union encouraged Catholicos Kevork V to change the hierarchical structure of the Echmiadzin See, a Supreme Spiritual Council replacing the time-honoured but more unwieldy Synod of Bishops.[26]

This situation changed somewhat when the Cilician See moved to Lebanon after World War I. Practical reasons favoured the sees' independence and the patriarchates' autonomy, and serious communication issues persisted. Many of the original refugees arriving from the Ottoman Empire learned Armenian. (Subsequent generations also became fluent in Arabic.) The ASSR's Armenians spoke – and still speak – a dialect known as Eastern Armenian, which is quite distinct from the dialect spoken by Armenians in the Arab Middle East and Turkey, known as Western Armenian. (Iranian Armenians' dialect is closer to Eastern Armenian).[27] What is more, the formation of nation-states after World War I further constricted movement and communication between the Echmiadzin and Cilician Sees, and created additional distinctions to do with citizenships. And yet, as Chapter 2 showed, the two sees set aside these issues when coordinating their efforts during the repatriation movement of 1946–1949.[28]

Return to the Mid-1950s

But by the early 1950s, the relationship between the two Sees had taken a definite turn for the worse. This was partly because of the altered Armenian political landscape in Lebanon, and partly due to the Cold War heating up.[29] The coordinated efforts of repatriation had past. With the drastic reduction of the leftist Hnchak and centrist Ramgavar Party rosters, many of whose members had repatriated to the ASSR, the nationalist/rightist Dashnak Party was able to consolidate its power among Lebanon's Armenians.[30] This change also affected Lebanese politics. By the 1950s, it was mostly Dashnak members who represented the Armenian community in Lebanon's parliament. In addition, its government, led by Chamoun, was ardently anti-communist and was supported financially, and in 1958 militarily, by the United States. Earlier, in 1955, Chamoun, while not signing the Baghdad Pact between Iraq, Pakistan, Turkey, Iran and the United Kingdom – the United States was unofficially involved – had shown public enthusiasm for this military alliance, triggering violent protests in Lebanon.

At a time when one's position vis-à-vis communism and the USSR was a key political litmus test, a natural alliance thus crystallised between Chamoun's government and the fervently anti-communist Dashnak Party – an alliance that was also convenient given the Dashnak's dominance in the Armenian community. And in this context, acting Catholicos Archbishop Khoren's known close relationship to Dashnak officials and to Chamoun meant that by early 1956, it became clear that elections could now be held and that a catholicos to the liking of both the Lebanese government and the Dashnak rightists would be elected; the person upmost on people's mind was Zareh (1915–1963), a staunch opponent of communism and the ASSR. Indeed, the maturation of the Chamoun–Dashnak and Dashnak–Antelias/Khoren relationships by the mid-1950s created an opportue moment to finally hold the catholicos election.

Catholicos Vasken's Arrival in Beirut

When Vasken landed in Beirut on 12 February, he was greeted by tens of thousands of Armenians lining the streets from the airport, just south of Beirut, to the monastery in Antelias that was about 15 kilometres away, in the capital's north. Indeed, in the volatile political atmosphere of the juncture, Vasken's visit elicited great interest among the city's Armenians. And while the Armenian population in Lebanon did not formally participate in the electoral process, many joined in with planned and spontaneous public activities throughout the capital city. Starting in the airport, they lined the streets welcoming Vasken, and followed him *en masse* to meetings with Armenian church officials and Lebanese politicians and officials. This unprecedented level of popular involvement by Armenians, together with continuing media coverage, highlighted that a decade into Lebanon's independence, the country's Armenians were at ease making the capital city's public space their own.[31] They did not really feel like marginal and weak subjects anymore; they had ceased thinking of themselves firstly as 'fresh off the boat' refugees who better keep a low profile in order not to attract undue attention. They showed up in force not only in their own neighbourhoods, places like Antelias and Bourj Hamoud, but also in supra-ethnic/religious, we may say secular, public

Figure 3.1 Crowds gathering at the airport to welcome Catholicos Vasken. *Zartonk*, 14 February, 1956.

spaces like Beirut's airport and the roads connecting the airport to Beirut's centre. (See Figures 3.1, 3.2 and 3.3.)

Did Vasken shift from being a Soviet authority into an Armenian one during his journey? It was unclear where the jurisdiction of his person as a Soviet authority ended and where the Armenian began. Be that as it may, the Armenian public's support of Vasken as either, or both, a Soviet or an Armenian official sidestepped the Lebanese nation-state. After all, while only some Armenians welcomed Vasken because they were leftists and he a

Figure 3.2 Crowds beside the road from the airport to the Cilician See to welcome Catholicos Vasken. *Aztag*, 14 February, 1956.

Figure 3.3 Crowds lining the roads to the Cilician See to welcome Catholicos Vasken. *Zartonk*, 14 February, 1956.

Soviet representative, most, if not all, of those who packed Beirut's airport and lined the city's streets on 12–14 February did so because Vasken's arrival was a rather momentous chapter in *Armenian* history. As noted above, this was the first time since the creation of the USSR that the catholicos of the Echmiadzin See was allowed to leave Soviet territory and to directly meet Armenians elsewhere. This was doubly crucial because the Echmiadzin See was not some unimportant, second-rank ecclesiastical unit, but rather the self-anointed Mother See, whose keystone church was the first cathedral built in post-conversion Armenia, in 301–303.[32]

Moreover, even as the Armenian response to Vasken's visit highlighted how much Armenians were comfortable using Lebanese public space, as just noted above, it simultaneously showed how much they thought it necessary to identify, and be identified, as Lebanese of Armenian confession rather than 'simply' as Armenians. To be sure, Armenian political party figures, newspapers and members of the public all participated in the spectacle of Vasken's visit. Armenian schools were closed; and the established 'Committee to Welcome Catholicos Vasken' encouraged students to line the streets from the National Museum of Lebanon to the bridges that lead into Bourj Hamoud, 'out of respect for' the catholicos.[33] But this directive was publicised by the Armenian newspapers along with five instructions. The third one announced, 'The only flag that is permitted to be held is the flag of the Lebanese state'.[34] Although the directive did not elaborate on the significance of alternative flags, it clearly deemed the Lebanese flag the only appropriate symbol for representing Lebanon's Armenians as they welcomed Vasken.[35] To give that metaphorical screw one more turn, one may argue that the Armenian citizens of Lebanon Armenianised the Lebanese flag. It became an *Armenian* symbol – albeit one loyal to Lebanon – that demonstrated their approval of the visit by an official of the Echmiadzin See who was simultaneously a Soviet official.

The events of 12–14 February, then, transcended the bounded notions of the nation-state.[36] Where the authority of Lebanon and the USSR began, ended and overlapped was ambiguous; and so was Lebanese Armenians' (self)-identification. Further, the events of 12–14 February did not simply *reflect* an already extent (complex) configuration of the complex religious-*cum*-national identities by Christian Armenian citizens of Lebanon. Rather, they helped shape the ways in which said multiple identities were expressed in public, including the ambiguity of using Lebanese flags and the self-confidence on display as Armenians thronged the airport and the avenues from there to Antelias.

The First Scheduled Election Day and Vasken's Involvement

The Cilician See rejected Vasken's involvement in the electoral process, its electoral committee snubbing his and the Soviet Union's authority over its own matters. But the Echmiadzin See was simply too honoured an Armenian institution for its catholicos to coldly be ignored by the Cilician See. A put-on warmth held forth; Antelias decided to invite Vasken to the electoral meeting; and on the morning of 14 February, the day of the election, acting Catholicos Archbishop Khoren opened the meeting with a 'friendly' invitation for Vasken to speak.[37] Vasken accepted, and in turn offered his personal wishes from the Echmiadzin See to the Cilician See.[38] Then, he made his move. He described the role of the elections as 'aiding in the advancement of Armenian diasporic church life'.[39] And he stressed how his presence was an opportunity 'to further strengthen the life of our churches and the national life in *these areas*'.[40] By talking of 'diaspora', he automatically implied, and highlighted, that he did *not* come from the diaspora but from Armenia 'itself', which presumably gave him a leg up vis-à-vis the Cilician See. And by connecting his person to 'these areas' – presumably those under the jurisdiction of the Cilician See – he also extended his authority from the Echmiadzin See in Soviet Armenia to Lebanon.

Then, Vasken dropped a bombshell. He announced the convention, that very week, of an emergency meeting of The Council of Bishops in Jerusalem, and requested that the election be rescheduled for 20 February.[41] This move was also meant to put him in the position of guardian of 'diasporic' church life and to question the authority of the Cilician See and its necessity as an institution separate from the Echmiadzin See. Was Vasken trying to place the Cilician See under his realm, and possibly under Soviet control as well? And yet, at the same time, the request to reschedule the election demonstrated the limitations of the Echmiadzin See's power. After all, a rescheduled election would mean he would not be present – as they would take place *after* he was scheduled to leave the country. While an absence of Vasken would convey at best an ambiguity towards the new catholicos, or at worst, its disapproval, it also demonstrated Vasken's inability to stop the election. Nevertheless, the committee acquiesced to his demands, and in so doing paradoxically both reinforced and thwarted his power.[42] Khoren adjourned the meeting and rescheduled the catholicos election for the morning of 20 February.[43]

The Lead Up to the First Scheduled Election Day

Vasken's ability to come to Lebanon and attend the electoral meeting only to ask it to be rescheduled showcased his power to both the Cilician See and the Armenian inhabitants of Lebanon. His meeting with President Chamoun, which had taken place also on 14 February, was an additional attempt to assert and show off his authority (see Figure 3.4). The photographs printed in the Lebanese papers on 15 February – the date of the elections – were an affront to the authority of the Cilician See.

But if Vasken used the Lebanese state to demonstrate his own importance to the Armenian population in Lebanon and to challenge Khoren and the Cilician See's authority, there was another side to this meeting with Chamoun. The Lebanese president's statement to the press, after the meeting, indicated that he wished to be seen as being more elevated than both Vasken and Khoren, and that his state-bound authority ultimately superseded the

Figure 3.4 Chamoun meeting Vasken at the presidential palace. *Aztag*, 15 February, 1956.

ecclesiastical power of both. He declared, 'Please consider yourself in your own home, since it is without exaggeration when I say Lebanon is a second Armenia'.[44] To be sure, Chamoun's statement can be interpreted as a gesture of friendship and goodwill between Lebanon and the USSR. But at the same time, it enveloped all Armenians, placing them under *his* tutelage – the tutelage of a sovereign nation-state – in Lebanon. He concluded his remarks with the following wish: 'I hope that the elections are held under normal circumstances and that I am given the honour to share in your happiness tomorrow evening and will have the pleasure to receive you and the Cilician See's catholicos-elect thereafter'.[45] Chamoun reframed the election and its outcome as a reaffirmation of his authority. The election was taking place within the borders of the sovereign nation-state whose head he was. And once the election was over, he reserved the right – that is, did not simply offer the courtesy – to 'officially' receive *both* Vasken and the catholicos-elect, as if to offer his 'final' approval, and as if his approval was necessary to validate the result: which of course was not the case.

Election Day

On Sunday, 19 February, 1956, the day before the rescheduled elections, Vasken made another, new, and this time squarely religious attempt to assert his authority and extend it over the congregations of the Cilician See. He did so by performing Sunday mass, including a sermon, in the very compound of the Cilician See in Antelias.[46] While the announcement that he would officiate mass was printed on the front page of all of Lebanon's Armenian newspapers, the newspaper affiliated with the Dashnak Party, *Aztag*, did not cover the event, signalling its disapproval.[47] At this point that newspaper also became more persistent in attacking Vasken's presence. It called him a foreigner and a Soviet pawn, implying he was neither privy to nor aware of the intricacies of Armenian life and politics in Lebanon.[48]

Indeed, the events following Vasken's meeting with Chamoun and his officiation of the Sunday mass in Antelias were anything but friendly. Not yet having secured a Jordanian visa to visit Jerusalem, yet aware that the catholicos elections would take place and that Zareh would indeed be elected, Vasken left for Paris. After Zareh was elected Catholicos Zareh I on 20 February under the protection of the Lebanese army (see Figures 3.5 and

Figure 3.5 Zareh I after his election. *Aztag*, 21 February, 1956.

3.6),[49] Vasken, from Paris, declared the entire election process illegal. Violent clashes erupted in Beirut between majority Zareh supporters, principally rightist Dashnak followers, and minority opponents of the new catholicos, mainly leftists.[50] Meanwhile, in Antelias about one hundred women, mainly leftists, had taken over the St Gregory Cathedral located in the Cilician See's compound, seeking to annul the election.[51] A general strike was declared in the Armenian neighbourhoods; and Armenian stores and schools closed in an attempt to deescalate the conflict.[52]

Opponents of the elections did not limit their action to Armenian structures. Others who also opposed the choice of Zareh took to the streets; some attacked archbishops, including Khoren; causing some to be hospitalised.[53] A number of women who had participated in the takeover of the monastery structure in the hopes of delaying the election also attempted to meet President Chamoun.[54] While they were unsuccessful, they did manage to deliver a letter explaining their opposition and imploring the president to take action and nullify the election.[55] In the letter, these women connected

Figure 3.6 The Cilician See monastery complex on election day. In the upper left corner, two armed Lebanese officers overlook the courtyard. *Zartonk*, 23 February, 1956.

their appeal to the Lebanese president to their legal status as Lebanese citizens, and declared the necessity for him to become involved as the leader of their 'homeland'.[56]

The Election's Aftermath

As the women's group attempted to use their legal status as Lebanese citizens to compel the state to intervene on their behalf, the Lebanese state too saw fit to do so. It did so, however, on the side of the party allied with Chamoun, the Dashnaks, who supported the anti-communist Zareh. The Lebanese state made an official declaration backing the new catholicos, and reinforced troops guarding the Antelias complex against Zareh's opponents. Other states also acted – and did so in a way that demonstrated how much an Armenian ecclesiastic election had become politicised, and how that politicisation reflected Cold War faultlines within and beyond the Armenian community. Numerous dignitaries from Western states including

Great Britain, France and the United States offered their congratulations, and Jordan continued to refuse Vasken an entry visa to Jerusalem.[57] By contrast, the Soviet Union and other Warsaw Pact countries expressed dismay. And yet another Middle Eastern state entered the fray. Cairo invited Vasken to organise his emergency Council of Bishops meeting, which he initially had planned to hold in Jerusalem, in Egypt's capital.[58] Lebanon, Jordan and Egypt's reactions to the election and their differing treatment of Vasken reflected their relationships with the USSR and the United States during the Cold War.

Three days after the election, on 22 February, 1956, President Chamoun received Zareh.[59] As did, in the following days, Syrian President Shukri al-Quwatli and other Syrian officials. All meetings were amply covered in the Armenian and Arabic press.[60] By receiving Zareh, Chamoun and al-Quwatli signalled that their governments approved the election result, which in turn communicated that they backed the Cilician See's autonomy and disapproved of the Echmiadzin See and the USSR meddling in Antelias' affairs. This was, certainly, how pro-Dashnak newspapers covered the event. A picture of Chamoun and Zareh's meeting in *Aztag* showed a smiling catholicos and an equally jovial president at the presidential palace sharing a drink. (See Figure 3.7.) Zareh's outfit, including the black headpiece worn by bishops and archbishops, complete with gold medallions bearing the crest of the Cilician See, indicated that the meeting was being held in an official capacity. *Aztag* described the conversation as follows: 'the Catholicos-elect and the honourable president exchanged views and had an intimate and tender conversation with one another'.[61] By not mentioning Zareh and Chamoun's names and by identifying them simply by their titles, *Aztag* implied that their personal identities were irrelevant. More important yet, it implicitly described the catholicos and the president as equals – as two elected, legitimate leaders of their respective flocks.

But there was another side to this picture. While both officials are smiling and sharing a drink – possibly champagne, judging by the glasses? – the catholicos is sitting erect on the side of the sofa. By contrast, the president is slightly reclining in the very middle of the sofa. This was *the president's* house, the two men's seating order and postures seemed to indicate; of the two, the president was more powerful. Indeed, the fact that the Cilician See

Figure 3.7 Zareh and Chamoun in the presidential palace. *Aztag*, 23 February, 1956.

was seeking Chamoun and al-Quwatli's approval by coming for an audience showed that the Lebanese and Syrian governments had some leverage over the see. (In Syria's case, the matter was yet more complex: by recognising Zareh's election and receiving him, Damascus signalled it had a stake in events beyond its sovereign borders.) Rank and file Armenians seemed to reflect that political reality. When Zareh's motorcade passed through Armenian neighbourhoods *en route* to Chamoun's presidential palace, community members along the road 'held Lebanese flags, in respect'.[62] If nothing else, this signalled a basic acceptance that the Lebanese state had a say vis-à-vis the Cilician See in general and the recent election in particular. Indeed, with anti-Zareh protests still ongoing, Antelias needed the Lebanese and Syrian states' approval to cement the election result. And it needed official pictures of that endorsement. Characteristically, newspapers opposed to Zareh like *Ararad or Zartonk* made a point of refusing to reprint those pictures, while pro-Zareh, pro-Chamoun papers – besides *Aztag* the Arabic *an-Nahar* and *The Daily Star* – did carry them.

Zareh received official support from other quarters as well. And these acts also had to be published to create the desired effect of buffering the

Cilician See election result. On 26 February, 1956, *Aztag* ran a front-page article publicising the congratulatory remarks the Archbishop of Canterbury offered to Zareh. The article also reported that 'various other countries, including France, the United States, Great Britain and Turkey' had congratulated Zareh.[63] And 'from yesterday morning onward', *Aztag* reported on 23 February, 'numerous state officials from all over Lebanon went to Antelias to offer their congratulations to the newly elected Catholicos'.[64] The president of the American University of Beirut and scholars of various universities also visited.[65] The new catholicos was thus firmly linked to Lebanese institutions just as he was being legitimised as the leader of the Lebanese Armenian community. And there was a crucial difference between these meetings and Zareh's visits to Chamoun and al-Quwatli. In the former he was stationery and was receiving, while in the latter he moved to make a visit, indicating that he needed these meetings more than Lebanon's and Syria's presidents and that those presidents outranked him at the end of the day.

As mentioned earlier, after Jordan refused to grant Vasken a visa to enter Jerusalem, Egypt invited Vasken to hold the emergency meeting of the Council of Bishops in Cairo.[66] On the face of it, this was a surprising move. Unlike Jordan, Egypt was not home to an Armenian Patriarchate like that of Jerusalem, and its Armenian population was insignificant.[67] But Cairo's move *did* make sense if we do not see the catholicos election as 'simply' an ecclesiastical event or as an affair 'purely' happening within Lebanon's borders. Cairo's move indeed showcased that nation-states paid attention to a purportedly 'only' internal Armenian issue, and how much states became interested in the election, its result, and the result's management, to defend their interests, broadcast their political and ideological alignments and/or assert their power. Egypt, which saw itself as, and indeed was, a central most player in the Arab state system, thus had no choice but to enter the fray and show that it had a stake and a position in this matter – and, to boot, the power and independence to advance its agenda.

This showed during Vasken's visit to Egypt's president, Gamal Abdel-Nasser. The catholicos first expressed his gratitude for being invited to visit 'this amazing country, and meet Egypt's refined people'.[68] He then recognised 'the bravery and genius' of its leader – a formulation referencing Nasser's anti-imperialist stance in the Arab world and the world of decolonising nations

– and thanked him for having 'always wholeheartedly supported Armenian matters'.⁶⁹ Nasser's reply was interesting. He lauded Armenians while signalling that the Egyptian nation-state had a claim on them. This made sense given that some Armenians in Egypt had started to be affected by (mainly economic) nationalisation campaigns from the mid-1950s. 'Armenians are not foreigners', the Egyptian president stated, 'but children of this country. Through their hard-work and commitment they have won-over the Egyptian people and its government and excelled in the country'.⁷⁰

The 'Vasken Cairo visit' episode of the 1956 catholicos election, like so many other episodes, also had a reverse side. Vasken's invitation to Cairo demonstrated that his authority could not be simply reduced to his being an official operating from the USSR. He was also, if not firstly, a supreme religious authority; he yielded tremendous respect and power in the world's Armenian community, the only one calling himself 'Catholicos of All Armenians' of 'the Mother See'.⁷¹ Uncharacteristically, the doggedly pro-Dashnak, pro-Zareh newspaper *Aztag*, also felt compelled to cover Vasken's Egyptian visit, and in a very positive vein at that. 'The [Cairo] church courtyard was completely packed and had a celebratory atmosphere', it reported. 'Vasken spent the entire day meeting and receiving both Armenian community members and dignitaries'.⁷² That Vasken's authority reached far showed also, and even, in his audience with Abd al-Nasser. The very fact that the Egyptian president made time to receive the catholicos acknowledged his tremendous significance to Armenians. Abd al-Nasser may have been in need of Vasken's embrace what with Egypt's Armenian community being somehow unsettled by the afore-mentioned economic nationalisation campaign. This showed also in Abd al-Nasser's reported answer to Vasken inviting him to the ASSR: 'it is with great pleasure that I accept your invitation. If I go to Moscow and if given the opportunity, I promise to visit you and Echmiadzin, because I really enjoy visiting religious centres'.⁷³

The Theft of the *Ach*

On 24 March, 1956, Armenian papers reported the theft of a handful of relics, including the Holy Right Arm of St Gregory, from the monastery of the Cilician See in Antelias.⁷⁴ It was reported that they were taken from the room of Archbishop Khat Achabahian, the former locum tenens, who was in Cairo attending the Council of Bishops Meeting called by Vasken.⁷⁵ The saint's arm, soon referred to simply as *the ach* by the Armenian press during the 1956 affair, embodied the see's glory and survival through the ages, including during the genocide in World War I.⁷⁶ It was understood as the very incarnation of the see's power, indeed. This also showed in its central symbolic use during the anointment of a newly elected catholicos.⁷⁷ In 1956, those opposed to Zareh's election argued that without it, his election was null and void.

When it became clear that the golden arm would not immediately be returned to the Cilician See, Zareh and other religious figures of the Cilician See reacted with supreme pragmatism and suppleness: They qualified the *ach*'s role as a representation of their authority. A characteristic text in this regard was an article by Father Der Melkonian that, published in *Aztag*, asserted that the Cilician See's authority did not depend on the *ach*. Der Melkonian quoted nobody less than the late Bishop Papken, who, he stated, had 'devoted his time to researching, and writing about, the dogmatic and emotional importance of the *ach*'.⁷⁸ Papken's expertise delineated the relevance of the *ach*. In Der Melkonian's words, 'the *so-called* arm of St Gregory is not regarded as a holy relic within [Armenian] history. In fact, the narrated tales that surround the *ach*, connecting it with the Cilician See, consistently consider the *ach* to be symbol, or remembrance, of His [God's] Illumination. Under no circumstances, however, is it considered to be connected to the existence of faith, hierarchal validity, or positioning [of the See]'. To be sure, the *ach* was crucial to the see. But the authority and power of the Cilician See did not rely or was dependent on its presence in Antelias.⁷⁹ Der Melkonian further underlined his argument by reminding *Aztag*'s readers that at least two Catholicoi had been consecrated without the *ach* being present, adding that one consecration was declared invalid on dogmatic grounds although the *ach* had been present. 'In reality', he concluded, 'the Illuminator's *ach* is neither obligatory in the rule of the see nor in its governance'.⁸⁰

This, incidentally, was not the only article published at this juncture by priests and bishops in *Aztag*. And another key topic of theirs was the history of the Armenian sees in general and their often-contentious relationship in particular. In an attempt to discredit the Echmiadzin See and Vasken, these religious authorities declared the Echmiadzin See a house of thieves. By detailing past stories of insurrections, defections, and – at present most crucially – theft, they implicated Echmiadzin, and by extension Vasken, in the *ach*'s theft. Der Melkonian's 'The Migration of the Armenian Catholicos Seat' asserted that because Echmiadzin had meddled in the Cilician See's affairs before, albeit hundreds of years ago, it was most certainly doing so again. The Echmiadzin See was pathologically treacherous.[81] To Der Melkonian, the prime example was the theft, in 1443, of the Right Arm of St Gregory from Sis – and the fact that it resurfaced in Echmiadzin.[82] More specifically, he added, the *ach* had been smuggled to Echmiadzin via the See of Aghtamar, in Van. In making this statement, Der Melkonian also hinted at the possible collusion of other sees or prelacies in the 1956 theft. If in 1443, the See of Aghtamar was involved, in 1956 it was Archbishop Karekin Khachadourian, the Patriarchate of Istanbul, he hinted. He rhetorically asked the reader why the Prelate of Istanbul had, he asserted, travelled from Istanbul to Beirut to Jerusalem to Cairo in early 1956. And the Istanbul Prelate's current friendly rapport with Vasken, he further insinuated, had to be understood against the background of his earlier sympathetic comments on the USSR and communism.[83]

Zareh's Sunday sermon that week, which was reprinted in *Aztag*, echoed Der Melkonian's article. 'This is not the first time that there have been thefts', the catholicos-elect reminded his flock. 'Similar thefts have occurred before. The *ach* can go missing. But no one can "really" take the Illuminator's *ach*. I have faith that the *ach* [and the other treasures that were stolen] will be found soon in their place, in this monastery. But still, I wish to pray not that we find them, but that this will be done through God's grace, and that the culprits return and put them in their place, at this church'.[84] Zareh also then asserted that his, and the Cilician See's, authority certainly did not depend on the *ach*'s presence, while delicately calling for its return.

The *Ach*'s Return

On 31 March 1957, over a year after its disappearance, the *ach* was 'found'. *Aztag* announced, 'The Holy *Ach* that was stolen from the Catholicosate is found: Archbishop Khoren arrives tomorrow, Sunday, at noon with the Holy Relics at the airport at Khalde'.[85] The details of the theft, including how the relics were stolen, where they were found, under what circumstances, or how they were delivered to Archbishop Khoren, were not immediately provided.[86] *Aztag* only disclosed that the relics were found 'in a neighbouring country', a claim echoed in the Lebanese French daily, *L'Orient*.[87] The very following issue, 2 April, 1957, *Aztag* covered the arrival of the relics, in 'The Stolen *Aches* Yesterday Arrived in Beirut'. *Aztag*'s front page was filled with pictures of Catholicos Zareh joyfully raising the *ach* to bless members of the community who lined the streets from the airport until the monastery.[88] Many of them were mimicking the gesture of the golden arm: their arms raised with their palms open and their thumb bent slightly towards the right.[89] (See Figures 3.8 and 3.9.)

Now the details of the theft were also finally provided. 'With names withheld in order to protect certain identities', *Aztag* described the *ach*'s theft and how it was smuggled out of Lebanon. On 19 February, 1956, once it

Figure 3.8 Zareh with the recovered *ach*, using it to bless the people gathered to celebrate its homecoming to Beirut. *Aztag*, 2 April, 1957.

Figure 3. 9 Crowds celebrating the return of the *ach* and mimicking the *ach*'s gesture. *Aztag*, 2 April, 1957.

had become clear that the election would take place the next day and that Zareh would be elected, Archbishop Karekin, the Prelate of Istanbul and Archbishop Diran Nersoyan, then residing in Jerusalem, orchestrated the burglary in order to invalidate or at least postpone Zareh's election.[90] 'That very night', *Aztag* recounted, 'cold hands stole the case of the golden *ach* [and other relics] from their room and smuggled them out of the monastery, to the home of a collaborator in Beirut'.[91] The following day, when word spread in the religious circles about the theft and that there would be door-to-door inspections, the thieves decided that the *ach* 'must vanish'.[92] The two collaborators, one of whom had stored the *ach* and the other relics in the house of a person loyal to them in Beirut, gave them to Patriarch Yeghishe, acting Prelate of Jerusalem – whose Patriarchate was historically aligned with the Echmiadzin more than with the Cilician See – with the 'demand' that they be taken outside of Lebanon to Jerusalem.[93]

According to *Aztag*, Patriarch Yeghishe then took the relics to Jerusalem and safeguarded them outside the monastery of St James in the Armenian Quarter, 'always thinking that one day he would be able to officially return them'.[94] When there was another attempt to steal the *ach*, this time from Jerusalem, *Aztag* reported that Patriarch Yeghishe eventually made a turnaround: He started to openly disagree with 'the authorities of Jerusalem', (a reference to Archbishop Nersoyan) 'believing the rightful holder of the golden arm and its associated treasures was the See of Cilicia, which must be returned to Beirut'.[95] Eventually, in early 1957, *Aztag* maintained, Yeghishe decided that the time had come to return the relics.[95] 'And so he sent word to Catholicos Zareh in Antelias to send a representative first to Amman and then to Jerusalem to receive the Golden Arm'.[97] With the return of the *ach*, the independence of the See of Cilicia, at least vis-à-vis the Echmiadzin See, was fully re-established.

Incidentally, this turn of events also beautifully showed how the Cilician See's authority crisscrossed various nation-state borders. In 'The Bewilderment of the Thieves of the *Ach*', on 4 April, 1957, *Aztag* stated, 'All of the Armenians of the Cilician See share in the true happiness of the Armenian People. Many hurry to Beirut to thank and congratulate the Catholicos and to see the Holy *Aches*. Antelias has become a place of pilgrimage since Sunday, where the Right Arm of St Gregory the Illuminator blesses all its flock'.[98] Antelias' authority shone far and wide, for all to see, as parishioners travelled there not only from Lebanon but also from the Syrian cities of Aleppo and Damascus and from the Jazira area, from Jordan's Amman and Jerusalem, and from Cyprus.[99]

Zareh reinforced this spectacle – and thereby the Cilician See's religious authority not only in Lebanon but across the Middle East – by expressly choosing the first Feast of St Gregory the Illuminator after the return of the *ach*, 9 April, 1957, to announce that there would be the Blessing of the Holy *Muron*, or chrism, in the fall of that year. (See Figure 3.10.)[100] The consecration of the chrism in Antelias was significant for four reasons. First, the chrism could only be consecrated at the see, reinforcing the monastery at Antelias as the centre of the Cilician See. Second, it could only be completed with the *ach* that blesses the oil. Third, the chrism could only be blessed and consecrated by the catholicos of the see, in this case Zareh, further securing his legitimacy. And finally, the chrism made at the centre

Figure 3.10 Zareh holds the *ach* while performing the ceremony of the consecration of the holy chrism. *Heghapoghagan Album*, 1963.

was then transported to the peripheral congregations which were under the jurisdiction of that see. No religious rite – including marriage, baptismal, or funerary – could take place without the chrism. The Cilician See imposed itself as the authority over its parishioners, who in turn legitimised this very authority.

But the Cilician See was not the only one whose actions were transnational, effectively transcending nation-state borders and dodging nation-state authorities and their power, in the *ach* theft episode of the catholicos election story. The actions of the Echmiadzin See and of the loyalist Istanbul and Jerusalem Prelates also did so. After all – if we are to believe *Aztag*'s account – the latter had succeeded in smuggling the *ach* out of Lebanon and into Jordan *although* the pro-Western authorities in Beirut and Amman were notoriously anti-Vasken and pro-Zareh. And they had succeeded in keeping the *ach* hidden for a good year, away from the preying eyes of the Jordanian authorities. In this case, then, nation-states were unable to control the Armenian struggle for power, and incapable of containing that struggle within their borders. The smuggling of the *ach* out of one country and into another happened at the behest and discretion of a religious figure; national spaces did not contain them.

Then again, the return of the *ach* and the other relics, and their coverage, highlighted the authority of the states that aided in the homecoming, affirming the control certain leaders exercised over the territory of the nation-state. While Archbishop Khoren Paroyan was given the order to collect the golden arm from Catholicos Zareh, he had to wait until the Jordanian authorities in Amman granted him permission to travel and collect the relic.[101] And his arrival in Beirut, together with the 25,000 gathered to welcome the *ach*, had to be sanctioned by Lebanese national authorities. Equally, it was not Catholicos Zareh, but the Lebanese authorities that, controlling the airport, ordered the arrival hall to be closed to secure the *ach*'s arrival and then allow many Armenians to be present outside.

Postscript

One ocean away and two decades before the events described in this chapter, in New York City, on 24 December, 1933, Archbishop Leon Tourian walked down the aisle of the Washington Heights Armenian church to begin evening mass.[102] Five rows in, he was surrounded and stabbed multiple times.[103] Bleeding profusely, he lurched forward, his weight bending his golden staff. Minutes later, he was dead. A murder weapon, an eight-inch butcher's knife wrapped in newspaper, was found on the altar.[104] Two people were arrested at the very scene of the crime; another three the following morning; eventually, nine were prosecuted.[105] All were found guilty, two of first-degree murder, the other seven of first-degree manslaughter.[106]

Tourian was assassinated by members of the Armenian nationalist Dashnak Party.[107] His death formed part of escalating tensions in interwar Armenian communities in the United States and elsewhere regarding Armenia's Sovietisation. An independent republic in 1918, Armenia had become part of the Transcaucasian Socialist Federative Soviet Republic (TSFSR) in 1920, and as such was a founding republic of the USSR in 1922. (In 1936, Moscow would dissolve the TSFSR, and its Armenian part would become the Armenian Socialist Soviet Republic (ASSR).) As a matter of fact, December 1933 was not the first time that Dashnak Party members had attacked Tourian. On 1 July that year, the archbishop was scheduled to address an Armenian Day meeting at the Chicago World's Fair. When he arrived, he found that Dashnak members had placed the flag of the former Armenian republic on the stage. 'Explaining that Armenia is no longer a republic, but a part of the Soviet Union', the *New York Times* later informed its readers, 'Archbishop Tourian insisted that the flag of the old republic be taken down and that the present flag, which bears the white hammer and sickle of the Soviets on a red background, be raised instead'.[108] Dashnak supporters and opponents clashed; chairs flew and other weapons were also used. Eventually, the Chicago police broke up the fights, the Soviet Armenian flag was raised and the archbishop gave his address.[109]

This event illustrated how, together with the Sovietisation of the land of Armenia, the Armenian church in Armenia, and specifically the Echmiadzin See whose base was located in the ASSR, had also come under Soviet oversight. And as the Echmiadzin See had administered US Armenian churches already before Russia's 1917 October Revolution, a fascinating situation arose after World War I in the United States. In this most determinedly capitalist country, the religious and community life of Armenians – many Dashnaks – was administered by a see whose hierarchy was under the ultimate control of the world's first communist country. While the Dashnak Party refused to recognise the ASSR and advocated the establishment of an independent Armenia within the boundaries of historical Armenia, it did not have the power to ecclesiastically challenge the Echmiadzin See. More than that: Ecclesiastically and religiously, that party and its members were at the mercy of the Echmiadzin See. And that see reacted with utter firmness to Tourian's assassination. In the following days, it excluded from US parishes nothing less than circa 300,000 Armenians for their alleged opposition to Armenia's Soviet status, denying them baptisms, marriages and death rites.[110]

This situation persisted for more than two decades.[111] Switching to the Cilician See was not a realistic option. Only recently relocated from the Ottoman Empire to Antelias/Beirut, that see was still somewhat weak; it was not willing to challenge Echmiadzin; and it operated overwhelmingly in the Middle East. But as we have seen in this chapter, by the 1950s, tensions with the Echmiadzin See increased and in 1956–1957 crystallised in the show-down over the 1956 catholicos election and the subsequent theft of the *ach*. These events provided an opening for excommunicated US Armenians to ask the Cilician See to start operating in the United States. Naturally, Washington had no objections; and as naturally, Antelias was delighted to respond in the positive, breaking the Echmiadzin See's monopoly on organised Armenian religious life there.[112]

Thus, in late 1957, Cilician See priests, bishops and archbishops were brought to the United States from monasteries and seminaries in Lebanon, and the Holy Chrism was also flown in from there. The ensuing competition, in the United States, between the Cilician and Echmiadzin See was not limited to the realm of the spiritual.[113] Money talked, as well. Armenians in the United States paid membership dues to their parish. These funds were needed to pay for church employees like secretaries, deacons, priests, bishops and archbishops, and secured the land on which monasteries and divinity schools were built. As such, they underwrote a see's legitimacy vis-à-vis Armenians and non-Armenians alike.

Obviously, this change was cause for much celebration not only among Dashnak Armenians in the United States but also in Lebanon, with *Aztag* declaring in October 1957 that 'from this day forward, the American–Armenian prelacy will enjoy the great guidance of the Holy See of the Catholicosate of Cilicia'.[114] Headquartered in New York City, the Cilician See's US prelacy maintained this ecclesiastical Armenian connection between the United States and Lebanon. It also acted as an embassy of sorts for Antelias in the United States. US politicians legitimised these developments, meeting the envoy sent from Lebanon, Archbishop Khoren. And the broader, Cold War dimension of this development was on full display when on 27 October, 1957, Archbishop Khoren met US Vice President Richard Nixon, who saluted the archbishop's work.[115]

In sum, while Antelias' US operation was of course welcomed by the US government, here as in the catholicos election crisis, Armenians deftly exploited the Cold War to their own ends. We can fully understand post-war, post-colonial Armenian history only if we *also* keep the Cold War in mind; but by the same token, we need to understand how Armenians were able to manipulate Cold War tensions – between the United States and the USSR globally as well as regional manifestations and versions – in order to advance their proper agendas.

Notes

1. For further details on the period between Karekin's death and Zareh's election, see Simon Payaslian, 'The Institutionalisation of the Catholicos of the Great House of Cilicia in Antelias', in *Armenian Cilicia*, ed. Richard G. Hovannisian and Simon Payaslian (Costa Mesa: Mazda, 2008), 557–92.
2. 'Atenagrut'iwn Patgamaworakan Zhoghovoy' [Minutes of the Meeting of Religious Representatives], *Hask* (Beirut, Lebanon) Nos. 1–4 (January–April 1956), 12. Before being chosen catholicos, Zareh was the archbishop of Aleppo.
3. Seta Dadoyan, *The Armenian Catholicosate from Cilicia to Antelias* (Antelias: The Armenian Catholicosate of Cilicia, 2003), 95–6.
4. '50 Women Capture Church; Armenians Elect Anti-Communist Patriarch', *The Daily Star* (Beirut, Lebanon), 15 February, 1956, 1; 'Two Armenian Merchants Knifed and Beaten', *The Daily Star*, 24 February, 1956, 1.
5. Given that the return of the *ach* was facilitated by the Jerusalem Patriarchate, it is impossible that the divisive Archbishop Yeghishe Derderian was not involved. This, even though he was residing in Amman at the time due to a crisis of legitimacy at the Jerusalem Patriarchate. For more on this internal struggle and how Israeli and Jordanian Cold War allegiances played a role in the politics of the Jerusalem Patriachate, see Ara Sanjian, 'The Armenian Church and Community of Jerusalem', in *The Christian Communities of Jerusalem and the Holy Land: Studies in History, Religion, and Politics*, ed. Anthony O'Mahony (Cardiff: University of Wales Press, 2003), 70–84; Bedross Der Matossian, 'The Armenians of Jerusalem in the Modern Period: The Rise and Decline of a Community', in *Routledge Handbook on Jerusalem*, eds Suleiman A. Mourad, Naomi Koltun-Fromm, and Bedross Der Matossian (New York: Routledge, 2019), 400–2.
6. Nikola Schahgaldian, 'The Political Integration of an Immigrant Community into a Composite Society: the Armenians in Lebanon 1920–74' (Ph.D diss., Columbia University, 1978), 203–4.
7. The election of Zareh was, in turn, used by other Armenian religious figures in order to articulate their own power. For example, Archbishop Yeghishe Derderian, the *locum tenens* of the Jerusalem Patriarchate, in the wake of Zareh's election, threatened to transfer the allegiance of the Jerusalem Patriarchate from the Echmiadzin See to the Cilician See if they did not heed his wishes. While such promises came to naught, demonstrating the savviness of Archbishop Derderian, who manipulated both sees and the Jordanian

government's fear of communism to win his own election and become the Patriarch of Jerusalem, they simultaneously reveal the continued impact of this election beyond Lebanon. For more on Archbishop Derderian see Sanjian, 'The Armenian Church', 71–84.

8. On an analysis of both direct and indirect interventions of the United States in Armenian affairs see James R. Stocker, 'The United States and the Armenian Community in Lebanon, 1943–1967', in *Armenians of Lebanon (II) Proceedings of the Conference (14–16 May 2014)*, ed. Antranik Dakessian (Beirut: Haigazian University Press, 2017) and 'An Opportunity to Strike a Blow? The United States Government and the Armenian Apostolic Church, 1956–1963', *Diplomacy & Statecraft* 29, no. 4 (2018): 590–612. On both the involvement and non-involvement of British and American officials in matters of succession in the Jerusalem Patriarchate see Sanjian, 'The Armenian Church', 71–84. Talin Suciyan also profiles the Istanbul Patriarchate's election crisis (1944–1950) and analyses how the Echmiadzin See, in interfering with the election, attempted to gain power under the auspices of the USSR. Nevertheless, she positions this struggle for power to analyse its imapct on anti-Armenianism in Turkey. Suciyan, *The Armenian in Modern Turkey*, 169–197.

9. Kamal Salibi, *A House of Many Mansions* (Berkeley: University of California Press, 1988); Fawwaz Traboulsi, *A History of Modern Lebanon* (London: Pluto Press, 2007); Caroline Attié, *Struggle in the Levant: Lebanon in the* 1950s (London: I. B. Tauris, 2004).

10. Payaslian does mention 'international pressure' referencing 'East–West polarisation', but does not elaborate further. Instead, he used the incident to comment on how the Cilician Catholicosate was 'sound enough' to withstand such tension. Payaslian, 'The Institutionalisation of the Catholicos', 591. Dadoyan, *Armenian Catholicosate*, 96, describes the event as an 'embarrassing episode', but does not fully address the implications of the 'media wars between various factions and parties'.

11. 'Kilikioy Kat'oghikosakan Untrut'iwnĕ Teghi Piti Unenay P'etruar 14–in' [The Elections of the Cilician See Will Take Place on February 14], *Aztag*, 9 February, 1956, 1.

12. Ibid.

13. 'Amenayn Hayots' Kat'oghikosĕ Pĕyrut' Kugay Shk'akhumbov' [The Catholicos of All Armenians Arrives in Beirut with Splendour], *Ararad*, 5 February, 1956, 1. The Cilician See's dioceses historically consisted of those

in Cilicia, Aleppo and Cyprus. By the 1930s, it had relocated and its jurisdiction presided over congregations throughout Syria, Lebanon and to an extent, Cyprus. (The authority over the diocese of Cyprus remained fluid between the Patriarchate of Jerusalem and the Cilician See.) Payaslian, 'The Institutionalisation of the Catholicosate', 571.

14. 'Barov Yekak' Vehap'aṛ Hayrapet' [Welcome Catholicos], *Zartonk* (Beirut, Lebanon), 12 February, 1956, 1.
15. 'Atenagrut'iwn Patgamaworakan Zhoghovoy' [Minutes of the Meeting of Religious Representatives], *Hask* No. 1–4 (January-April 1956), 12.
16. Of course, also before Vasken's announcement, practice often differed. Thus, every parish of the Catholicosate of Cilicia prayed for the catholicos of Echmiadzin during Sunday mass. (Those from the Catholicosate of Echmiadzin did not reciprocate.)
17. For an overview of the establishment of the Armenian Church and its surviving sees, see Hratch Tchilingirian, 'The Catholicos and the Hierarchical Sees of the Armenian Church' in *Eastern Christianity: Studies in Modern History, Religion and Politics*, ed. Anthony O'Mahony (London: Melisende, 2004), 140–59.
18. Dickran Kouymjian, 'Cilicia and its Catholicosate from the Fall of the Armenian Kingdom to 1915', in *Armenian Cilicia*, ed. Richard Hovannisian and Simon Payaslian (Costa Mesa: Mazda, 2008), 299.
19. On the establishment of the Cilician See and the Kingdom of Cilicia see amongst others, Azat A. Bozoyan, 'Armenian Political Revival in Cilicia', in *Armenian Cilicia*, 67–78; Gérard Dédéyan, 'The Founding and Coalescence of the Rubenian Principality, 1073–1129', 79–92; and Robert Hewsen, 'Armenia Maritima: The Historical Geography of Cilicia', 33–65; on the period between the fall of the Cilician Kingdom in 1375 until the Armenian Genocide, see Kouymjian, 'Cilicia and its Catholicosate', 297–307.
20. For more on how relations between the Cilician Kingdom and the Papacy affected the Cilician Catholicosate see Peter Halfter, 'Papacy, Catholicosate, and the Kingdom of Cilician Armenia', in *Armenian Cilicia*, 111–29. For more on the relationship between the sees and patriarchates see Malachia Ormanian, *The Church of Armenia: Her History, Doctrine, Rule, Descipline, Liturgy, Literature, and Existing Condition* (London: Forgotten Books, 2012).
21. This fact was not lost on Russian and Ottoman authorities, and there were attempts to curtail the breadth of the Armenian Church's authority and have its power abide by specific boundaries.
22. For more on the history of the Armenian Church in Istanbul and how the

tanzimat challenged its power, see Richard Edward Antaramian 'In Subversive Service of the Sublime State: Armenians and Ottoman State Power, 1844–1896' (Ph.D diss., University of Michigan, 2014); Bedross Der Matossian, *Shattered Dreams of Revolution: From Liberty to Violence in the Late Ottoman Empire* (Stanford: Stanford University Press, 2014); Raymond Kévorkian, *The Armenian Genocide: A Complete History* (New York: I. B. Tauris, 2011), 691–698. For more on the history of Armenians in Jerusalem see Bedross Der Matossian, 'The Armenians of Palestine 1918–48', *Journal of Palestine Studies* 41, No. 1 (Autumn 2011): 24–44; Avedis Sanjian, *The Armenian Communities in Syria Under Ottoman Domination* (Cambridge, MA: Harvard University Press, 1965), 114, 257–258. On the Jerusalem Patriachate and the Cold War, see Sanjian, 'The Armenian Church', 71–84.

23. While the Patriarchate of Istanbul represented the entirety of the Armenian *millet* to the Ottoman government, it was, with regards to hierarchy, lower in rank than the Catholicoi of Cilicia, Aghtamar, or Echmiadzin. That the vast majority of the Armenians under jurisdiction of these Catholicoi were peasants, while the parishioners in Istanbul were more landed and educated gentry, suggests the Ottoman government privileged (social) class over the (religious) hierarchy of the institution of the Armenian Apostolic Church. For more on the Patriarchate of Istanbul see Kevork Bardakjian, 'The Rise of the Armenian Patriarchate of Constantinople' in *Christian and Jews in the Ottoman Empire*, vol. 1: *The Central Lands*, ed. Benjamin Braude (New York: Holmes and Meier, 2014), 97.

24. Der Matossian, 'The Armenians of Palestine', 24–44.

25. For example, in 1916, Jemal Pasha met with Cilician See Catholicos Sahag in Aleppo and informed him that the Aghtamar and Cilician Sees were to be abolished, along with the Jerusalem and Istanbul Patriarchates (the CUP had already cut off ties with the Catholicosate of Echmiadzin), in favour of the establishment of a single Armenian religious authority, or patriarch-catholicos. While the CUP proclaimed Catholicos Sahag (of the Cilician See) its new head in 1916, this never really came into fruition. Kouymjian, 'Cilicia and its Catholicosate', 306–7.

26. Eduard Oganessyan, 'The Armenian Church in the USSR', *Religion in Communist Lands* 7, No. 4 (2008): 238–242. Edward Alexander, 'The Armenian Church in Soviet Policy', *The Russian Review* 14, No. 4 (October, 1955), 358–9.

27. While the differences are not insurmountable, variances remain. In a conver-

sation held with Archbishop Kegham Khajerian, the head of the Armenian Patriarchate in Lebanon in 2008 at the Lebanese Prelacy in Bourj Hamoud, Khajerian stated that the centre of the Western Armenian language was in Beirut, Lebanon. Accordingly, he explained, he and the Armenian Church of Lebanon had a duty to protect it from being replaced by Arabic in Lebanon. He also added that it was his responsibility, as the head of the Lebanese Armenian community, to defend it against the growing prowess of Eastern Armenian in the form of television and publishing from the Republic of Armenia. Interview with author, Beirut, Lebanon, 20 February, 2009. For more on the role of Armenian in the construction of Armenian identity in Lebanon and the diaspora see Arda Jebejian, 'Patterns of Language Use Among Armenians in Beirut in the Last 95 Years', *Haigazian Armenological Review* 31 no. 1 (2011): 453–69 and Shoushan Karapetian, 'Opportunities and Challenges of Institutionalising a Pluricentric Diasporic Language: The Case of Armenian in Los Angeles', in *The Routledge Handbook of Heritage Language Education: From Innovation to Program Building*, eds Olga Kagan, Maria Carreira, and Claire Chick (New York: Routledge, 2017), 145–60.

28. There was not a single record of opposition by priests, bishops, or archbishops of the Cilician See to Catholicos Karekin's position, even as thousands of their members were leaving their authority permanently. While this movement reduced the Cilician See's membership base by thousands and inevitably contributed to a decline in its power, it did not foster a greater power struggle between the Cilician See in Lebanon and the Echmiadzin See in Soviet Armenia.

29. For more on the US involvement in the Middle East during the Cold War, see Rashid Khalidi, *Sowing Crisis: The Cold War and American Dominance in the Middle East* (Boston: Beacon Press, 2009); on the 1950s, see also Salim Yaqub, *Containing Arab Nationalism: The Eisenhower Doctrine in the Middle East* (Chapel Hill and London: University of North Carolina Press, 2004).

30. Schahgaldian, 'The Political Integration', 203–4.

31. It is interesting to note that *The Daily Star*, the country's English language press, covered Vasken's visit with the headline 'Patriarch Visit May Unite Armenians Here' indicating that it saw Armenians as a divided community, saw Vasken's visit solely as an internal (Armenian) affair, and as a hopeful development. *The Daily Star*, 14 February, 1956, 1.

32. On the election of 1441 and the 'transfer' of the Cilician See 'back' to Echmiadzin and the institutionalisation of the use of the terms and titles

'Mother See' and 'Catholicos of All Armenians'', see Dickran Kouymjian, 'Cilicia and its Catholicosate', 299–303.
33. 'Koch' Hay Zhoghovurdin' [A Call to the Armenian People], *Aztag*, 11 February, 1956, 1.
34. Ibid. The others included the request for Armenian school students to line the route from the National Museum to Corniche al-Nahr, the expected crowds to facilitate the passage of the motorcade, not to gather en masse at the entrance to the Antelias monastery complex, and for all Armenians to act in an 'orderly and respectful' manner.
35. While there are different readings of flag holding, indicating the fluidity of identity, I agree with Robert John Foster's assertion that 'all [are] within, against, or at least in dialogue with the nation, and understood as a salient frame of reference for delineating personal and collective identities', in *Materializing the Nation: Commodities, Consumption, and Media in Papua New Guinea* (Bloomington: Indiana University Press, 2002), 17.
36. Vasken arrived in Beirut on Sunday, 12 February, and was greeted by acting Catholicos Archbishop Khoren. He met with additional Cilician See officials on 13 February and held meetings with President Chamoun on 14 February.
37. 'Kilikioy Kat'oghikosakan Ěndrut'yan Patgamaworakan Zhoghově Bats'uets'aw Erěk ew Ěndrets' ir Mnayun Diwaně Khap'anararneru Bolor Dawerě Dzakhoghets'an' [Yesterday the Meeting of the Election Representatives of the Cilician See Opened and Elected a Permanent Panel; The Naysayers' Ruses to Sabotage these Efforts Failed], *Aztag*, 16 February, 1956, 1.
38. Ibid.
39. Ibid.
40. Ibid. Emphasis added.
41. Ibid. For more on the Council of Bishops see Ormanian, *The Church of Armenia*.
42. 'Ējmiatsnay Kat'oghikosě Irawunk' Ch'uněr Patgamawor Zhoghovi Hedadzgumě Pahanjelu' [The Unjustified Request to Reschedule the Meeting of the Election Representatives by the Echmiadzin Catholicos], *Aztag*, 17 February, 1956, 1, 4. Buzand Yeghiayan, *Zhamanakakits' Padmut'yun Kat'oghikosut'yan Hayots' Kilikioh 1914–1972* [The Contemporary History of The Armenian Catholicosate of Cilicia] (Antelias: The Catholicosate of Cilicia, 1975), 675.
43. 'Pashtōnakan Zekoyts' Kilikioy Kat'oghikosakan Ěndrut'yan Patgamawor

Zhoghovi Diwanēn' [The Official Minutes from the Election Representatives of the Cilician See], *Aztag*, 17 February, 1956, 1.
44. 'Vehapʻaṛin Aytsʻĕ N.V. Hanrpetin Nakhagahin' [The Catholicos' Visit to the President], *Aztag*, 15 February, 1956, 1, 4.
45. Ibid.
46. 'Vehapʻaṛ Vazgēn I Hayrapet Ays Kiraki Kĕ Kʻarozē Antʻiliasi Mēj' [Catholicos Vasken I Gives the Sermon at Antelias This Sunday], *Aztag*, 18 February, 1956, 1.
47. Ibid.
48. 'Vehapʻarʻin Aytsʻĕ N.V. Hanrpetin Nakhagahin' [The Catholicos' Visit to the President], *Aztag*, 15 February, 1956, 1.
49. While the election of the catholicos took place on 20 February, he was not consecrated until 2 September. This lag between election and consecration was not entirely unusual, however.
50. '50 Women Capture Church; Armenians Elect Anti-Communist Patriarch', *The Daily Star*, 21 February, 1956, 1; 'Two Armenian Merchants Knifed and Beaten Here', *The Daily Star*, 24 February, 1956, 1.
51. 'Ov Hay Kin' [O Armenian Woman], *Aztag*, 24 February, 1956, 1. '50 Women Capture Church; Armenians Elect Anti-Communist Patriarch', *The Daily Star*, 21 February, 1956, 1. 'Armenian Women Demonstrate', *The Daily Star*, 25 February, 1956, 1.
52. 'Aztag'i Pʻoghotsʻayin Vayrahachʻutʻiwnnerĕ Barepasht Kineru Hastsʻēin' [*Aztag*'s Disreputable Terrorist Activities Against the Virtuous Armenian Women] *Zartonk*, 28 February, 1956, 1.
53. 'Erkushapdi Ōruan Srbapights Ararkʻnerĕ' [Monday's Abusive Endeavors], *Aztag*, 24 February, 1956, 1; 'Kiraki Ōruan Zhoghovrdayin Hskay Mitʻinkĕ ew Tsʻoytsʻĕ' [Sunday's Popular Meeting and Demonstration], *Zartonk*, 23 February, 1956, 3.
54. 'Tesaran Mĕ Barepasht Hayuhineru Sahagyani Mitʻinkēn' [A View of the Virtuous Women at the Sahagyan Meeting], *Zartonk*, 26 February, 1956, 1.
55. The letter was printed in full on the front page of *Zartonk*, 26 February, 1956. 'Barepasht Hayuhineru Khōskʻĕ N.V. Nakhagah Shamunin' [The Virtuous Armenian Women's Communiqué to the Honourable President Chamoun], *Zartonk*, 26 February, 1956, 1.
56. Ibid.
57. *Aztag*, the Dashnak paper, reports on the snub with tempered glee: '*We hear that that the Jordanian government has refused to grant a visa to the Catholicos*

of All-Armenians [his official title], Vasken I, and his entourage, who, for ten days, have been in Egypt waiting for their visa to travel to Jerusalem. It is said that Echmiadzin's head will now go to Rome'. In 'Hordanan Merzhats ē Ējmiatsnah Katʻoghikosin' [Jordan Has Refused to Grant a Visa to Echmiadzin's Catholicos], *Aztag*, 2 March,1956, 1. Emphasis added.
58. 'Jordan Slams Door in Face of Armenian Patriarch', *The Daily Star*, 11 March, 1956, 1.
59. 'Surioy Vsemashukʻ Nakhagah Shukʻri Kʻuatʻli Kě Shnorhaworē N.S. Zareh I Kʻatʻogh.i Ěntrutʻyuně' [His Eminence the Syrian President Shukri al-Quwatli Congratulates Zareh I on his Election], *Aztag*, 24 February, 1956, 1; see also the front page of *Aztag's* February 28, 1956 issue.
60. Ibid.
61. 'Norěndir Vehapʻarʻ D.D. Zareh I Katʻoghikos Artakarg Patiwnerov Ěndunewtsʻaw Libanan Hanrapetutʻyan Vsemashukʻ Nakhagahin Koghmē' [Newly Elected Catholicos Zareh I was Met with Great Honour by His Eminence the President of the Lebanese Republic], *Aztag*, 23 February, 1956, 1.
62. Ibid.
63. Catholicos Zareh I's personal papers, 25–1(16) February 1956, Archives of the Catholicosate of Cilicia, Antelias, Lebanon.
64. 'Azg. Pashdōnakan Marminer, Usuchʻichʻner, Usanoghner, ew Azgayinnyer Kě Shnorhaworen Norěndir Katʻoghikosě' [Official National Organisations, Teachers, Scholars, and Nationals Congratulate the Newly Elected Catholicos], *Aztag*, 23 February, 1956, 1.
65. Ibid.
66. 'Hortanan Merzhats ē', 1.
67. Egypt's Armenian population fell dramatically as a result of the repatriation movement 1946–1949. It experienced a further decrease during the presidency of Gamal Abd al-Nasser. By the late 1950's the number of Armenians had dwindled from 40,000 in 1920 to around 15,000. For more on the history of Armenian Egyptians in the modern era, see Dawn Chatty, *Displacement and Dispossession in the Modern Middle East* (Cambridge: Cambridge University Press, 2010) and Otto F. A. Meinardus, *Christians in Egypt: Orthodox, Catholic and Protestant Communities Past and Present* (Cairo: The American University in Cairo Press, 2006).
68. 'N.S. Ō. Vasken I Yegiptosi Varchʻin Mōt' [N.S.O. Vasken I Close to Egypt's Governor], *Aztag*, 7 March, 1956, 1.

69. What types of 'Armenian matters', Vasken did not made clear. 'N.S. Ō. Vasken I Yegiptosi Varch'in Mōt', 1.
70. Ibid.
71. Kouymjian, 'Cilicia and its Catholicosate', 302–3.
72. 'Amenayn Hayots' Kat'oghikosĕ Gahirēi Mēj' [The Catholicos of All Armenians in Cairo], *Aztag*, 24 February, 1956, 1.
73. 'N.S. Ō. Vasken I Yegiptosi Varch'in Mōt', 1.
74. 'Oronk' Goghts'an Lusaworich'i Ajĕ Ew Inch'u' [Who Stole the Illuminator's Aches and Why?], *Aztag*, 24 March, 1956.
75. While the Armenian press first reported on the theft on 24 March, the theft itself took place about ten days prior, on 13 March, 1956. Zaven Arzoumanian, *The Armenian Apostolic Church in Recent Times: A Path to the 21st Century* (Burbank: Issued Privately, 2010), 30.
76. The golden arm of the right hand of St Gregory was moved to Cilicia when the Kingdom of Ani fell in the eleventh century. It was then transported to Echmiadzin when the Kingdom of Cilicia fell in 1441, only to be brought back to Sis, today's Kozan, a few years later. See Dickran Kouymjian, 'The Right Hand of St. Gregory and other Armenian Arm Relics', in *Les objets de la mémoire. Pour une approche comparatiste des reliques et de leur culte*, ed. Philippe Borgeaud and Youri Volokhine (Geneva: Peter Lang, 2005), 215–40. During the Armenian massacres and the chaos of World War I, the *ach*, along with other relics, was transported by ox-cart from Sis to Aleppo. Once Catholicos Sahag had secured the Antelias compound as the home of the Cilician See, these relics, including the *ach*, were brought to Beirut. For more on the rescue operation and movement of the relics from Sis to Antelias, see Hermann Goltz and Klaus E. Göltz, *Rescued Armenian Treasures from Cilicia: Sacred Art of the Kilikia Museum Antelias, Lebanon* (Wiesbaden: Reichert, 2000).
77. It was also used to prepare the Holy Chrism (*muron*). This consecrated oil is used in various religious services including the administration of baptism, marriage, and death rites in addition to serving in other sacraments and ecclesiastical functions.
78. Father Ter Melgonyan, 'Hay Kat'oghikosakan At'or'in Teghap'okhutynnerĕ' [The Migration of the Armenian Catholicos Seat], *Aztag*, 21 March, 1956, 1.
79. Ibid. Emphasis added.
80. Ibid.
81. Ibid.
82. Ibid. In detailing this theft, Der Melkonian tells of how it was smuggled to

Echmiadzin via the See of Aghtamar in Van (which had been disbanded since the massacres during the Ottoman Empire). In doing so, he exposes the precedence of an accessory See or prelacy that aids in the theft, suggesting it as a precondition for its success. In 1443 it was the See of Aghtamar that was its co-conspirator, and it would not be a stretch for the reader in 1956 to replace Aghtamar with Istanbul (or Jerusalem for that matter). It was the Prelate of Istanbul's movements from Istanbul to Beirut to Jerusalem to Cairo that were covered with suspicion. And as his travels were scrutinised (though, it should be noted, not analysed), his past comments on the USSR and communism were juxtaposed with his current friendly rapport with Vasken I on the front pages of *Aztag*. ('Yerēk ew Aysōr' [Yesterday and Today], *Aztag*, 29 March, 1956).

83. Ibid. While it is unclear if Patriarch Karekin did play a role in the theft, this particular reasoning does not hold much merit, if one considers it in the context of the relationship of the Patriarchate of Istanbul and the Echmiadzin See. The crisis that affected the Istanbul Patriarchate between 1944 and 1950 had soured relations between Istanbul and Echmiadzin, with Vasken's predecessor, Catholicos Kevork VI, stating that Patriarch Karekin was 'misguided and dishonourable'. For more on the crisis see Suciyan, *Armenians in Modern Turkey*, 169–97. That being said, it is possible that Patriarch Karekin wanted to improve the situation with Catholicos Kevork VI's successor, Vasken I. The accusation that Patriarch Karekin was a communist sympathiser is also odd, as he was accused of supporting the Dashnak Party since the 1940s. Suciyan, *Armenians in Modern Turkey*, 196–7.
84. 'Vehap'ar' D. D. Zareh I-i Hogeshunch' K'arozĕ' [The Moving Sermon of Zareh I], *Aztag*, 22 March, 1956, 1.
85. 'Kat'oghikosaranēn Goghts'uats S. Ajerĕ Gdnuets'an' [The *Aches* Stolen from the Catholicosate Have Been Found], *Aztag*, 31 March, 1957, 1.
86. Ibid.
87. Ibid.
88. 'Goghts'uats Ajerĕ Yerēk Hasan Pēyrut'' [The Stolen *Aches* Yesterday Arrived in Beirut], *Aztag*, 2 April, 1957, 1. This scene could be juxtaposed with that of the arrival of Vasken I, 14 months earlier.
89. Ibid.
90. 'Voronk' ew Inch'pēs Goghts'an Masunk'nerĕ' [Who and How They Stole the Relics of the Saint], *Aztag*, 2 April, 1957, 1. Archbishop Diran Nersoyan was the most senior and influential member of the Brotherhood of St James,

the Armenian monastic order in Jerusalem. While he was also the Primate of the Eastern Diocese of North America (under the tutelage of the Echmiadzin See), he had been in Jerusalem since 1955 to demand an investigation into the finances of the Jerusalem Patriarchate and to hold elections for a new Patriarch. For more on Archbishop Diran, the delayed election in Jerusalem, and the *locum tenens* Yeghishe Derderian see Der Matossian, 'Armenians of Jerusalem in the Modern Period', 400–2; and Sanjian, 'The Armenian Church and Community', 71–84. If Archbishop Nersoyan was involved in the theft, it could have been in order to gain favour with Catholicos Vasken I and further move against Archbishop Yeghishe, whom he was attempting to remove from office.

91. 'Voronkʻ ew Inchʻpēs Goghtsʻan Masunkʻnerě' [Who and How They Stole the Relics of the Saint], *Aztag*, 2 April, 1957, 1.
92. Ibid.
93. It is unclear who made this 'demand', and what exactly it looked like. *Aztag* correspondences suggested that Archbishop Yeghishe had no choice in the matter and that he did so in order to safeguard the relics and prevent the already tense situation from descending into further chaos that could have led to the 'permanent loss' of the relics. The newspaper likewise noted that Patriarch Yeghishe considered the *aches* to be 'the property of and belonging to the Cilician Catholicosate", taking care not to accuse him in the crime. 'Voronkʻ ew Inchʻpēs Goghtsʻan Masunkʻnerě' [Who and How They Stole the Relics of the Saint], *Aztag*, 2 April, 1957, 1. And yet, one cannot forget that Archbishop Yeghishe was embroiled in a battle with Archbishop Diran over legitimacy and succession. In fact Archbishop Yeghishe consistently threatened to reorient the allegiance of the Jerusalem Patriarchate to the Cilician See in order to pressure the Echmiadzin See to legitimise his rule, pardon his past misdeeds and remove Archbishop Diran from Jerusalem. Accordingly his involvement in 'safeguarding' and returning the *aches* may have been collateral to use against either see in order to restore his power in Jerusalem as he (and his supporters) saw fit. In fact, Archbishop Yeghishe notified the Cilician See authorities of the whereabouts of the *ach* from Amman, just a few days after Archbishop Diran was elected Patriarch of Jerusalem, and after he himself was expelled from the Jerusalem Brotherhood and suspended from all religious and ecclesiastical functions by a decree of Vasken I. By 1960, Archbishop Diran was deported, the punishments against Archbishop Yeghishe were reversed, and he was elected Patriarch of Jerusalem. Sanjian, 'The Armenian Church

and Commnuity', 71–84. A subtext of this story therefore exists that can demonstrate how Archbishop Yeghishe subverted the powers of the Cilician and Echmiadzin Sees along with the Cold War superpowers and used their proxies, most notably that of Jordan, of which he held citizenship, in a struggle for power.

94. 'Voronk' ew Inch'pēs', 1.
95. Ibid.
96. Ibid.
97. Ibid.
98. 'Ajagoghnerĕ Sahmrkats' [The Bewilderment of the Thieves of the *Ach*], *Aztag*, 4 April, 1957, 1.
99. Ibid.
100. 'Lusavorich'i Tōnĕ Ant'eliasi Mēj' [The Feast of St Gregory in Antelias], *Aztag*, 9 April, 1957, 1.
101. 'Goghts'uats S. Masunk'nerĕ Yerēk Hasan Pēyrut'' [Yesterday the Stolen Holy Relics Arrived in Beirut], *Aztag*, 2 April, 1957, 1.
102. 'Slain in the 187th St. Church', *The New York Times*, 25 December, 1933, 1.
103. Ibid.
104. Ibid.
105. 'Killing of Prelate Laid to Five Rebels', *The New York Times*, 26 December, 1933, 1; '2 More held in Killing', *The New York Times*, 19 January, 1934, 42; '4 Jurors Chosen for Tourian Trial', *The New York Times*, 8 June, 1934, 22; 'Nine Found Guilty in Church Murder', *The New York Times*, 14 July, 1934, 1; 'Lehman Spares Lives of Tourian's Slayers', *The New York Times*, 10 April, 1935, 12.
106. 'Nine Found Guilty', 1; 'Lehman Spares Lives', 12.
107. 'Killing of Prelate', 1.
108. 'Slain', 13.
109. Ibid. Another incident occurred in August 1933 at a church picnic in Westboro, Massachusetts. Here, Tourian himself was assaulted, together with other parishioners. As he 'rose to pronounce his blessing on 1,500 communicants', the *New York Times* accounted, 'a truckload of younger members' also from the Dashnak Party struck him. Following yet another 'free-for-all' fight, local police were called in, and were 'finally' able to halt the violence. 'Beaten at Church Picnic', *New York Times*, 25 December, 1933, 3.
110. Over 5,000 Armenians attended the funeral of Tourian. In addition to the significant police presence, Tourian's body was guarded by four New York City

Patrolmen, demonstrating the level of anxiety and tension that surrounded the murder and funeral. 'Thousands Honour Slain Archbishop', *The New York Times*, 2 January, 1934, 11.

111. Tension in the immediate aftermath of the assassination often resulted in violence. The *New York Times* reported that those arrested were attacked by an 'angry mob of more than 500 adherents of the Archbishop'. 'Tourian Suspects Saved From Mob', *The New York Times*, 11 January, 1934, 42. See also 'Five Hurt in Clash of Armenians Here', when a group of Armenians attacked a Dashnak meeting in the auditorium of the Metropolitan Life Building in New York City, *The New York Times*, 26 February, 1934, 38. Violence spread to other cities with Armenian populations as well, including Boston and Chicago. 'Armenian Rivals Riot in Two Cities', *The New York Times*, 9 April, 1934, 36.

112. John H. Fenton, 'Armenian Church Cuts Russian Link', *The New York Times*, 17 October, 1957, 55.

113. Russell Porter, 'Armenian Cleric Assails Prelate', *The New York Times*, 20 October, 1957, 78.

114. 'Lkʻuats Ēin Tēr Unetsʻan' [Abandoned, Then Saved] *Aztag*, 18 October, 1957, 1.

115. Khoren was also the guest of honour at a well-attended dinner-reception by the Lebanese Ambassador to Washington, DC, Charles Malek. 'Khorēn Srbazan Erkushabtʻi Piti Ĕndunui Amerikayi Pʻokh-Nakhagahin Koghmē' [Archbishop Khoren Will Meet with the Vice President of the United States], *Aztag*, 27 October, 1957, 1.

4

MAKING ARMENIANS LEBANESE: THE 1957 ELECTION AND THE ENSUING 1958 CONFLICT

Introduction

From the mid-1950s, Lebanese President Camille Chamoun's (1952–1958) openly pro-Western orientation created considerable political tensions in Lebanon. As noted in Chapter 3, in 1955 this showed in his support of the Baghdad Pact. Two years later, in 1957, Chamoun positively answered the US Eisenhower Doctrine, which was directed against the USSR in the Middle East and against presumably pro-Soviet Arab nationalist regimes, firstly Egypt. His divisive stance, together with increased social disparities in the wake of the Gulf oil boom and the influx of Palestinian refugees, created a toxic social, political and economic environment in Lebanon. In this fraught situation, and in a desperate attempt to hold on to power, in 1957 he used the irregular and corrupt parliamentary elections, in which his party and its allies – including the Dashnak Party – triumphed, to push through an unpopular bid to extend his presidency by an additional term starting the following year. While the election's outcome did not trigger violence, political rivalries hardened. The assassination of Nassib Matni, the editor of the major opposition newspaper, *al-Telegraph*, on 8 May, 1958, led to a nationwide general strike that escalated into a civil war that lasted until October.[1]

Figure 4.1 *The Daily Star*'s coverage of Chamoun, 22 May, 1958, 1.

With the exception of parts of Beirut and the Mount Lebanon governorate, Lebanon was under 'rebel' control for five months.[2]

While US Secretary of State John Foster Dulles initially refused to provide requested military assistance, the violent coup d'état in Iraq in July 1958 changed the American stance. By mid-July, 15,000 US troops were present in Lebanon, backed by another 40,000 on 70 warships of the US Navy's sixth fleet.[3] Beirut and the airport were 'secured' within days, essentially ending the civil strife.[4] Negotiations to end the fighting between government figures and the opposition were predicated upon the agreement to choose an acceptable successor to Chamoun. Fouad Chehab, the head of the Lebanese army, emerged as the best choice, garnering support from all sides of the conflict. A national pact was signed on 17 October, 1958, and American troops left the country by the end of October.[5]

Armenian parties participated in, and contributed to, the events of 1957 and 1958. Simultaneously, they used their position within the Lebanese political system to jostle for power within the Armenian community. This development turned violent and came to a close only in December 1958, almost two months *after* the Lebanese mini-civil war had ended, when the Lebanese army intervened. These tensions and violent confrontations between Armenian parties and their armed men had a crucial spatial effect: they unprecedentedly territorialised parts of Beirut. To be sure, parts of Lebanon were already organised by sects and classes. By relative contrast, it was according to political party affiliation that in 1957–1958 many Armenians of Mar Mikael, Sin el Fil, Bourj Hamoud and Corniche al-Nahr were re-sorted and relocated, often by force. This was the second time in less than a decade that, especially in Beirut, the political profile of Lebanese Armenians changed considerably. As Chapter 2 showed, tens of thousands of Armenians from Lebanon, many from Beirut, had answered the USSR's call to repatriate to the Armenian Socialist Soviet Republic (ASSR) in 1946–1949. In consequence, as Chapter 3 noted, Armenian leftists became weaker while the right-wing nationalist Dashnak Party, affiliated with President Chamoun, grew stronger. However, until 1958, Armenian neighbourhoods continued to be home to people with contrasting political convictions.

This chapter tells the story of Armenians' stance in the 1957 elections and in the 1958 mini-civil war – both in the 'general' Lebanese one and in the intra-Armenian one. In the process, it makes three interrelated points. First, a good decade after the 1945–1946 transition from the French Mandate to post-colonial independence, Armenians were firmly part of, and ensconced in, Lebanese politics. As Chapter 1 demonstrated, Armenians' (re)-positioning vis-à-vis Lebanon's imminent post-colonial independence in the mid-1940s included a fair share of double-entendres, tensions and contrasts. But already at that point it was clear that Armenians in Lebanon were indeed part of that country – and also that they *wished* to be so. This fact showed up again in the events and processes analysed in Chapters 2 and 3. And they showed in the clearest (and most painful) fashion possible in 1957 and 1958, analysed in this chapter: Lebanese Armenians were divided along the right–left faultlines that divided Lebanese politics and society in general at that point. They were Lebanonised, one may say.

Secondly, and at the same point, the Lebanese state was somehow Armenianised, in that it started to pay more attention to Armenian matters than before, intervening directly and by military force in Armenian neighbourhoods by December 1958 in order to end the internecine Armenian confrontation. And thirdly, while Armenians were Lebanonised, they also, more than other confessions in Lebanon, were very strongly – by 1958 indeed mortally – internally divided along political lines. This division was not new, of course. It dated back to before World War II, as the postscript of Chapter 3 illustrated. It had been manifest in the 1946–1949 repatriation and in the 1956 catholicos election, as Chapters 2 and 3 showed. But it came to a boil in 1958. This was the case not only because of the general Lebanese context, i.e. the accentuating right–left political polarisation that at this point in time mapped on roughly, though by no means fully, on the country's Muslim–Christian confessional landscape. It was the case also because the Cold War – left-wing versus right-wing politics and ideologies globally – was felt with particular acuity in the Armenian case, principally for the simple reason that the Soviet Union included the ASSR, that is, that Armenia formed part of one Cold War superpower. In turn, this meant that leftist, and especially communist, Armenians had an especially direct connection to the Soviet Union. Vice versa, it was of supreme importance for right-wing Armenians to criticise that connection, to reject the 1920 Sovietisation of Armenia, which overthrew the independent republic (1918–1920) and the ruling Dashnak Party, and to assert the right to speak for Armenians despite the existence of Soviet Armenia.

Lebanon as a Site of Armenian Political Identity

Armenian political parties were engaged in heated rhetoric prior to and in the aftermath of the 1957 Lebanese parliamentary elections, attacking their Armenian rivals. In the case of the nationalist Dashnak Party, whose very world headquarters were in Beirut, this was done in four ways. First, the Dashnak mouthpiece *Aztag* rhetorically separated Armenians from the Lebanese population as a whole to produce a space where it could attack its Armenian rivals. Second, it addressed Armenians as Lebanese, but as a specific, if not marginal, bloc, whose duty in consequence it was to support the Lebanese government in power, i.e. President Chamoun. Third, it sought to strip anti-Dashnak Armenians from both their Armenian and Lebanese identifications, turning them into foreigners who were loyal to outside powers rather than to Lebanon or the Armenian nation. And fourth, it claimed that its Armenian rivals had a history of acting immorally. In this multipronged attack, Lebanon was not then just some diaspora for Armenians. Rather, it became *the* vital site for Armenians to act out power struggles and articulate belonging.

On 4 June, 1957, less than a week before the parliamentary elections, *Aztag* pleaded with its readership to stay uninvolved in the national crisis of Lebanon, and maintained that the instability in the country was temporary and would pass.[6] This indicated that the political and social tension did not concern the Armenians in Lebanon, even though *Aztag* self-identified Armenians as citizens of Lebanon.[7] Not surprisingly, it did not address how this status and *Aztag*'s subsequent call for neutrality was itself a type of involvement in both the daily affairs in Lebanon and the larger political sphere. What's more, it subsequently separated Armenians from Arab citizens: 'we are happy to assert that the Armenians living within Lebanon's borders are aware of their responsibilities and always trust in their Arab hosts and their governments'.[8] This established a hierarchy of citizenship, and designated Arabs as more authentic to Lebanon, suggesting that Armenian presence was temporary, or at least a status guaranteed by a more legitimate group.[9] It also portrayed Armenians as indebted to both the Arabs and to the state of Lebanon.

While this dismissed the potential impact of Armenians within Lebanese society, on a closer look, it served a purpose: the Dashnak political party used its affiliated newspaper to claim the Armenians in Lebanon.[10] Yes, labelling Lebanon as a host linked belonging to another location or physical space. But in so doing, *Aztag* also identified the Armenian inhabitants as a community and separated them from the Arab inhabitants. When warning of 'seditious elements ... intent on carrying out their threats to harm the brotherly relationship between Armenians and Arabs', it went on to designate the Dashnak Party as the leader who would ensure the harmonious relationship between Armenians and Arabs.[11] Armenians had the responsibility to uphold the authority of the Lebanese state that had been generous enough to 'host' them, but could not participate in this 'Lebanese' crisis.[12] And because the Dashnak Party represented only the loyal and honourable, its opponents were clearly the contrary. This rhetoric also served the Lebanese state. The Dashnak Party portrayed the community as a docile population, its rivals as potentially seditious.

If this was the case, supporters of President Chamoun had found their

Armenian ally, as his opponents had found theirs. Accusations that the Hnchak and Ramgavar parties wanted to 'break the bond between Armenians and Arabs and destabilise Lebanon' displaced ideological rivalry amongst Armenian parties struggling over power.[13] *Aztag* accused *Ararad* and *Zartonk* of having spent over 25 years, roughly the length of time the majority of Armenians had been in Lebanon, 'sharpening their axe against the tree of the Armenian nation'.[14] Lebanon was the site of a power struggle between competing authorities of the Armenian nation.

Lebanon's contested national elections presented Armenians with an additional medium to attack one another. They used the national crisis to separate 'true' Armenians (read: its supporters) from others, and sharpened a power struggle between the Armenian parties. According to *Aztag*, these guilty parties were 'once again, *our* city's *Zartonk* and *Ararad* newspapers, whose provocative and inflammatory news broadcasts are an invitation to go to war'.[15] *Aztag*'s claim of Beirut as 'our' city made Beirut Armenian, affirming both Armenian belonging and Beirut as a site to articulate this belonging.[16]

Most of *Aztag*'s issues in 1957 followed a similar construction: they affirmed Armenians as Lebanese citizens, but then told them to distance themselves from the 'Lebanese' crisis. This would have served the Dashnak Party well – they firmly supported the president and stridently opposed any dissent. *Aztag* used the purported involvement of Dashnak Party rivals to substantiate its claims that they were violent and even more virulent than their 'native' opponents.[17] They depicted Armenian rivals as zealous troublemakers: 'if they were really concerned with our people's security and happiness here, in the host country of Lebanon, how could they say such things?'[18] And even though *Aztag* identified Lebanon once again as a 'host', it did so to place Armenians within the sectarian structure of Lebanon, and to herald the Dashnak Party as the true 'leader' of the community.[19] The Dashnak Party had no choice then but to engage with Lebanese politics. It had to do so to limit the power of its rivals and protect the Lebanese state. *Aztag*'s rivals were indeed a danger not only to Armenians in Lebanon, but rather, to all Lebanese. It was in the national interest of *Lebanon* to defeat Dashnak Party rivals. The end result of this distance was to de-Armenianify them. *Zartonk* and *Ararad*, *Aztag* explained, were not even Armenian, but 'newspapers merely written in Armenian script'.[20]

While *Aztag* reminded Armenians of their non-native standing in Lebanon, it also told them what types of Lebanese nationals to be, i.e. whom to support in the upcoming parliamentary elections. The nationalist paper reminded its readers of the 'civic duty' of voting, linking this action to responsible citizenship.[21] Since the Dashnak Party's rivals in Lebanon supported the ASSR, it also juxtaposed the right of voting with the 'irrelevance' of voting under authoritarian regimes.[22] Lebanon was the 'land where freedom reigns, citizen rights are respected, and most importantly – the right to vote is private'.[23]

And since Armenians were reportedly happy to live in such a place, they had a duty to preserve its 'unrestrictive political environment' and participate in the Lebanese parliamentary elections as Lebanese citizens.[24] 'Every Lebanese, and accordingly, we too, should head to the ballot box', *Aztag* stated.[25] While Armenian suffrage was neither novel to the political structure of Lebanon nor unprecedented in their participation, *Aztag*'s desperation demonstrated how this election became a space to both claim Armenian belonging in Lebanon and triumph over rival Armenian political parties.

The Dashnak Party made Armenian and Lebanese interests synonymous with one another and distanced opposing Armenians from the larger Armenian community. It declared through its newspaper *Aztag* 'With the exception of a few who have become agents for others, we are sure that Armenians will vote with one heart, one soul and one voice for freedom, independence and the pursuit of security and rights ... this Sunday the elections will result in the victory of our delegates who are dedicated to the success of the Lebanese and the Armenians'.[26] Through voting, Armenians assured the accuracy and legitimacy of the political process of Lebanon.

And yet, Armenians were not only ordered to vote in exchange for their privilege as Lebanese. The Dashnak Party also instructed its followers to defer to other Lebanese, whose 'native' citizens supported President Chamoun.[27] Armenians were fashioned as a particular type of Lebanese citizen, one that had to participate in elections, but only if they voted in accordance with the Dashnak Party's wishes. Only through this type of deed could they truly demonstrate their appreciation for Lebanon. There was no evidence, however, that Armenians needed to prove to the native Lebanese that they were worthy of the civic rights granted to them decades prior.[28] And there is no record of non-Armenian Lebanese making such an accusation or calling on them to support Chamoun's government. It was the Dashnak Party that created this anxiety and used it to tell its supporters to vote in accordance to their political alliances.

By voting according to the Dashnak Party's agreements, the Armenian 'would prevent the Hnchak and Ramgavar parties' plot of eliminating opportunity for the people of Lebanon'.[29] What is more, a vote for rival Armenian parties encouraged 'lawlessness, mutiny, and endangered the country's peace'.[30] An Armenian's vote in 1957 had the power to ensure the continuation of the state of Lebanon: 'A vote for any of the evil-minded Ramgavars, Hnchaks, or Bolsheviks means abandoning our principled duties, challenging Lebanon's supreme order, and would present a calamitous opportunity for the feeble-minded to mobilize their destructive forces'.[31] As the Dashnak Party battled against its Armenian rivals, it continued to hone the power of the Armenian inhabitants to shape the political system in Lebanon to its liking. For the Dashnak Party, these elections were 'the culmination of two opposing forces and the demonstration of the seminal power of the Lebanese–Armenian vote . . .'[32] Lebanese Armenians, whom *Aztag* labelled the 'free-thinking', would cast their votes for the government lists and 'out of their respect for Lebanon's independence and the safeguarding of its citizenry'.[33]

The Dashnak Party also used the office of the presidency to demonstrate its superiority and reinforce its supremacy over rival Armenian parties. Its followers synchronised the platform of the party with the actions of the Lebanese president. On 11 March, 1958, President Chamoun visited the Armenian monastery at Antelias and bestowed the National Order of the Cedar, the highest medal awarded to a Lebanese civilian, upon Catholicos Zareh.[34] This visit coincided with the second anniversary of Zareh's election, legitimising it and Zareh's Dashnak supporters. Through its backing of the Cilician Catholicosate, the president of the republic's presence and the bestowal of such an honour upon their supported catholicos, the Dashnak Party flaunted its power to its supporters and detractors (Armenian and non-Armenian alike).[35] The Dashnak Party used Chamoun, the head of the Lebanese state and the National Order of Cedar, its state prize, to reinforce its authority over the Armenian community in Lebanon (and beyond) and endorse how it imagined Armenians to behave in the country. At the same time, the bestowal of such a prize upon the catholicos dually served the president's and his own interests, as it showed the harmonious relationship between the president and the spiritual, cultural and religious head of the Armenian community that extended beyond the border of Lebanon. This relationship also identified for President Chamoun his supporters and opponents within the Armenian community. Being an Armenian member in good standing was dependent upon supporting a Lebanese political figure. In contrast, those who wavered in their support for the president were undertaking 'feeble attempts to destabilise the country', according to the Dashnak Party.[36]

The Dashnak Party also referred to how crowds reportedly lined the streets until the Antelias monastery complex to flaunt its power against its rivals. The Hnchak and Ramgavar parties could not generate the same level of spectacle that Zareh's supporters produced in the streets of Beirut. *Aztag* reported that 'the entire way to Antelias, starting from the bridge at Dora, was decorated with the colours of the Lebanese flag. Triumphant arches were constructed along the road, under which the presidential motorcade would pass on its way to Antelias. The scouts of HMEM (Armenian General Athletic Union), formed in military discipline impatiently awaited the arrival of the president at the monastery'.[37] Armenians used urban space in Beirut to mark Armenianness – which, in turn, supported Lebanon's sitting president.

Similarly when, after the crisis of spring and summer 1958 the new cabinet was announced on 7 September, *Aztag* printed a message to 'Lebanon's Armenian People'.[38] It pledged the Dashnak Party's support for President Chehab, declaring that it 'stands with our beloved homeland, Lebanon, to ensure it peace and security'.[39] The Dashnak position was consistent with the Cilician See's Archbishop Khoren's call to heed their 'responsibility as citizens and to do all they could to resolve the crisis, keeping the Armenian name pure'.[40] And it further questioned the rival Hnchak and Ramgavar parties' Armenianness and Lebaneseness. The Dashnak declaration stated 'the Armenian People have always been respected individuals of peace, aware of their responsibilities as citizens, and faithful to this country's traditions and laws'.[41] Involvement in Lebanese affairs was an obligation for the Armenians, but it was the Dashnak Party that determined acceptable methods of participation. The Dashnak press went on to publish a series of editorials reinforcing their representations of Lebanon as the Armenian homeland. They congratulated their involvement in its recovery while accusing their Hnchak and Ramgavar rivals of contributing to Lebanon's breakdown.[42]

As a matter of fact, the Dashnak Party had made a habit of questioning the Armenianness of its rivals and of questioning their loyalty as Lebanese citizens. Ramgavar and Hnchak supporters were 'the minions of meddlers of the Middle East' referring to them as powerless proxies of greater – and foreign – powers.[43] They were thereby deemed unworthy of Lebanese citizenship rights, and were responsible for jeopardising the peace and security of Lebanon. 'They belong not in Lebanon, but in the Soviet Union'.[44]

At stake here was the representation of Armenians in Lebanon. Armenian transnational connections became a liability in 1957, an opportunity for political rivals to accuse one another of loyalty to another state. By associating their rivals with another national space, the Dashnak Party concluded that it was the sole (and ethical) representative for Armenians in Lebanon. The insecurity present in 1957 was an opportunity for the Dashnak Party to claim power – via the Armenian community – within the Lebanese political sphere. In turn, this meant it upheld the sectarian system of Lebanon, as it helped facilitate its own presence within its structure.

The Dashnak Party continued to separate its rivals from *its* (read: the) Armenian nation as the elections approached. When Hnchak and Ramgavar parties broadcast Yerevan radio programmes in Beirut, the Dashnak Party called these foreign transmissions, whose aim was to use the Armenian people to propagate a communist agenda.[45] Its newspaper's designation of Soviet Armenia as a foreign entity and of its rivals as Soviet pawns, marked Lebanon as a vital site of Armenian identity production and maintenance. With 'irrefutable proof' it accused the Hnchak and Ramgavar parties of attempting 'to use the Armenian people as a tool to serve the communist propaganda project in the Middle East'.[46]

Aztag asked 'Moscow's agents', 'What right do you have to interfere in Lebanon's domestic election matters?'[47] For the Dashnak Party in 1957, Yerevan's presence in Lebanon – even if only in the form of a radio broadcast – was a cause for concern. The Armenian capital became conceived of as a foreign presence that threatened the Armenian nation and challenged Lebanon's sovereignty.[48] The only way to protect both the Armenian nation and Lebanon was to vote for the Dashnak-supported candidates in the upcoming elections. 'The Armenian people will counter the communist informers and the scheming enemies of Lebanon with their votes. As the law-abiding citizens of this country, we will declare to the meddlers that they do not represent the Armenian people'.[49] In this battle of good versus evil, the mouthpiece of the Dashnak Party did not mince words: 'We must punish these people by not giving them our vote. We will not give our vote to the Bolshevik whose authentic and sole homeland is not Lebanon, but the USSR. We will not give our vote to the sly Hnchak, whose only homeland is his own pocket. And we will not give our vote to the charlatan Ramgavar whose homeland is neither Lebanon nor Armenia, but the Soviet regime'.[50] Not only did the Dashnak Party associate its rivals with foreign powers, thus suggesting a non-Armenian quality about them, it also located the safekeeping of the Armenian nation and Lebanon within the outcome of this Lebanese parliamentary election.

In the crisis of 1958, the Dashnak Party employed a similar language. For example, it used undated statements made by Soviet Armenian officials to shame its rivals in Lebanon and to elevate its own political and ideological principles. It used an unnamed Soviet Armenian official who spoke against the Armenian church allegedly claiming it did not belong in 'our homeland, our schools, or even in our moral register' who likened the church to 'human excrement, that needed to be thrown into the sea'.[51] It did so to uphold Lebanon as a safer home for Armenians than the Soviet Republic of Armenia. In so doing, the Dashnak Party also legitimised its support for Camille Chamoun who it considered to be the guarantor of the sovereignty of the Catholicosate of Cilicia.[52] It went on to attack its Armenian opponents for 'singing the praises of the notorious Stalin, that very monster who destroyed our churches in our homeland'.[53] Again not offering further contextualisation, the statement attempted to appropriate activities in Lebanon. The purported support of the Hnchak and Ramgavar parties for Stalin denoted not only opposition to the Armenian church in Lebanon, but the destruction of their institutions. The Dashnak Party went on to express its disgust that its opponents had the audacity to then organise their activities in Armenian churches in Lebanon. 'These same opponents use church halls and invite religious speakers to celebrate 29 November, the official black day of an enslaved Armenia, as the "Independence Day of Armenia".[54] It attempted to separate its rivals from Armenian institutions, making their gathering there unlawful. It used its newspaper to remind the reader that the Hnchak and Ramgavar parties celebrated the establishment of the Soviet Republic of Armenia as national independence day of Armenia, even though its Soviet authorities worked against the national religion.[55]

Back in 1957, not surprisingly, the electoral triumph of the Dashnak and pro-government lists only exacerbated the tension between the political parties. Still, the division of Armenians in Lebanon continued after the elections. To the Dashnaks, their rivals were no longer Armenians but 'carpetbaggers and traitors' while the genuine Armenians 'possessed high moral value' and were the true champions of freedom, the Armenian nation and the Lebanese state.[56] These attacks likewise demonstrated that the power struggle to articulate Armenianness belonged in Lebanon. By maintaining that the membership rosters of the Hnchak and Ramgavar parties were full of liars and cheats, and that these characteristics were part of the essence of the Hnchak and Ramgavar parties and their supporters, the Dashnak Party continued to question their moral compass and place them outside the realm of both Armenian and Lebanese belonging.[57] The Dashnaks also began to link their rivals with Turkey, that perpetual enemy of the Armenian nation. *Aztag* contended that the Hnchak and Ramgavar parties, by supporting the Soviet Union that had ties with Turkey, also bonded with Turks.[58] This continued de-Armenianification of its rivals was necessary to consolidate the Dashnak Party's power.[59]

Regarding the United States, and specifically the 1957 Eisenhower Doctrine, the Dashnak Party relayed to its followers through its newspaper that the doctrine would not interfere 'in Lebanese domestic issues or politics'.[60] In fact, *Aztag* stated that the Eisenhower administration in its entirety 'is one of friendliness'.[61] This echoed Chamoun's position, i.e. his declarations of loyalty to the United States. Typical in this regard was a speech regarding Lebanon's domestic and international policies that Chamoun gave in Der al-Qamar less than a month after the elections, on 5 August, 1957. He prepared the public for his decision to seek American assistance, explaining its necessity by highlighting the dangers of communism. The recent events, Chamoun continued, in reference to the 1956 Suez crisis and the political instability in Jordan, only further demonstrated Lebanon's international role.[62] It was the United States, he reminded the public, which immediately realised the terrifying repercussions to Middle East peace if Jordan 'fell' to communism.[63]

Rival Armenian political parties continued to be othered through the Armenian language media. The Dashnak Party consistently accused supporters of the Hnchak and Ramgavar parties of backing foreign interests intent on damaging the Armenian nation. In this way, transnational attributes of Armenians became a liability. While this is not a novel accusation against diaspora communities, it is not regularly one that is adopted by members of the community itself. In this way, the Dashnak Party fought against the diaspora identification, associating it with disloyalty to the Armenian nation and the Lebanese state. In an effort to claim power over its rivals, it localised Armenians and cast connections to Soviet Armenia as a problem. Characteristic of their rivals' lack of commitment to Lebanon, the Dashnaks maintained, was their unethical and criminal behaviour in Lebanon.

Thus, after the assassination of Nassib Matni, the editor of the oppositional *al-Telegraph* newspaper, on 8 May, 1958, the Dashnak newspaper 'exclusively' published the printed instructions that opponents of President Chamoun allegedly distributed to one another: 'Scuffle and fire upon the police. Wreak havoc upon Souq Touwil, Hamra Street and Sadat Street. Kill anyone who bothers you. Drop bombs and grenades from roofs onto the streets. Burn a few cars, preferably at night to generate terror. Erect barricades on the roads. Aim to replicate what happened in Tripoli in Beirut'.[64]

Furthermore, when intra-Armenian tensions turned violent, the *Aztag* mouthpiece of the Dashnak Party systematically blamed and accused its rivals. In November 1958, after the Dashnak member Jirayr Khrimyan was murdered in Beirut, the Dashnaks immediately accused 'Hnchak-communists' of the deed.[65] And when the Dashnak Party called for a general strike in protest, it did so, it said, not to disrupt the Lebanese economy for sinister reasons, but to show its fellow (Lebanese) countrymen the danger of its Armenian rivals.[66] Lebanon had fully transformed into a space for Armenians to battle over their ideological differences. The Minister of Interior had set out immediately for Bourj Hamoud in an attempt to mediate between the parties, and elite security forces were stationed in the Armenian populated neighbourhoods to prevent further unrest.[67]

In the following days, *Aztag* continued to report on the situation in Hajin, placing the conflict under the 'Domestic State of Affairs' section of the newspaper.[68] Lebanese officials were becoming increasingly involved in the violence between Armenian political party members and affiliates. Prime Minister Rashid Karami and Minister of the Interior Raymond Eddé both announced that the government would intervene and suppress any actions that undermined the public's security.[69] As Armenians were resolving their ideological differences by clashing in Beirut's Armenian neighbourhoods, officials became ever more aware and concerned about the territorialisation underway in these urban spaces. By the fall of 1958 intra-Armenian violence had become a Lebanese matter. In fact, by late 1958 intra-Armenian competition had become so intense that the Lebanese government and military was needed to restore calm. *Aztag* reported that army forces searched houses in Hajin to locate and seize weapons, making numerous arrests.[70]

The Dashnak Party also described attacks against them as premeditated criminal hits. 'Four criminals, in all likelihood emerging from the den of Hajin, stopped in front of the store of Comrade Simon Hagopian in the neighbourhood of San Michel. Using the excuse of purchasing cigarettes, they opened fire upon the comrade, who received three fatal shots to the head, dying immediately'.[71] Identifying the neighbourhoods – both those of the alleged perpetrators, and of the victim – marked those streets as enemy and ally locations, respectively. Maps of Beirut were redrawn in accordance with the Dashnak Party's understanding of the city's political geography. 'The den of Hajin' was the site of the Hnchak Communists, while San Michel located southwest of Hajin, was home to comrades.

The Dashnaks used Simon's death to reinforce their own manufactured division between the idealised Armenian and the Armenian to be expelled from the nation. 'This heinous crime has caused a deep fury in the Armenian neighbourhoods. Comrade Hagopian was loved by all. A serious and loving man, he fell victim to a conspiracy of uncivilised and brutish individuals'.[72] By reminding its readership of the continued presence of the Lebanese army in Hajin, the ongoing searches of individuals entering and exiting the neighbourhood, and the 'huge quantity of weapons and ammunition that were found', the Dashnak Party represented those inhabitants as enemies of the people – both Lebanese and Armenian.[73] In fact, it encouraged the army to fire upon 'combatants' who did not cooperate or attempted to escape, recognising the primacy of the Lebanese state: 'We hope that the security forces will be able to restore calm within the Armenian neighbourhoods, and impose rule-of-law upon these professional agitators, who for months have taken advantage of the nation's exceptional state of affairs, creating a criminal atmosphere'.[74]

The Dashnak Party continued to advance its own platform and to use the Lebanese government's push to reestablish order. When *Aztag* reported that Interior Minister Raymond Eddé had a meeting with Father Boghos Aris, the mayor of Bourj Hamoud, it went on to declare the loyalty of that neighbourhood, associated with the Dashnak Party, to the Lebanese government. Father Aris, the newspaper reported, 'dutifully explained to Minister Eddé that the Armenian community members do not want to create any agitation but only desire the return of peace, and encourage the government to take any means necessary to ensure security and to severely punish all perpetrators'.[75] The absence of the neighbourhood of Hajin and of the Hnchak and Ramgavar parties identified them and their populace as Bourj Hamoud's – and the Lebanese state's – territorial and ideological counterpart.

Two days after Eddé's proclamation, *Aztag* reported that arrangements were underway to find a permanent resolution to 'the clashes that have stained the name of the Armenian Nation'.[76] *Aztag* also included, in the same issue, the decree made by Catholicosate of Cilicia's Archbishop Khoren, and added that the declaration would surely be heeded by all, since it was administered by the 'supreme fatherly counsel'.[77] The archbishop reflected the 'happy and peaceful life Armenians have lived in this hospitable Homeland, the beautiful Lebanon, for thirty years', and the many accomplishments of the Armenian community, including the construction of the monastery at Antelias, the prelacies of the see, its organisations, its schools and its cultural programmes.[78] For its part, the Dashnak Party told its supporters that the Hnchak and Ramgavar parties aimed to destroy these accomplishments.[79] It used the words of Archbishop Khoren to maintain its attacks on the Hnchak and Ramgavar parties, and continued to identify Armenianness with Lebanon.

While Archbishop Khoren framed Lebanon's Armenians as subservient to the Lebanese state, he simultaneously buttressed the Dashnak ideology. 'Dear Armenian people! You are well aware of what kind of circumstances we are living in, as citizens of a Free Lebanon and part of a civilised collective'.[80] He also distinguished an Armenian 'civilized collective', a segment of 'Free Lebanon', from other Armenians, most notably those loyal to foreign powers and ideologies.[81] 'Instead of contributing to this sacred recovery', he chided the latter, 'you drove yourself to savage fratricide with lustful hatred towards your brethren'.[82] The archbishop's decree also, and at the same time, exposed Armenians' changing status in Lebanon. While he celebrated their achievements separately from Lebanon's development at large, he also spoke of their duty to the state, and categorised them as Lebanese nationals. Armenians used this flexibility for their own promotion of Armenian belonging and idealised Armenian behaviour. These in turn served to reinforce the power of specific Armenian institutions: including the Armenian church, *Aztag* and the Dashnak Party.

In sum, Armenians used Lebanese civil institutions to claim power in Lebanon in four sometimes contradictory ways: by separating Armenians from the Lebanese, by making Armenians Lebanese, by stripping fellow Armenians of their Armenian identification and rendering them foreign, and by demonstrating that their rivals were not committed to Lebanon and criminalising them collectively. The rhetoric of protecting both the Armenian nation and the Lebanese state defined Lebanon as the prime site for this nation-building.

Making Beirut Armenian

By the 1950s, Armenians lived in various neighbourhoods of Beirut. These ranged from the upper middle-class neighbourhoods of Zarif and Zokak al-Blat in Ras Beirut to the lower middle- and working-class areas around St Sarkis Patriarchate near the Serail. Armenians also resided in Furn al-Shabak and Geitawi. Outside of the centre, Armenians lived in the working and lower-class neighbourhoods of Karantina, Mar Mikael, Corniche al-Nahr, Bourj Hamoud and Sin el-Fil. Within Karantina, some Armenians still lived within the confines of the original Armenian refugee camp. The original camp of Sanjak also continued to house Armenians of more meager means.[83]

While these neighbourhoods were roughly segregated by class, Armenians of different political and religious persuasions lived in them. Armenian Orthodox and Catholic churches were established within walking distance from one another in Bourj Hamoud and Downtown. Armenian schools, administered by the headquarters of either the Armenian Orthodox, Catholic and Protestant Churches, also enjoyed a diverse student body. For example, the majority of students at the Armenian Evangelical College, an Armenian Protestant institution located in Qantari, were members of the Armenian Catholic and Orthodox churches. The community centres of Armenian political parties were no different. Located near one another, they attracted children and adults from the neighbourhood, and were not always rigid regarding membership and affiliation. Thus, while youth from the neighbourhood often joined a sports team affiliated with a political party, they or their parents were not necessarily party members; rather, they chose a team for its sportive success and quality.[84]

This situation, however, was affected by the violence following the 1957 elections and again in 1958. In 1957, according to Dashnak reports, Hnchak members attacked polling stations and threw rocks on the voters and fired on them.[85] That this attack took place 'at the entrance of Hajin' coded and compartmentalised a bit of Beirut's urban space, separating it from the city as a whole. This move was sharpened by the descriptions of how the victims and perpetrators experienced and moved throughout the incident. There were attacks at the 'entrance' of the neighbourhood, 'passers-by' were also affected, and inhabitants 'returned' to the neighbourhood during the attacks to seek 'refuge'.[86] They were also 'forced inside' due to violence.[87] These descriptions demonstrated the struggle for power not only within but between Beirut's Armenian populated neighbourhoods (in effect treating them as separate from a larger Beirut).

As part of Lebanon's broader crisis in 1957 and 1958, then, *specific* Armenian Beiruti neighbourhoods began to stand for *particular* imaginations of belonging and articulating citizenship in Lebanon. This territorialisation, as it were, of Armenian neighbourhoods like Mar Mikael, Bourj Hamoud, Sin el-Fil and Rmeil was new. Prior to 1958, Beirut's Armenian, Arabic and Francophone press alike collectively described these areas as 'the Armenian neighbourhoods'. But by early 1958, the Armenian press talked of 'the sullied Bourj Hamoud', 'the violent Bourj Hamoud', 'the suffering Corniche al-Nahr', 'the infiltrated Hajin' – the last a reference to alleged Dashnak attacks – or a 'Nor Hajin under siege'.

Arabic Lebanese newspapers did not reproduce these fissures, but continued to use the generic term 'the Armenian areas'.[88] The armed blockade of these neighbourhoods made it hard for outsiders to enter them, at least temporarily marginalising them within Beirut and setting them off from other quarters in the readers' imagination. Even when the Lebanese military was deployed, the obstruction of movement continued. For example, in January 1958, the Armenian church in Rmeil was forcefully closed, allegedly by Dashnak Party adherents, irrespective of the presence of Lebanese military and police forces who were supposed to aid in its reopening.[89]

As for Armenians' treatment of Beiruti Armenian spaces, it was not only the Dashnaks who segregated them discursively. The Ramgavar press also did so. It reoriented and reclassified Bourj Hamoud as non-Armenian. For *Zartonk*, Hajin and the neighbourhoods of its readership were 'Armenian neighbourhoods', separating them from Bourj Hamoud, which it labelled as 'the base of the terrorists'.[90] *Zartonk* also noted that while it was [its] Armenian neighbourhoods blockaded by the Dashnak Party, it should be 'Bourj Hamoud under seige ... by the Lebanese state'.[91] At the same time, neither *Zartonk* nor presumably its readership felt the need to explicitly identify or state where the borders of 'the Armenian neighbourhoods' or Bourj Hamoud were located, demonstrating that Armenian Beirutis shared an understanding of where neighbourhood borders lay in their city.

Armenian parties also used the editorial pages to lambast one another and accuse one another of murdering 'true Armenian patriots'.[92] For the Ramgavars, 'the Dashnak Party held the Armenian people hostage', and even 'the Lebanese military cannot save them'.[93] Perhaps the inability of the Lebanese state institutions to do so, however, was related to their lack of knowledge of the entry and exit points of their new demarcations. On the other hand, to the Dashnak Party, the Lebanese state was working on behalf of its supporters. After the murder of Dashnak member and athlete Kevork Voskerichian, in Hajin, *Aztag* reported that the Lebanese army arrived at the scene and transported him to the Hotel Dieu hospital.[94] The intervention of the Lebanese army – and not of a Lebanese civil service such as the police or ambulatory services – indicated that the state feared the political nature and fallout from the intra-Armenian violence. As for the Dashnaks, it framed the state's intervention as a validation of their campaign against their Armenian rivals. The army, they said, came in to save the Armenian athlete, and in so doing intervened on behalf of the Dashnak political party and against the aggression of its rival political party members who allegedly staged the operation.[95] Indeed, *Aztag* reported that the army was forced to surround the entire neighbourhood of Hajin to 'conduct arrests'.[96]

In fact, the Dashnak Party began to rely more and more on the Lebanese army. When Hagop Kushgerian was murdered in Hajin the day after Vosgerichian's death, the Lebanese army once again 'negotiated' for Hagop's body to be released and brought to Nor Sis, in Bourj Hamoud.[97] The army arbitrated the removal of the victim's body.[98] It had entered a district where its power, while respected, was also somewhat foreign. It indeed had sought permission to enter, and then was compelled to barricade the area in order to do so, treating the neighbourhood as a hostile and autonomous space. The act of moving the body also shows how quarters had become territorialised. The attack occurred in Hajin, just south of Bourj Hamoud and in Mar Mikael, and the body was meant to be moved to Nor Sis, in Bourj Hamoud. While less than a kilometre apart, these two quarters were identified as very different Armenian centres.

As the Ramgavar press described the 'conquest' of the Armenian neighbourhoods as complete, it also covered the 'Independent Armenian Community', a group that came together in 1956 to contest – and distance itself from – the Cilician Catholicosate and the Dashnak Party.[99] While this group eventually disappeared, its members met with President Fouad Chehab (1958–1964) when he attempted to restore order to the neighbourhoods.[100] The Ramgavar press termed the meeting 'cordial and good-natured', and described how the newly-elected president 'understood the gravity of the situation, and had requested information on the current crisis and intended to evaluate the current situation, ending the meeting with a pledge "to try to resolve the problems and conduct an objective examination if need be"'.[101] Although this request could be seen as an attempt to consider the various aspects of the violent outbursts, it also demonstrated his limited knowledge of the goings-on in the Armenian community. Relatedly, Chehab's subsequent announcement that he was 'independent' seemed to suggest that he considered himself an outsider even though he was the president of Lebanon.[102]

But Chehab did not completely forfeit his claim of authority over the Armenian community. Printed alongside the meeting coverage, *Zartonk* detailed the ongoing and intensified Lebanese military presence in Armenian neighbourhoods, describing how many rooftops were occupied by the Lebanese military, and that house to house searches were commonplace.[103]

Meanwhile, the violence continued – for weeks.[104] Armenian newspapers continued to reinforce the distinction between the violent Armenian and restive non-Armenian populated neighbourhoods and amongst the peace-loving Armenian ones. For the Hnchak and Ramgavar press, the inhabitants of Nor Hajin were victims of the oppressive Dashnak Party and Bourj Hamoud housed their criminals.[105] For the Dashnak press, the opposite was the case.[106] The violence was so pervasive that *Zartonk* was forced to halt the publication of its newspaper for three weeks in late September, returning on 17 October.[107] By November, Nor Hajin was completely blockaded. The Ramgavar Party reported that the inhabitants were 'living in a quarter of fear'.[108] While the violence between spaces continued for approximately two months after the larger national cessation of hostilities, it ended by early December with additional negotiations and declarations amongst Armenian parties brokered by the Minister of Interior Raymond Eddé.[109]

Figure 4.2 Page in *Ayk*: 'Raymond Eddé-i Hrashk'-Gortsoghut'iwnĕ' [Raymond Eddé's Miraculous Operation] *Ayk*, 9 December, 1958, 1.

The Lebanese state was eventually able to placate the warring parties, demonstrating its power. Eddé's official declaration reinforced the authority of the Lebanese state by invoking the Armenian neighbourhoods' proximity to and in Beirut, *its* capital.[110] Beirut was not to be further factionalised. Or: even if factionalised and polarised, the different Armenian quarters still fell under the jurisdiction of the state. Still, new facts had been created; damage had been done. Eddé's declaration also acknowledged the creation of bounded neighbourhoods. Eddé's call for the immediate return of inhabitants to 'their own neighbourhoods', contradictorily acknowledged both the separation of Armenians vis-à-vis non-Armenians in Lebanon and an internal displacement.[111]

The End and Aftermath of the Intra-Armenian confrontation

On 12 December, 1958, Minister Eddé announced that an official ceasefire had been brokered by the national government between the Dashnak, Hnchak and Ramgavar Armenian political parties.[112] *Aztag* printed the agreement in full:

> The Minister of the Interior is pleased to announce that the Hnchak, Ramgavar, and Dashnak Armenian political parties have decided to put an end to the bloody clashes between their members and supporters, and to carry on instead via practical means; to permanently resolve inciting actions and violence, and to restore security and peace in the neighbourhoods and areas which have been horrifically impacted during the recent clashes.[113]

Eddé also thanked the negotiating parties for working with one another and the government to resolve the tension and violence in the community.[114] He then addressed the Armenian people, referring to them as 'the Armenians of the Lebanese family'.[115] Pleading with them to 'follow the actions of their representatives', he appealed to them to 'condemn violence, terrorism, meddling, incitement and to trust the people's government to solve their ideological differences through compromise and reason'.[116] Placing the clashes between Armenians within a Lebanese context, he also bemoaned the loss of life. 'Every drop of their blood wounds the government, all of the Lebanese, and damages this country's creative capability'.[117]

The next day, the Armenian parties collectively issued a statement pledging their support for Eddé's declaration.[118] Dashnak, Hnchak and Ramgavar representatives agreed to five shared pledges: the condemnation of all terrorist activity and criminal offences against their compatriots; the right for all those who fled their homes, to return, without delay or provocation; the end to all incendiary writings in the press, which could threaten the established peace; the cooperation with the government to search and arrest all criminally guilty parties; and the submitting of lists of the victims and of the disappeared, to help the government determine compensation.[119]

The order to end incendiary writing in the press was the first instance where all political parties identified the power of the press and the resultant responsibilities. On 14 December, two days after Minister Eddé's proclamation and the day after the Armenian political parties' pledge, *Aztag*'s lead editorial addressed this pledge.[120] For the Dashnak Party, the agreement offered it the opportunity to go on record that its newspaper 'has always been careful during our national, religious and political struggles to use journalistic moderation and to avoid inappropriate language'.[121] And while it chided a few newspapers for confusing 'the press with the street', it stated that *Aztag* had always 'worked against provocative writings'.[122]

Aztag also acknowledged, and deferred to, the Lebanese government's desire for the Armenians to resume the normalcy of their daily life. It stated 'it is our people's responsibility to stand in support of the government'.[123] In making such a vow, the Dashnak Party simultaneously confirmed itself as the representative of the Armenian people to the Lebanese state. To further consolidate its power and stake in Lebanon, the Dashnak Party also asked Armenians not to emigrate from Lebanon.[124] It attempted to calm their nerves after the recent hostility, reassuring them that the violence was indeed over. Lebanon was the only country, the party continued to insist, where Armenian life was 'this advanced and progressive'.[125] Despite the violence of 1957 and 1958, Lebanon remained the centre of Armenian life worldwide to the Dashnaks. 'There is no other place where our national life is organised so well, and where it works so well'.[126]

Conclusion

The 1957 elections became an opportunity for the Dashnak Party to continue its virulent attacks against its rivals. Its success in a however corrupt election process allowed both its supporters and detractors to use urban space in Beirut to seize Lebanese territory. While these enclaves challenged the sovereignty of Lebanese state power, reliance on the Lebanese military to restore order simultaneously reaffirmed the power of the Lebanese state. And yet, the interventions of the state demonstrated its role in 'Armenian' affairs, making these conflicts far more local than merely 'Armenian'. The participation of the Lebanese state along with ideological demographic changes further oriented the Armenian inhabitants of Lebanon to Lebanon itself. The actions by Armenians and non-Armenian alike in 1957–1958 showcase how Armenians lived as local Lebanese citizens, undercutting both diasporic categorisations and a refugee past. Cold War rivalries manifest in the support and opposition to the Lebanese president and to the Dashnak Party became opportunities for Armenians to claim and struggle for power, all the while articulating their belonging and citizenship.

Notes

1. Samir Khalaf, *Civil and Uncivil Violence in Lebanon* (New York: Columbia University Press, 2004), 114.
2. Fawwaz Traboulsi, *The History of Modern Lebanon* (London: Pluto Press, 2007), 134.
3. Ibid., 136.
4. Ibid.,137.
5. '"National" Salvation', *The Daily Star*, 18 October, 1958, 1. Traboulsi, *History*, 137.
6. 'Khrovararnerĕ Anzōr en Hay ew Arab Eghbayrut'yan Vnaselu' [The Troublemakers are Feeble in their Attempt to Harm the Fraternity between Armenians and Arabs], *Aztag*, 4 June, 1957, 1.
7. 'In this situation, our people, like in all crises, must act as ordered, vigilant, and civil citizens'. Ibid.
8. Ibid.
9. Ibid.
10. Ibid.
11. Ibid.
12. Ibid.
13. 'Mijazgayin Khrovarneru Hay Gortsakalnerĕ' [The Armenian Agents of the Troublemakers of the Middle East], *Aztag*, 5 June, 1957, 1.

14. Ibid.
15. 'Khr̲ovararnerĕ Anzōr en', 1. (Emphasis added.)
16. Ibid.
17. For *Aztag*, Arabic newspapers at least had 'a moderate tone' as opposed to *Ararad* and *Zartonk*. 'Mijazgayin Khr̲ovarneru', 1.
18. Ibid.
19. 'Khr̲ovararnerĕ Anzōr en', 1.
20. 'Mijazgayin Khr̲ovarneru', 1.
21. 'Mer T'eknatsneru Hed' [With Our Candidates], *Aztag*, 6 June, 1957, 1.
22. Ibid.
23. Ibid.
24. Ibid.
25. Ibid.
26. Ibid.
27. 'Libanahay Keghts K'aghak'ats'in' [The Fake Lebanese-Armenian Citizen], *Aztag*, 6 June, 1957, 2.
28. *Aztag* stated 'Our civic rights become worthy in the eyes of the natives as Lebanon grows and thrives'. Ibid.
29. 'K'uēn Iravunk' Ē' [Voting is a Right], *Aztag*, 9 June, 1957, 2.
30. Ibid.
31. Ibid.
32. Ibid.
33. Ibid.
34. 'N. V. Nakhagah K'amil Shamun Ant'iliasi Mēj' [His Eminence President Chamoun in Antelias], *Aztag*, 11 March, 1958, 1.
35. *Aztag* described the occasion: 'The crowd of believers had a joyous occasion to express their happiness, because the Cilician Chair [Zareh I] and the Armenian people became worthy of the presence of His Eminence, the President of the Lebanese Republic. They became worthy of the bestowal of the highest Lebanese medal, the National Order of the Cedar, which was decorated upon the chest of the Vehapar [Zareh I] by His Eminence Camille Chamoun and in warm appreciation by the solicitous Lebanese government'. Ibid.
36. 'Khaghagh Ts'oyts'er T'rip'olii Mēj' [Peaceful Demonstrations in Tripoli], *Aztag*, 22 March, 1958, 1.
37. 'N. V. Nakhagah K'amil Shamun Ant'iliasi Mēj' [His Eminence President Chamoun in Antelias], *Aztag*, 11 March, 1958, 1. HMEM is the organisation of scouts of the Armenian Dashnak Party.

38. 'Koch' Hay Zhorghovrdin' [Declaration to the Armenian People], *Aztag*, 19 September, 1958, 1.
39. Ibid.
40. 'Artagin Koch'' [External Call] *Aztag*, 7 September, 1958, 1.
41. 'Koch' Hay Zhorghovrdin', 1.
42. 'Mēk Sirt Mēk Hogi' [One Heart, One Soul], *Aztag*, 11 October, 1958, 1.
43. 'Khrovararnerĕ Anzōr en',1.
44. 'Libanahay Keghts K'aghak'ats'in' [The Fake Lebanese-Armenian Citizen], *Aztag*, 6 June, 1957, 2.
45. 'Dimaknerĕ Var' [The Removal of Masks], *Aztag*, 9 June, 1957, 1.
46. Ibid.
47. Ibid.
48. Ibid.
49. Ibid.
50. 'K'uēn Iravunk' Ē', 2.
51. 'Dashnakts'akannerĕ ew Ekeghets'in' [The Dashnaks and the Church], *Aztag*, 3 May, 1958, 2.
52. Ibid.
53. Ibid.
54. Throughout the 1940s, the catholicos of the Cilician See would have been present at such celebrations as well. Ibid.
55. Ibid.
56. 'Haght'anakēn Etg'' [After the Victory], *Aztag*, 12 June, 1957, 1.
57. 'Hayut'yan Azatatench' Vogin Anparteli Uzh Měn Ē' [The Armenian Nation's Yearning Spirit for Freedom is an Undefeatable Force], *Aztag*, 13 June, 1957, 1.
58. 'Kamawor Struknerĕ' [The Willing Slaves], *Aztag*, 4 October, 1957, 1. As *Aztag* branded its Hnchak and Ramgavar rivals agents of the Soviet Union and worked to strip their followers of their Armenian identification, its rivals embarked on similar projects. *Zartonk* branded Dashnak loyalists as non-Armenians and as 'foreign plants' of the Turkish state. This was not the first time that the Ramgavar Party had made such an accusation. By referencing the support of the Dashnak Party for the Ottoman constitutional movement and the CUP before the latter dissolved into a ultra nationalist distrustful organisation, and by then treating the modern Turkish state as its heir, it accused the Dashnak Party of having collaborated with the Turkish Republic. Aside from these accusations that simultaneously defined the contours of the community and Armenian identification, these representations upheld differing views on

how to engage with the Lebanese political sphere and how to articulate citizenship and belonging in Lebanon. See for example, 'Dashnakneru Vtangawor Kortsunēut'iwn Mijinarewelyan Erkirneru Mēj' [The Dangerous Actions of the Dashnaks in the Middle East], *Zartonk*, 6 June, 1957, 3. With the victory of the Dashnak Party and its position in Lebanese politics, *Zartonk*'s rhetoric against them only sharpened. By the end of the year, they also accused the Dashnak Party of being agents of the United States of America. See for example, 'Dashnakts'akan Karō-i Arkatsnerĕ' [The Accidents of Dashnak Garo], *Zartonk*, 11 October, 1957, 1. This cartoon also shows the Dashnak Party as Nazi stooges in 1941 and literally arm and arm with the Turkish state in 1921.
59. 'Kamawor Struknerĕ' [The Willing Slaves], *Aztag*, 4 October, 1957, 1.
60. 'Nakhagah Shamuni Karewor Charĕ' [President Chamoun's Important Address], *Aztag*, 6 August, 1957, 1, 4.
61. Ibid.
62. Ibid.
63. Ibid.
64. '25 Spannyal ew Bazmat'iw Viraworner Pēyrut'i Mēj' [25 Dead and Numerous Wounded in Beirut], *Aztag*, 15 May, 1958, 1.
65. 'Hnch'ak-Hamaynavarneru Erkrord Zohn al Meṛaw Erek' [The Second Victim of the Hnchak-Communists Died Yesterday], *Aztag*, 15 November, 1958, 4. *Aztag* did not detail the victim's political leanings. Nevertheless, it noted that the crowds sang 'Verkerov Li Chan Fedayi', as they were leaving the cemetery. The singing of this traditional revolutionary song indicated that Jirayr was a member of the Dashnak political party. This reference would not have been lost upon any of *Aztag*'s readers – party member or not. The message of its final stanza is, 'And now I finally lie in comfortable ground/ You, my comrades, are my hope now/ Continue our sacred work/ Brave heroes of the Dashnaks'. *Armenian National and Revolutionary Songs* (Watertown: Armenian Revolutionary Federation, 1983), 16.
66. 'Hnch'ak-Hamaynavarneru', 4.
67. Ibid.
68. Banakayin Udzer Pasharets'in Hachĕn ew Rmēyl T'agherĕ' [Army Forces Surrounded the Neighbourhoods of Hajin and Rmeil], *Aztag*, 19 November, 1958, 4. Hajin is the name of the neighbourhood used and given by Armenians. In the 1920s, when it became inhabited, most were refugees from Hajin, in Southern Cilicia. For Arab–Lebanese, the names Corniche al-Nahr or Badawi are used.

69. Ibid.
70. Ibid.
71. 'Hnch'ak-Hamaynavarnerĕ Vochir mĕ Ews Gortsets'in' [The Hnchak-Communists Commit Yet Another Crime], *Aztag*, 20 November, 1958, 4.
72. Ibid.
73. Ibid.
74. Ibid. The Lebanese government met to discuss domestic security on 21 November, 1958. Minister of Interior Raymond Eddé stated that progress had been made to calm the neighbourhoods of Nahr and Bourj Hamoud, adding that stockpiles of weaponry and ammunition were confiscated. In addition, he issued a special decree specifically to the Armenian political parties, their members, and their officials, so that 'the security situation would not deteriorate even further'. 'Ts'awali Mijatēperĕ Gĕ Sharunakuin Haykakan T'agheru Mēj' [Unfortunate Clashes Continue in the Armenian Neighbourhoods], *Aztag*, 21 November, 1958, 4.
75. 'Haykakan T'agherĕ Handart Mnats'in Erēk' [The Armenian Neighbourhoods Remained Calm Yesterday], *Aztag*, 22 November, 1958, 4.
76. 'Andorrut'iwnĕ Gĕ Verahastatui Haykakan T'agherēn Ners' [Calm Restored in the Armenian Neighbourhoods], *Aztag*, 23 November, 1958, 1.
77. Ibid.
78. 'Srtagin Koch' Libanani Hay Zhoghovurdin' [Heartfelt Declaration to Lebanon's Armenian People], *Aztag*, 23 November, 1958, 1.
79. Ibid.
80. Ibid.
81. Ibid.
82. Ibid.
83. Joanne Randa Nucho, *Everyday Sectarianism in Urban Lebanon: Infrastructures, Public Services, and Power* (Princeton: Princeton University Press, 2016), 54.
84. Nicola Migliorino, *(Re)constructing Armenia in Lebanon and Syria: Ethnocultural Diversity and the State in the Aftermath of a Refugee Crisis* (Oxford: Berghahn Books, 2008), 64–5.
85. 'Moskua Mijamtets' Libanani Ĕntrut'iwnnerun' [Moscow Interfered in Lebanon's Elections], *Aztag*, 16 June, 1957, 1.
86. Ibid.
87. Ibid.
88. See for example, 'Eddé ya'qdu muaalaha bayna ahzab al-Arman' [Eddé Holds

Reconciliation Between Armenian Parties], *al-Nahar* (Beirut, Lebanon), 9 December, 1958, 1.
89. 'Azgayin Kronik' [National Chronicles], *Zartonk*, 10 January, 1958, 1, 2.
90. 'Dashnak Ahabekichʻneru Vayragutʻiwnnerĕ Haykakan Tʻagherēn Ners' [The Horrifying Activities of the Terrorist Dashnaks], *Zartonk*, 18 November, 1958, 1.
91. Ibid.
92. 'Vochirneru Sharkʻĕ Gĕ Sharunakui Haykakan Tʻaghamaserēn Ners' [The Criminals' Streak Continues Inside the Armenian Neighbourhoods], *Zartonk* (Beirut, Lebanon), 19 November, 1958, 1.
93. Ibid.
94. 'Anarg Vochragortsner Gĕ Spannen HMEMakan Marzik Shamin ew Gĕ Viraworen Grigor Sēraytaryanĕ' [Vile Criminals Murder HMEM Athlete Shami [Kevork Voskerichian] and Wound Krikor Seraidarian], *Aztag*, 28 August, 1958, 4.
95. Ibid.
96. 'Hay Hamaynavarnerĕ Nor Zoh mĕ ews Khletsʻin' [Armenian Communists Claimed Another Victim], *Aztag*, 29 August, 1958, 2.
97. Ibid.
98. Ibid.
99. 'Haydararutʻiwn Ankakh Azgayinneru Hamakhmbumin' [Announcement of the Independent National Committee], *Zartonk*, 11 March, 1956, 1; 'Haydararutʻiwn' [Announcement], *Zartonk*, 15 June, 1957, 4.
100. 'Aytsʻelutʻiwn N.V. Norĕntir Naghagah Zōr. Fuat Shehapin' [The Visit of the Newly Elected Honourable Fouad Chehab], *Zartonk*, 27 August, 1958, 1; 'Kochʻ Libanahay Zhoghovurdin' [Decree to the Lebanese Armenian People], *Zartonk*, 19 September, 1958, 1.
101. 'Aytsʻelutʻiwn N.V. Norĕntir Naghagah Zōr. Fuat Shehapin', 1; 'Ankakh Hay Hamaynkʻi Patuirakutʻyan Shnorhaworagan Aytsʻelutʻiwnĕ Libanani Norĕntir Nakhagah N.V. Zōr. Fuat Shehapin' [The Newly Elected Fouad Chehab's Visit to the Independent Armenian Community], *Zartonk*, 30 August, 1958, 1.
102. 'Ankakh Hay Hamaynkʻi', 1.
103. 'Katsʻutʻunĕ Pēyrutʻi Haykakan Tʻagherēn Ners' [The Situation in Beirut's Armenian Neighbourhoods], *Zartonk*, 30 August, 1958, 1.
104. 'Eghbayraspan Ochirner Haykakan Tʻagherēn Ners' [Fratricidal Crimes in the Armenian Neighbourhoods], *Zartonk*, 28 August, 1958, 1; 'Katsʻutʻunĕ', 1;

through 'Haykakan T'agheru Mēj Kargĕ Verahastatelu Hamar' [Reestablishing Order in the Armenian Neighbourhoods], *Aztag*, 13 December, 1958, 1.

105. See for example, 'Eghbayraspan Ochirner', 1. 'Dashnak Ochramit K'aghak'akanut'yan Aghitaber Hetewank'nerĕ' [The Disastrous Political Results of the Criminal Minded Dashnaks] *Zartonk*, 29 August, 1958, 1.

106. See for example, 'Banakayin Uzher Pasharets'in Hachĕn ew R̆ĕmēyl T'agheruĕ' [Army Forces Have Surrounded Hajin and Rmeil Neighbourhoods], *Aztag*, 19 November, 1958, 2.

107. 'Mer Ĕnt'erts'oghnerun' [To Our Readership], *Zartonk*, 17 October, 1958, 1.

108. Ibid.

109. 'Nerk'in Nakhararhi Koch'ĕ Libanahayut'yan' [The Minister of Interior's Declaration to Lebanese-Armenians], *Aztag*, 12 December, 1958, 1.

110. Ibid. Emphasis mine.

111. Ibid.

112. Ibid.

113. Ibid.

114. Ibid.

115. Ibid.

116. Ibid.

117. Ibid.

118. 'Haykakan T'agheru', 1.

119. Ibid.

120. 'Mer Derĕ' [Our Role], *Aztag*, 14 December, 1958, 1.

121. Ibid.

122. Ibid.

123. Ibid.

124. 'Anteghi Mtahogut'iwnner' [Absurd Worries], *Aztag*, 18 December, 1958, 1.

125. Ibid.

126. Ibid.

CONCLUSION

This book has told the story of the Armenian inhabitants of Lebanon in the first decade and a half following its independence in 1943–1946 and in the increasingly bifurcated environment of the Cold War. My analysis has showcased Armenians' manifold sociopolitical activities and power struggles. The Armenians who have emerged from the pages of the past four chapters are much more than 'simply' downtrodden, oppressed, powerless refugees. They time and again used Lebanon and the Cold War tensions playing out in that country to explore and assert their own agency – and thus to reaffirm, and indeed redefine, their own identity not simply as objects but also as subjects of history. This also meant that the Armenians who we have encountered here engaged with Lebanon and the Cold War powers by meddling in them as their very *own* locales. This has not been a history of loss or simple rebirth, then: two perspectives omnipresent in writings on modern Armenian history. Rather, it has been a history of power. I have focused on how Armenians experienced the everyday in early post-colonial, Cold War Lebanon, making it their own, and how they manipulated and managed loss and renewal. I have pursued this inquiry by closely analysing Armenian language newspapers published in Beirut, examining what they said and how they did so. These often ideologically-opposed newspapers reflected how

Armenians in Lebanon re-situated themselves and re-imagined their place in that Middle Eastern country and in the world more broadly during a sensitive, transitional time of change, the early post-colonial period.

With this approach, *Armenians Beyond Diaspora* contests previous scholarship of Armenians, Lebanon and the Cold War. Historians of Lebanon have largely ignored Armenians in their local and national histories; and if including them, have treated them as a fixed foreign and refugee community, a choice aligned with worn-out, if not cliché, understandings of Lebanon as an abnormal country. They are invested in showing that due to its demographic composition, the Lebanese nation-state barely holds itself together and is always on the brink of violence and warfare. Scholarship on Lebanon's Armenian community has reinforced this picture. It considers Armenians intrinsically and fundamentally as part of other Armenian communities worldwide, united in a desire to return to a homeland and traumatised by violence. Both of these literatures fail to consider Armenians as active members of local, regional and global communities independently of their being Armenian. On a related note, this book advocates for a history that fundamentally differs from, and thus challenges, Armenian historiographies, including and particularly Diaspora Studies. The latter ultimately always define Armenians vis-à-vis a lost homeland, reducing them to that presumably clear-cut dimension of their existence. In consequence and in parallel, those studies also assert and enshrine notions of Armenian victimhood.

Armenians Beyond Diaspora has challenged these assumptions. It thereby contributes to a growing body of scholarship that aims to move marginal elements in society to the centre-stage. These histories effectively challenge macro-histories that privilege the nation-state and its principal power holders and brokers. They also reveal power dynamics internal to groups that have far too often been seen as homogenous and harmonious. Armenian histories have certainly not been at the forefront of works that detail the inner workings of Armenian communities and tensions in their ranks. It is not, of course, that this book advocates for, or is, a tabloid tell-all. But it does show how Armenians, just like other inhabitants of Lebanon, engaged in power struggles whose analysis highlights their own agency.

Moreover, this book has not sought to merely insert the Armenian story into a larger, set narrative of Lebanon. Its ultimate aim has not simply been to render Lebanese history more inclusive and complete. It adds texture to recent works that focus on how the Cold War shaped the region, also amongst minority groups. In doing so, it has demonstrated how Armenians used the bifurcated environment of the Cold War. While the United States and the Soviet Union attempted to advance their national interests through proxies, including the Armenian community, Armenians in turn articulated their own power locally and transnationally. Just as – and indeed because – Armenians were invested on both sides of the ideological differences between the Soviet Union and the United States, they used their respective beliefs and representations to attack Armenian political and religious rivals. The Cold War, then, was both a cloak to articulate these differences and an opportunity to battle for power over representations of the Armenian community.

In locating Lebanon as a site of these power struggles, *Armenians Beyond Diaspora* challenges an Armenian historiography that aims to connect Armenians in Lebanon to other Armenian communities worldwide and to an external homeland. By letting Lebanon become the centre of the story, we have the opportunity to investigate the inner workings of a segment of the Lebanese population that, while legally Lebanese, has not been considered as an actor in its history (only as a passive beneficiary). What these examinations have found is the Armenians engaged with their environment as Armenians and Lebanese, varying concepts of belonging and identification depending on the historical moment. These changes demonstrate the activity amongst Armenian inhabitants of Lebanon and show how they participated and were incorporated in local, regional and global power struggles. For Armenians in Lebanon, the centre of Armenian life was in Lebanon, and not some distant or imagined homeland, although the Armenian press and the associate political parties upheld these representations. While some Armenians connected to a diasporic understanding of themselves, they simultaneously used these representations to articulate their own power in Lebanon. These exercises took place in the form of violence and reordering of Beirut's urban space, as well as through heated disputes between newspapers; analysing the news coverage and debates in the Armenian press in the years following Lebanese independence thus explores how Armenians performed as Lebanese citizens in an independent Lebanon. While these newspapers showcased a certain viewpoint, more often than not connected to an Armenian political party ideology, the discussions between and amongst the papers highlight the changes influencing Armenians, brought about by Armenians, within a larger social, political and economic context of Lebanon.

I have explored four principal aspects of the above reality. Setting the scene, Chapter 1 examined how Armenians lived in the everyday in Lebanon: their lives' debates, concerns and interests, partly mediated through Beirut's rich universe of Armenian newspapers. This chapter investigated Lebanese Armenians' triangulations and balancing acts vis-à-vis the Lebanese state, its wider Arab environment and the Armenian Socialist Soviet Republic (ASSR). I studied four themes. The first was Armenians' position in and vis-à-vis the Lebanese polity, as well as vis-à-vis Syria. A second concerned language, and specifically the multiple roles of Arabic and its relationship with Armenian. The next one had to do with the ambiguities of spaces relevant for Armenians in and beyond Lebanon, including the ASSR. And a last one concerned the fascinating political positioning of the church that, although conservative, felt forced to support communist Armenia and the USSR as the ASSR's protector.

Chapter 2 dealt with the 1945–1947 organised Soviet repatriation drive and, specifically, the Lebanese Armenian political-cultural understandings of it. The emerging Cold War was more than a backdrop to this story. The very divergent readings of, and responses to, the repatriation initiative among Lebanese Armenians – reinforced tensions between Armenian rightists and leftists. The Lebanese example showed that Armenians' response to repatriation did not simply reflect their extant political–cultural positions. Rather, repatriation sharpened those positions.

While the excitement and success of the repatriation movement was a public relations victory for the USSR supported by local Armenian institutions and assisted by Lebanese and Syrian governments, the 1956 catholicos election in Lebanon, profiled in Chapter 3, became a site of contestation by Cold War powers and by their state and non-state allies and proxies in the Middle East. This election allows us to look at the Cold War in the Middle East not from the top down, through the eyes of Washington or Moscow (or Lebanon's or Egypt's state authorities, for that matter) during flashpoints like the 1958 US intervention in Lebanon or the US and Soviet reactions to the Tripartite Aggression against Egypt in 1956. Rather, in that election, Armenians made use of Cold War tensions to designate a leader of the Armenian church who was seen to suit the community's interests. That story also expands historians' and social scientists' understanding of Lebanon's Armenians: from refugees and outsiders in national politics to true participants, whose own internal politics, moreover, were also of interest to Lebanon's authorities, and who by now felt free to invade and use public spaces beyond their own neighbourhoods to make political statements.

Finally, Chapter 4 investigated Armenians' stance in the 1957 elections and in the 1958 mini-civil war – both in the 'general' Lebanese one and in the intra-Armenian one. Coming a good decade after the 1945–1946 transition from the French Mandate to post-colonial independence, Armenians were firmly part of and ensconced in, Lebanese politics. Lebanese Armenians aligned along the right–left faultlines that divided Lebanese politics and society in general at that point: they were Lebanonised, one may say. At the same point, the Lebanese state was Armenianised, as it were, in that it started to pay more attention to Armenian matters than before, intervening directly and by military force in Armenian neighbourhoods by December 1958 in order to finally end the internecine Armenian confrontation. These tensions and violent confrontations between Armenian parties and their armed men had a crucial spatial effect: they unprecedentedly territorialised parts of Beirut. Whereas parts of Lebanon were already organised by sects and classes, by relative contrast, it was according to political party affiliation that in 1957–1958 many Armenians of Mar Mikael, Sin el Fil, Bourj Hamoud and Corniche al-Nahr were re-sorted and relocated, often by force.

These investigations allow me to reflect upon additional struggles for power after 1958, including the Lebanese Civil War and the post-Taif Period.[1] The 1975–1990 Civil War dominated studies on Lebanon for a good decade. More recently, there has been a surge of historical and anthropological works that shifted the focus more towards marginalised inhabitants, every day experiences, and sectarianism.[2] Many explain this (re)emergence by framing their contributions as a way to understand the 'outcome' (as if it were a process and now complete) of the uprisings of the 2010s and/or the so-called ensuing 'explosion of sectarianism' in Lebanon and throughout the Middle East.[3] These lines of inquiry once again confine Lebanon to the paradigm of violence and conflict, but this time, do so to demonstrate its familiarity and ease with a sectarian rubric. Familiar tropes are thereby adopted, disregarding the everyday, the marginal and experiences that may challenge this understanding in favour of ever-profiling its more recognisable 'divides'.[4] Not surprisingly, they rarely, if ever, mention Armenians.

Armenians Beyond Diaspora, through its explorations of the concurrent Lebanonisation of Armenians and the Armenianisation of Lebanon pierces these understandings as well. It forces the reconsideration of additional power struggles that have been excluded by design, in order to reinforce a particular rendering of Lebanon, its inhabitants and the region. For example, considering Armenian involvement in the Lebanese Civil War and especially since the Taif accords could force a recategorisation of the Lebanese political realm's so-called 'major players' and (re)construct Lebanon's recent history. Ohannes Geukjian, for example, discusses how leaders of the three main Armenian political parties in Lebanon adopted a policy of 'positive neutrality' in 1975.[5] In discussing their motives, Geukjian argues that such a term does not mean that they avoided participation in internal Lebanese politics, but rather engaged in 'effective communication, consultation and negotiation at the state and party levels'.[6]

And yet, while Armenians did not participate in battles in a sustained manner, their presence in the public realm as he describes it, and also in combat (Geukjian mentions how Armenian quarters in Beirut were shelled from all sides in October 1978) are fundamentally active forms of engagement that simultaneously demonstrate membership in Lebanon.[7] Defensive participation is still participation. In addition, disruption, relocation and permanent immigration were all sustained engagements with the Lebanese Civil War. That the Armenian Evangelical College in Qantari was used by different militias and its buildings damaged and renovated testifies to a prolonged involvement in the war. So does the drop in Armenian student enrollment in Armenian schools during this time period, the 'migration' of schools from Beirut's centre to Sin el-Fil and Fanar and the permanent migration of entrepreneurs and capital.[8] While measured as observation or loss, these moments are also additional examples of the redrawing of boundaries of Beirut and beyond. They are likewise additional articulations of being and living as Lebanese.

Armenian participation, involvement, presence and absence must be released from the confines of loss, defeat and reticence.[9] Such an approach is not a result of a desire to make Lebanese (or Armenian) history more complete, to reconfigure the experiences of Armenians as more 'positive', or to construct an account of Armenians in a more nationalist vein. Rather, it is a way to go beyond extraordinary or exceptional moments and capture what is routine.[10] It is perhaps the only way to engage with both Armenians in Lebanon and Lebanon as a site apart from the lens of 'catastrophe' – be it the Armenian Genocide or the Lebanese Civil War – and engage with daily practices that hold the potential to reveal additional sites of power and activity.[11]

Finally, post-Taif historiography often characterises the Dashnak, Hnchak and Ramgavar parties as unable or failing to reach an agreement on their political representation in the Armenian community.[12] But Armenian political parties have also been shown to engage, shift and actively react to a variety of political realities and pressures.[13] These actions are often seen 'only' as responses to the authority of Lebanese state, or rather, the success of Rafiq Hariri's political ambition. But they can also be understood as evidence of the Lebanese state's engagement with its Armenian inhabitants and its further 'Armenianisation'. They likewise reveal how active the 'pact of neutrality' in fact was and may have even threatened the Lebanese state's – and in particular Hariri's – own aims.[14] And yet, reductions and divisions cannot be the only way to view contemporary Armenian presence in Lebanon. Cases like the 2007 Metn by-election exemplify the Lebanonisation of Armenians. They used their representation as overlooked inhabitants to articulate power[15] – even in the wake of 'splits' amongst political parties and racist and angry taunts targeting them.[16]

Armenians Beyond Diaspora has registered how both Armenian and non-Armenian Lebanese fashioned each others' belonging and identity. It is my hope that this account will help us understand post-genocide Armenian histories, including everyday life, beyond nationalist, insular and diasporic stories.

Notes

1. The 1989 Taif agreement, drafted in Saudi Arabia, supported by Syria and the United States, effectively ended the Lebanese Civil War. Ohannes Geukjian,

'From Positive Neutrality to Partnership: How and Why the Armenian Political Parties Took Sides in Lebanese Politics in the Post-Taif Period (1989–present), *Middle Eastern Studies* 45, no. 5 (September 2009): 739.

2. The current resurgence of using sectarianism as a frame to structure alleged conflict is not limited to Lebanon. It dominates recent studies on the Middle East, simultaneously claiming to both 'explain' while constructing that very dynamic. In fact, sectarianism is often posited to be native to Lebanon, and then revealed to have 'spread', like an infectious disease, to other sites. See for example Geneive Abdo, *The New Sectarianism: The Arab Uprisings and the Rebirth of the Shi'a–Sunni Divide* (New York: Oxford University Press, 2017); Rola El-Husseini, *Pax Syriana: Elite Politics in Postwar Lebanon* (Syracuse: Syracuse University Press, 2012); Nader Hashemi and Danny Postel, eds, *Sectarianisation: Mapping the New Politics of the Middle East* (Oxford: Oxford University Press, 2017); Paul W. T. Kingston, *Reproducing Sectarianism: Advocacy Networks and the Politics of Civil Society in Postwar Lebanon* (Albany, NY: State University of New York Press, 2013); Bassel Salloukh, Rabie Barakat, Jinan S. Al-Habbal, Lara W. Khattab, and Shoghig Mikaelian, eds, *Politics of Sectarianism in Postwar Lebanon* (London: Pluto Press, 2015); and Ken Seigneurie, *Standing By the Ruins: Elegiac Humanism in Wartime and Postwar Lebanon* (New York: Fordham University Press, 2011).

3. Abdo, *The New Sectarianism*, 1. Hashemi and Postel, *Sectarianisation*, 2; Salloukh, Barakat, Al-Habbal, Khattab, and Mikaelian, *Politics of Sectarianism*, 2.

4. See for example, Bassel Salloukh, 'The Architecture of Sectarianism in Lebanon', in *Sectarianisation*, 218.

5. Ohannes Geukjian, 'The Policy of Positive Neutrality of the Armenian Political Parties in Lebanon during the Civil War, 1975–1990: A Critical Analysis', *Middle Eastern Studies* 43, no. 1 (January 2007): 65–73.

6. Ibid., 69–71.

7. Ibid., 69.

8. Nicola Migliorino, *(Re)Constructing Armenia in Lebanon and Syria: Ethno-Cultural Diversity and the State in the Aftermath of A Refugee Crisis* (New York: Berghahn Books, 2008), 161, 162, 170.

9. Many works on Armenians engage in such themes. See for example Bedross Der Matossian, 'The Armenians of Jerusalem in the Modern Period: The Rise and Decline of a Community', in *Routledge Handbook on Jerusalem*, eds Suleiman A. Mourad, Naomi Koltun-Fromm, and Bedross Der Matossian (New York: Routledge, 2019), 396–407; Darren Logan, 'A Remnant Remaining: Armenians

amid Northern Iraq's Christian Minority", *Iran and the Caucasus* 14, no. 1 (2010): 143–57; Susan Pattie, 'Paradise Lost and Regained in Kessab: Narratives of Rebuilding and Migration', in *Armenian Communities of the Northeastern Mediterranean: Musa Dagh–Dört-Yol–Kessab*, ed. Richard Hovannisian (Costa Mesa: Mazda, 2016), 453–78; Simon Payaslian, 'Diasporan Subalternities: The Armenian Community in Syria', *Diaspora: A Journal of Transnational Studies* 16, vol. 1–2 (2007): 92–132; Vahram L. Shemmassian, 'Vakef Köy of Musa Dagh: The Sole Armenian Village Remaining in Turkey', in *Armenian Communities of the Northeastern Mediterranean*, 287–308. Hratch Tchilingirian, 'The "Other" Citizens: Armenians in Turkey between Isolation and (Dis)Integration', *Journal of the Society for Armenian Studies* 25, no. 4 (2017): 123–55; Hagop Tcholakian, 'Kessab as a Diasporan Community', in *Armenian Communities of the Northeastern Mediterranean*, 409–52.

10. Liesel Olsen, 'Introduction', in *Modernism and the Ordinary* (Oxford: Oxford University Press, 2014), 6.
11. I am appropriating *Alltagsgeschichte* here. Paul Steege, Andrew Stuart Bergerson, Maureen Healy, and Pamela E. Swett, 'The History of Everyday Life: A Second Chapter', *The Journal of Modern History* 80, no. 2 (2008): 358.
12. Geukjian, 'From Positive Neutrality to Partnership', 739.
13. See for example, the 1992 joint Dashnak-Hnchak communiqué, the refusal of Ramgavar Party to take part, the speech made by President Elias Hraoui defending the lack of Armenians in civil servant posts, the growing involvement of the Republic of Armenia in Lebanese Armenian affairs as an attempt to weaken the Dashnak Party and the 'splitting of the Armenian bloc' through the political manoeuvering of Prime Minister Rafik Hariri. Geukjian, 'From Positive Neutrality to Partnership', 745–47.
14. Geukjian notes how Hariri preferred not to work with strong allies. Ibid., 748–49.
15. The by-elections were held on 5 August, 2007 with the Dashnak Party supporting the Free Patriotic Movement's candidate Camille Khoury against Amin Gemayal, the leader of the Phalange Party and former Lebanese president. The resulting win of Khoury unleashed a barrage of accusations against the Dashnak Party and Armenians, but also revealed the potential 'value' of the Armenian vote. Geukjian, 'From Positive Neutrality to Partnership', 757–9.
16. 'Hoss: Metn Polls Prove Democracy in Lebanon is an "Illusion"', *The Daily Star*, 7 August, 2007, 3.

BIBLIOGRAPHY

In the main body of the book, I have not used diacritics, and used more common spellings of Western and Eastern Armenian names and spoken Lebanese Arabic dialects. Also, I have added an *s* to indicate plurals to aid the reader unfamiliar with Western Armenian. In the endnotes, the transliteration of all Armenian sources is based on the *Armenian Review* key (modelled on the Eastern Armenian pronunciation), and includes diacritics. Names of the Armenian political parties have been given in the Armenian. The transliteration of Arabic is based on the *International Journal of Middle Eastern Studies* (*IJMES*) transliteration chart.

Newspapers and Periodicals

al-Nahar, Beirut.
Ararad, Beirut.
Ayk, Beirut.
Aztag, Beirut.
Aztarar, Beirut.
The Daily Star, Beirut.
Hask, Beirut.
Joghovourti Tzain, Beirut.
L'Orient, Beirut.
Marmnamarz, Istanbul.

The New York Times, New York.
Zartonk, Beirut.

Books and Articles

Abu-Rish, Ziad. 'Conflict and Institution Building in Lebanon, 1946–1955'. Ph.D. diss., University of California, Los Angeles, 2014.

Abu Izzedin, Nejla M. *The Druzes: A New Study of Their History, Faith, and Society*. Leiden: Brill, 1993.

Abdo, Geneive. *The New Sectarianism: The Arab Uprisings and the Rebirth of the Shi'a–Sunni Divide*. New York: Oxford University Press, 2017.

Al-Hardan, Anaheed. *Palestinians in Syria: Nakba Memories of Shattered Communities*. New York: Columbia University Press, 2016.

Al-Rostom, Hakem. 'Rethinking the "Post Ottoman": Anatolian Armenians as an Ethnographic Perspective'. In *A Companion to the Anthropology of the Middle East*, edited by Soraya Altorki, 452–79. Oxford: Wiley–Blackwell, 2015.

Alajaji, Sylvia. *Music and the Armenian Diaspora: Searching for Home in Exile*. Bloomington: Indiana University Press, 2015.

Alexander, Ben. 'The American Armenians' Cold War: The Divided Response to Soviet Armenia'. In *Anti-Communist Minorities in the U.S.: Political Activism of Ethnic Refugees*, edited by Ieva Zake, 67–86. New York: Palgrave, 2009.

Alexander, Edward. 'The Armenian Church in Soviet Policy'. *The Russian Review* 14(4) (October, 1955): 358–9.

Ambrust, Walter. 'History in Arab Media Studies, A Speculative Cultural History'. In *Arab Cultural Studies: Mapping the Field*, edited by Tarik Sabry, 32–54. New York: I. B. Tauris, 2012.

Ang, Ien. 'Together-in-Difference: Beyond Diaspora, into Hybridity'. *Asian Studies Review* 27(2) (2003): 141–54.

Antaramian Richard, Edward. 'In Subversive Service of the Sublime State: Armenians and Ottoman State Power, 1844–1896'. Ph.D. diss., University of Michigan, 2014.

Armenian National and Revolutionary Songs. Watertown: Armenian Revolutionary Federation, 1983.

Armstrong, John. *Nations Before Nationalism*. Chapel Hill: University of North Carolina Press, 1982.

Arsan, Andrew and Cyrus Schayegh, eds, *The Routledge Handbook of the History of the Middle East Mandates*. New York: Routledge, 2015.

Arzoumanian, Zaven. *The Armenian Apostolic Church in Recent Times: A Path to the 21st Century*. Burbank: Issued Privately, 2010.
Aslanian, Sebouh David. 'From "Autonomous" to "Interactive" Histories: World History's Challenge to Armenian Studies'. In *An Armenian Mediterranean: Words and Worlds in Motion*, edited by Kathryn Babayan and Michael Pifer, 81–125. London: Palgrave Macmillan, 2018.
Attié, Caroline. *Struggle in the Levant: Lebanon in the 1950s*. London: I. B. Tauris, 2004.
Babikian Assaf, Christine, Carla Eddé, Lévon Nordiguian, and Vahé Tachjian, eds, *Les Arméniens du Liban: Cent ans de presence*. Beirut: Presses de l'Université Saint-Joseph, 2017.
Bardakjian, Kevork. 'The Rise of the Armenian Patriarchate of Constantinople'. In *Christian and Jews in the Ottoman Empire,* vol. 1: *The Central Lands*, edited by Benjamin Braude, 87–98. New York: Holmes and Meier, 2014.
Barrett, Roby C. *The Greater Middle East and the Cold War: US Foreign Policy Under Eisenhower and Kennedy*. London: I. B. Tauris, 2009.
Barry, James. *Armenian Christians in Iran: Ethnicity, Religion, and Identity in the Islamic Republic*. Cambridge: Cambridge University Press, 2019.
Barsoumian, Hagop. 'The Eastern Question and the Tanzimat Era'. In *The Armenian People from Ancient to Modern Times (Volume 2) From Dominion to Statehood: The Fifteenth Century to the Twentieth*, edited by Richard Hovannisian, 175–202. London: Macmillan, 1997.
Bashkin, Orit. *New Babylonians: A History of Jews in Modern Iraq*. Stanford, CA: Stanford University Press, 2012.
Bedoyan, Hratch. 'The Social, Political, and Religious Structure of the Armenian Community in Lebanon'. *The Armenian Review* 32(2) (1979): 119–30.
Berberian, Houri. *Armenians and the Iranian Constitutional Revolution of 1905–1911: The Love for Freedom Has No Fatherland*. Boulder: Westview Press, 2001.
Betts, Robert Brenton. *The Druze*. New Haven: Yale University Press, 1990.
Bilal, Melissa. 'Lullabies and the Memory of Pain: Armenian Women's Remembrance of the Past in Turkey'. *Dialect Anthropology* (2018):1–22. https://doi.org/10.1007/s10624-018-9515-8.
——. 'Longing for Home at Home: The Armenians of Istanbul'. In *Diaspora and Memory: Figures of Displacement in Contemporary Literature, Arts and Politics*, edited by Marie-Aude Baronian, Stephan Besser and Yolande Jansen, 55–66. Amsterdam: Brill | Rodopi, 2007.

Boudjikanian, Aida. ed., *Armenians of Lebanon: From Past Princesses and Refugees to Present-Day Community*. Beirut: Haigazian University Press, 2009.

Bournoutian, George. 'Eastern Armenia From the the Seventeenth Century to the Russian Annexation'. In *A History of the Armenian People*, vol. II: *Pre-History to 1500 AD*, edited by Richard Hovannisian, 81–108. Costa Mesa: Mazda, 1993.

Bozoyan, Azat A. 'Armenian Political Revival in Cilicia'. In *Armenian Cilicia*, edited by Richard Hovannisian and Simon Payaslian, 67–78. Costa Mesa: Mazda, 2008.

Björklund, Ulf. 'Armenians of Athens and Istanbul: the Armenian Diaspora and the "Transnational" Nation'. *Global Networks* 3(3) (2003): 337–54.

Bobelian, Michael. *Children of Armenia: A Forgotten Genocide and the Century-Long Struggle for Justice*. New York: Simon and Schuster, 2009.

Brubaker, Rogers. 'The "Diaspora" Diaspora'. *Ethnic and Racial Studies* 28(1) (2005): 1–19.

Butler, Kim. 'Multi-Layered Politics in the African Diaspora: The Metadiaspora Concept and Minidiaspora Realities'. In *Opportunity Structures in Diaspora Relations: Comparisons in Contemporary Multilevel Politics of Diaspora and Transnational Identity*, edited by Gloria Totoricagüena, 19–51. Reno, NV: Centre for Basque Studies, University of Nevada, 2007.

Cammett, Melani. *Compassionate Communalism: Welfare and Sectarianism in Lebanon*. Cornell: Cornell University Press, 2014.

Chamberlin, Paul Thomas. *The Cold War's Killing Fields: Rethinking the Long Peace*. New York: HarperCollins, 2018.

Chatty, Dawn. *Displacement and Dispossession in the Modern Middle East*. Cambridge: Cambridge University Press, 2010.

Clifford, James. 'Diasporas'. *Cultural Anthropology* 9(3) (1997): 302–38.

Cohen, Julia Phillips. *Becoming Ottomans: Sephardi Jews and Imperial Citizenship in the Modern Era*. New York: Oxford University Press, 2014.

Cohen, Robin. *Global Diasporas: An Introduction*. New York: Routledge, 2008.

Corley, Felix. 'The Armenian Orthodox Church'. In *Eastern Christianity and the Cold War, 1945–91*, edited by Lucian Leuștean, 189–203. London: Routledge, 2010.

Dadoyan, Seta. *The Armenian Catholicosate From Cilicia to Antelias*. Antelias: The Armenian Catholicosate of Cilicia, 2003.

de Waal, Thomas. *Great Catastrophe: Armenians and Turks in the Shadow of Genocide*. Oxford: Oxford Unversity Press, 2015.

Dédéyan, Gérard. 'The Founding and Coalescence of the Rubenian Principality, 1073–1129'. In *Armenian Cilicia*, edited by Richard Hovannisian and Simon Payaslian, 79–92. Costa Mesa: Mazda, 2008.

Deeb, Lara. *An Enchanted Modern: Gender and Public Piety in Shi'i Lebanon*. Princeton: Princeton University Press, 2006.

Der Matossian, Bedross. 'The Armenians of Jerusalem in the Modern Period: The Rise and Decline of a Community'. In *Routledge Handbook on Jerusalem*, edited by Suleiman A. Mourad, Naomi Koltun-Fromm and Bedross Der Matossian, 396–407. New York: Routledge, 2019.

———. 'Explaining the Unexplainable: Recent Trends in the Armenian Genocide Historiography'. *Journal of Leventine Studies* 5(2) (Winter 2015): 143–66.

———. *Shattered Dreams of Revolution: From Liberty to Violence in the Late Ottoman Empire*. Stanford: Stanford University Press, 2014.

———. 'The Armenians of Palestine 1918–48'. *Journal of Palestine Studies* 41(1) (Autumn 2011): 24–44.

Dougherty, Roberta L. 'Badi'a Masabni, Artiste and Modernist: The Egyptian Print Media's Carnival of National Identity'. In *Mass Mediations: New Approaches to Popular Culture in the Middle East and Beyond*, edited by Walter Ambrust, 243–68. Los Angeles: University of California Press, 2000.

Ekmekcioglu, Lerna. *Recovering Armenia: The Limits of Belonging in Post-Genocide Turkey*. Stanford: Stanford University Press, 2016.

El-Husseini, Rola. *Pax Syriana: Elite Politics in Postwar Lebanon*. Syracuse: Syracuse University Press, 2012.

Farah, May. 'Palestinian Refugees in Lebanon: Worthy Lives in Unworthy Conditions', In *Diasporas of the Modern Middle East: Contextualising Community*, edited by Anthony Gorman and Sossie Kasbarian, 274–300. Edinburgh: Edinburgh University Press, 2015.

Firro, Kais. *A History of the Druzes*. Leiden: Brill, 1992.

Fisk, Robert. *Pity the Nation: The Abduction of Lebanon*. New York: Nation Books, 2002.

Foster, Robert John. *Materializing the Nation: Commodities, Consumption, and Media in Papua New Guinea*. Bloomington, IN: Indiana University Press, 2002.

Gabaccia, Donna R. *Italy's Many Diasporas*. Seattle: University of Washington Press, 2000.

Geukjian, Ohannes 'From Positive Neutrality to Partnership: How and Why the Armenian Political Parties Took Sides in Lebanese Politics in the Post-Taif

Period (1989–present)'. *Middle Eastern Studies* 45(5) (September 2009): 739–67.

———. 'The Policy of Positive Neutrality of the Armenian Political Parties in Lebanon during the Civil War, 1975–1990: A Critical Analysis'. *Middle Eastern Studies* 43(1) (January 2007): 65–73.

Gilroy, Paul. *There Ain't no Black in the Union Jack: The Cultural Politics of Race and Nation*. Chicago: University of Chicago Press, 1991.

Golan, Galia. *Soviet Policies in the Middle East: From World War Two to Gorbachev*. Cambridge, Cambridge University Press, 2009.

Gorman, Anthony and Sossie Kasbarian, 'Introduction'. In *Diasporas of the Modern Middle East: Contextualising Community*, edited by Anthony Gorman and Sossie Kasbarian, 1–30. Edinburgh: Edinburgh University Press, 2015.

———. 'The Italians of Egypt: Return to a Diaspora'. In *Diasporas of the Modern Middle East: Contextualising Community*, edited by Anthony Gorman and Sossie Kasbarian, 138–170. Edinburgh: Edinburgh University Press, 2015.

Halfter, Peter. 'Papacy, Catholicosate, and the Kingdom of Cilician Armenia'. In *Armenian Cilicia*, edited by Richard Hovannisian and Simon Payaslian, 111–29. Costa Mesa: Mazda, 2008.

Hanf, Theodor. *Coexistence in Wartime Lebanon: Decline of a State and Rise of Nation*. New York: I. B. Tauris, 2015.

Hanssen, Jens. *Fin de Siècle Beirut: The Making of an Ottoman Provincial Capital*. Oxford: Oxford University Press, 2005.

Hasanli, Jamil. *Stalin and the Turkish Crisis of the Cold War, 1945–1953*. Lanham: Rowman & Littlefield, 2011.

Hashemi, Nader and Danny Postel, eds *Sectarianization: Mapping the New Politics of the Middle East*. Oxford: Oxford University Press, 2017.

Hermann Goltz and Klaus E. Göltz, *Rescued Armenian Treasures from Cilicia: Sacred Art of the Kilikia Museum Antelias, Lebanon*. Wiesbaden: Reichert, 2000.

Hewsen, Robert. 'Armenia Maritima: The Historical Geography of Cilicia'. In *Armenian Cilicia*, edited by Richard Hovannisian and Simon Payaslian, 33–65. Costa Mesa: Mazda, 2008.

Hilal, Jamil. 'Reflections on Contemporary Palestinian History'. In *Across the Wall: Narratives of Israeli-Palestinian History*, edited by Illan Pappé and Jamil Hilal, 177–215. New York: I. B. Tauris, 2010.

Hiro, Dilip. *Lebanon Fire and Embers: A History of the Lebanese Civil War*. London: Weidenfeld & Nicolson, 1993.

Hirst, David. *Beware of Small States: Lebanon, Battleground of the Middle East.* New York: Nation Books, 2011.
Holslag, Anthonie. *The Transgenerational Consequences of the Armenian Genocide: Near the Foot of Mount Ararat.* New York: Palgrave Macmillan, 2018.
Hourani, Albert. *Syria and Lebanon: A Political Essay.* London: Oxford University Press, 1946.
Hovannisian, Richard G., ed. *Armenian Communities of the Northeastern Mediterranean: Musa Dagh–Dört-Yol–Kessab.* Costa Mesa: Mazda, 2016.
_____. 'The Postwar Contest for Cilicia and the "Marash Affair"'. In *Armenian Cilicia*, edited by Richard Hovannisian and Simon Payaslian, 495–518. Costa Mesa: Mazda, 2008.
_____ ed. *The Armenian People from Ancient to Modern Times (Volume 2) From Dominion to Statehood: The Fifteenth Century to the Twentieth.* London: Macmillan, 1997.
_____. 'The Ebb and Flow of the Armenian Minority in the Arab Middle East'. *Middle East Journal* 28(1) (1974): 19–32.
_____ and Simon Payaslian, eds, *Armenian Cilicia.* Costa Mesa: Mazda, 2008.
Ilias, M. H. 'Malayalee Migrants and Translocal Kerala Politics in the Gulf: Re-conceptualising the "Political"'. In *Diasporas of the Modern Middle East: Contextualising Community*, edited by Anthony Gorman and Sossie Kasbarian, 303–37. Edinburgh: Edinburgh University Press, 2015.
Jebejian, Arda. 'Patterns of Language Use Among Armenians in Beirut in the Last 95 Years'. *Haigazian Armenological Review* 31(1) (2011): 453–69.
Kalpakian, Seta. 'The Dimensions of the 1958 Inter-Communal Conflict in the Armenian Community in Lebanon'. MA thesis, American University of Beirut, 1983.
Karapetian, Shoushan. 'Opportunities and Challenges of Institutionalizing a Pluricentric Diasporic Language: The Case of Armenian in Los Angeles'. In *The Routledge Handbook of Heritage Language Education: From Innovation to Program Building*, edited by Olga Kagan, Maria Carreira, and Claire Chick, 145–60. New York: Routledge, 2017.
Kasbarian, Sosse. 'Between Nationalist Absorption and Subsumption: Reflecting on the Armenian Cypriot Experience'. In *Cypriot Nationalisms in Context*, edited by Thekla Kyristi and Nikos Christofis, 177–97. New York: Palgrave Macmillan, 2018.
_____. 'The "Others" Within: The Armenian Community in Cyprus'. In *Diasporas of the Modern Middle East: Contextualising Community*, edited by Anthony

Gorman and Sossie Kasbarian, 241–73. Edinburgh: Edinburgh University Press, 2015.

Katchadourian, Herant. 'Culture and Personality: The Case of Anjar'. In *Armenian Communities of the Northeastern Mediterranean: Musa Dagh–Dört-Yol–Kessab*, edited by Richard Hovannisian, 237–251. Costa Mesa: Mazda, 2016.

Kelidar, Abbas. 'The Political Press in Egypt 1888–1914'. In *Contemporary Egypt: Through Egyptian Eyes: Essays in Honour of P. J. Vatikiotis*, edited by Charles Trip, 1–21. New York: Routledge, 1993.

Kingston, Paul W. T. *Reproducing Sectarianism: Advocacy Networks and the Politics of Civil Society in Postwar Lebanon*. Albany, NY: State University of New York Press, 2013.

Kévorkian, Raymond. *The Armenian Genocide: A Complete History*. New York: I. B. Tauris, 2011.

Khalaf, Samir. *Civil and Uncivil Violence in Lebanon: A History of the Internationalization of Communal Conflict*. New York: Columbia University Press, 2004.

Khalidi, Rashid. *Sowing Crisis: The Cold War and American Dominance in the Middle East*. Boston: Beacon Press, 2009.

Khoury, Philip S. *Syria and the French Mandate: The Politics of Arab Nationalism, 1920–1945*. Princeton: Princeton University Press, 1987.

Kinzer, Stephen. *The Brothers: John Foster Dulles, Allen Dulles, and Their Secret World War*. New York: St Martin's Griffin, 2014.

Kokot, Waltraud, Khachig Tölölyan and Carolin Alfonso, 'Introduction'. In *Diaspora, Identity, and Religion: New Directions in Theory and Research*, edited by Waltraud Kokot, Khachig Tölölyan and Carolin Alfonso, 1–8. New York: Routledge, 2004.

Kouymjian, Dickran. 'Cilicia and its Catholicosate from the Fall of the Armenian Kingdom to 1915'. In *Armenian Cilicia*, edited by Richard Hovannisian and Simon Payaslian, 297–308. Costa Mesa: Mazda, 2008.

_____. 'The Right Hand of St. Gregory and other Armenian Arm Relics'. In *Les objets de la mémoire. Pour une approche comparatiste des reliques et de leur culte*, edited by Philippe Borgeaud and Youri Volokhine, 215–40. Geneva: Peter Lang, 2005.

Kunth, Anouche and Claire Mouradian, *Les Arméniens en France*. Toulouse: Attribut, 2010.

Lang, David Marshall. *The Armenians: A People in Exile*. London: Unwin Hyman, 1988.

Laycock, Joanne. 'Belongings: People and Possessions in the Armenian Repatriations 1946–1949'. *Kritika* 18(3) (2017): 511–38.

———. 'Soviet or Survivor Stories? Repatriate Narratives in Armenian Histories, Memories and Identities'. *History and Memory* 28(2) (2016): 123–51.

———. 'Armenian Homelands and Homecomings, 1945–9'. *Cultural and Social History* 9(1) (2012): 103–23.

———. 'The Repatriation of Armenians to Soviet Armenia, 1945–49'. In *Warlands, Population Resettlement and State Reconstruction in the Soviet-East European Borderlands, 1945–50*, edited by Peter Gatrell and Nick Baron, 140–61. London: Palgrave Macmillan, 2009.

Little, Douglas. *American Orientalism: The United States and the Middle East since 1945*. Chapel Hill: University of North Carolina Press, 2008.

Logan, Darren L. 'A Remnant Remaining: Armenians amid Northern Iraq's Christian Community'. *Iran & the Caucasus* 14(1) (2010): 143–57.

Makdisi, Usamma. *The Culture of Sectarianism*. Berkeley: University of California Press, 2000.

Maksoudian, Krikor. 'Armenian Communities in Eastern Europe'. In *The Armenian People from Ancient to Modern Times (Volume 2) From Dominion to Statehood: The Fifteenth Century to the Twentieth*, edited by Richard Hovannisian, 51–80. London: Macmillan, 1997.

Maksudyan, Nazan. *Orphans and Destitute Children in the Late Ottoman Empire*. Syracuse: Syracuse University Press, 2014.

McCormick, Jared. 'Hairy Chest, Will Travel: Tourism, Identity, and Sexuality in the Levant'. *Journal of Middle East Women's Studies* 7(3) (November 2011): 71–97.

Meinardus, Otto F. A. *Christians in Egypt: Orthodox, Catholic and Protestant Communities Past and Present*. Cairo: The American University in Cairo Press, 2006.

Meouchy, Nadine and Peter Sluglett, eds, *The British and French Mandates in Comparative Perspectives/Les Mandats français et anglais dans une perspective comparée*. Leiden: Brill, 2004.

Messerlian, Zaven. *Armenian Participation in the Lebanese Legislative Elections 1934–2009*. Beirut: Haigazian University Press, 2013.

Migliorino, Nicola. *(Re)constructing Armenia in Lebanon and Syria: Ethno-cultural Diversity and the State in the Aftermath of a Refugee Crisis*. Oxford: Berghahn Books, 2008.

Mills, Amy. 'Becoming Blind to the Landscape: Turkification and the Precarious National Future in Occupied Istanbul'. *Journal of the Ottoman and Turkish Studies Association* 5(2) (2018): 99–117.

Moumdjian, Garabet K. 'Cilicia Under French Adminstration: Armenian Aspirations, Turkish Resistance, and French Stratagems'. In *Armenian Cilicia*, edited by Richard Hovannisian and Simon Payaslian, 457–89. Costa Mesa: Mazda, 2008.

Nalbantian, Tsolin. 'Articulating Power Through the Parochial'. *Mashriq and Mahjar* 2(1) (2013): 41–72.

———. 'Going Beyond Overlooked Populations in Lebanese Historiography: The Armenian Case'. *History Compass* 11(10) (2013): 821–32.

Ndhlovu, Finex. 'A Decolonial Critique of Diaspora Identity Theories and the Notion of Superdiversity'. *Diaspora Studies* 9(1) (2016): 28–40.

Nucho, Joanne Randa. *Everyday Sectarianism in Urban Lebanon: Infrastructures, Public Services and Power*. Princeton: Princeton University Press, 2016.

Oganessyan, Eduard. 'The Armenian Church in the USSR'. *Religion in Communist Lands* 7(4) (2008): 238–42.

Olsen, Liesel. *Modernism and the Ordinary*. Oxford: Oxford University Press, 2014.

Ormanian, Malachia. *The Church of Armenia: Her History, Doctrine, Rule, Discipline, Liturgy, Literature, and Existing Condition*. London: Forgotten Books, 2012.

Ouahes, Idir. *Syria and Lebanon Under the French Mandate: Cultural Imperialism and the Workings of Empire*. New York: I. B. Tauris, 2018.

Ozbek, Esen Egemen. 'Commemorating the Armenian Genocide: The Politics of Memory and National Identity'. Ph.D. Diss., Carleton University Ottawa, 2016.

Pakhdigian, Nerses Apeghia. Hratarakutʻiwn HMĚM-i Surwoy, Libanani, ew Hordanani Shrjanayin Varchʻutʻean Hushamatean 1918–1958 [A Publication of the HMEM Regional Governing Board of Syria, Lebanon, and Jordan: A Registry 1918–1958]. Beirut: n.p., 1958.

Panossian, Razmik. *The Armenians: From Kings and Priests to Merchants and Commissars*. New York: Columbia University Press, 2006.

Papkova, Irina. 'The Three Religions of Armenians in Lebanon'. In *Armenian Christianity Today: Identity Politics and Popular Practice*, edited by Alexander Agadjanian, 171–96. Burlington, VT: Ashgate, 2014.

———. 'The Lebanese Armenian Church and Its Milieu'. In *Armenians of Lebanon (II) Proceedings of the Conference (14–16 May 2014)*, edited by Antranik Dakessian, 51–62. Beirut: Haigazian University Press, 2017.

Parikian, Vayk, and Hovnan Varzhapetian. *Patmutʻiwn Surioy hay tparanneru* [The History of Syrian Armenian Printing Houses]. Syria: Bibliothèque Violette Jébéjian-UGAB, 1973.

Pasura, Dominic. 'Competing Meanings of the Diaspora: The Case of Zimbabweans in Britain'. *Journal of Ethnic & Migration Studies* 36(9) (2010): 1445–61.
Pattie, Susan. *The Armenian Legionnaires: Sacrifice and Betrayal in World War I.* New York: I. B. Tauris, 2018.
_____. 'Paradise Lost and Regained in Kessab: Narratives of Rebuilding and Migration'. In *Armenian Communities of the Northeastern Mediterranean: Musa Dagh–Dört-Yol–Kessab*, edited by Richard Hovannisian, 453–78. Costa Mesa: Mazda, 2016.
_____. 'From the Centres to the Periphery: "Repatriation" to an Armenian Homeland in the 20th Century'. In *Homecomings: Unsettling Paths of Return*, edited by Fran Markowitz and Anders H. Stefansson, 109–24. Oxford: Lexington Books, 2004.
_____. *Faith in History: Armenians Rebuilding Community.* Washington, DC: Smithsonian Institution Press, 1997.
Payaslian, Simon. 'The Institutionalisation of the Catholicosate of the Great House of Cilicia in Antelias', in *Armenian Cilicia*, edited by Richard Hovannisian and Simon Payaslian (Costa Mesa: Mazda, 2008), 557–92.
_____. 'Diasporan Subalternities: The Armenian Community in Syria'. *Diaspora: A Journal of Transnational Studies* 16(1/2) (Spring/Autumn 2007): 92–132.
_____. *History of the Armenian People.* Costa Mesa: Mazda, 1993.
Perra, Antonio. *Kennedy and the Middle East: The Cold War, Israel and Saudi Arabia.* London: I. B. Tauris, 2017.
Picard, Elizabeth. *Lebanon: A Shattered Country.* New York: Holmes & Meier, 2002.
Pitts, Graham Auman. 'Fallow Fields: Famine and the Making of Lebanon'. Ph.D. diss., Georgetown University, 2016.
Primakov, Yevgeny. *Russia and the Arabs: Behind the Scenes in the Middle East from the Cold War to the Present.* New York: Basic Books, 2009.
Robson, Laura. 'Refugees and the Case for International Authority in the Middle East: The League of Nations and the United Nations Relief and Works Agency for Palestinian Refugees in the Near East Compared'. *International Journal of Middle East Studies* 49(4) (2017): 625–44.
Safran, William. 'Diasporas in Modern Societies: Myths of Homeland and Return'. *Diaspora* 1(1) (1991): 83–99.
_____. 'Deconstructing and Comparing Diasporas'. In *Diaspora, Identity, and Religion: New Directions in Theory and Research*, edited by Waltraud Kokot, Khachig Tölölyan and Carolin Alfonso, 9–30. New York: Routledge, 2004.

Sahakyan, Vahe. 'Between Host-Countries and Homeland: Institutions, Politics and Identities in the Post-Genocide Armenian Diaspora (1920s to 1980s)'. Ph.D. diss., University of Michigan, 2015.

Salibi, Kamal. *Crossroads to Civil War: Lebanon 1958–1976*. Delmar, NY: Caravan Books. 1976.

_____. *A House of Many Mansions: The History of Lebanon Reconsidered*. Los Angeles: University of California Press, 1990.

Salloukh, Bassel, Rabie Barakat, Jinan S. Al-Habbal, Lara W. Khattab and Shoghig Mikaelian, eds *Politics of Sectarianism in Postwar Lebanon*. London: Pluto Press, 2015.

_____. 'The Architecture of Sectarianism in Lebanon'. In *Sectarianisation: Mapping the New Politics of the Middle East*, edited by Nader Hashemi and Danny Postel, 215–34. London: Pluto Press, 2015.

Sanjian, Ara. 'The Armenian Church and Community of Jerusalem'. In *The Christian Communities of Jerusalem and the Holy Land: Studies in History, Religion, and Politics*, edited by Anthony O'Mahony, 57–89. Cardiff: University of Wales Press, 2003.

Sanjian, Avedis. *The Armenian Communities in Syria Under Ottoman Domination*. Cambridge, MA: Harvard University Press, 1965.

Sayed, Linda. 'Sectarian Homes: The Making of Shi'i Families and Citizens under the French Mandate, 1918–1943'. Ph.D. diss., Columbia University, 2013.

Sayigh, Yezid and Avi Shlaim, eds. *The Cold War and the Middle East*. Oxford: Oxford University Press, 2003.

Sbaiti, Nadya. '"If the Devil Taught French": Strategies of Language and Learning in French Mandate Beirut'. In *Trajectories of Education in the Arab World: Legacies and Challenges*, edited by Osama Abi-Mershed, 59–79. New York: Routledge, 2010.

Schahgaldian, Nikola B. 'The Political Integration of an Immigrant Community into a Composite Society: the Armenians in Lebanon 1920–74'. Ph.D. diss., Columbia University, 1978.

Schayegh, Cyrus. *The Middle East and the Making of the Modern World*. Cambridge, MA: Harvard University Press, 2017.

Schwalgin, Susanne. 'Why Locality Matters: Diaspora Consciousness and Sedentariness in the Armenian Diaspora in Greece'. In *Diaspora, Identity and Religion: New Directions in Theory and Research*, edited by Carolin Alfonso and Waltraud Kokot, 72–92. New York: Routledge, 2004.

Seigneurie, Ken. *Standing By the Ruins: Elegiac Humanism in Wartime and Postwar Lebanon*. New York: Fordham University Press, 2011.

Shafiyev, Farid. *Resettling the Borderlands: State Relocations and Ethnic Conflict in the South Caucasus*. Montreal: McGill-Queen's University Press, 2018.

Sharkey, Heather. *A History of Muslims, Christians, and Jews in the Middle East*. Cambridge: Cambridge University Press, 2017.

Shemmassian, Vahram. 'The Settlement of Musa Dagh in Anjar, Lebanon, 1939–1940'. In *Armenians of Lebanon (II) Proceedings of the Conference (14–16 May 2014)*, edited by Antranik Dakessian, 129–54. Beirut: Haigazian University Press, 2017.

_____. 'Vakef Köy of Musa Dagh: The Sole Armenian Village Remaining in Turkey'. In *Armenian Communities of the Northeastern Mediterranean: Musa Dagh–Dört-Yol–Kessab*, edited by Richard Hovannisian, 287–308. Costa Mesa: Mazda, 2016.

_____. 'The Repatriation of Armenian Refugees from the Arab Middle East, 1918–1920'. In *Armenian Cilicia*, edited by Richard Hovannisian and Simon Payaslian, 419–56. Costa Mesa: Mazda, 2008.

Steege, Paul, Andrew Stuart Bergerson, Maureen Healy, and Pamela E. Swett. 'The History of Everyday Life: A Second Chapter'. *The Journal of Modern History* 80(2) (2008): 358–78.

Stocker, James R. 'The United States and the Struggle in the Armenian Patriarchate of Jerusalem, 1955–1960'. *Jerusalem Quarterly* 71(2) (2017): 19–21.

_____. 'The United States and the Armenian Community in Lebanon, 1943–1967'. In *Armenians of Lebanon (II) Proceedings of the Conference (14–16 May 2014)*, edited by Antranik Dakessian, 155–81. Beirut: Haigazian University Press, 2017.

_____. 'An Opportunity to Strike a Blow? The United States Government and the Armenian Apostolic Church, 1956–1963'. *Diplomacy & Statecraft* 29(4) (2018): 590–612.

Suciyan, Talin. *The Armenians in Modern Turkey: Post Genocide Society, Politics, and History*. New York: I. B. Tauris, 2016.

Suny, Ronald Grigor. *'They Can Live in the Desert but Nowhere Else': A History of the Armenian Genocide*. Princeton: Princeton University Press, 2015.

_____, Fatma Müge Goçek, and Norman M. Naimark, eds *Question of Genocide: Armenians and Turks At the End of the Ottoman Empire*. Oxford: Oxford University Press, 2011.

_____. 'Eastern Armenians Under Tsarist Rule'. In *The Armenian People from Ancient to *Modern Times (Volume 2) From Dominion to Statehood: The Fifteenth Century to the Twentieth*, edited by Richard Hovannisian, 109–37. London: Macmillan, 1997.

———. *Looking Towards Ararad*. Indianapolis: Indiana University Press, 1993.

Tachjian, Vahé. *Daily Life in the Abyss: Genocide Diaries, 1915–1918*. New York: Berghahn Books, 2017.

———. 'L'établissement définitif des réfugiés arméniens au Liban dans les années 1920 et 1930'. In *Armenians of Lebanon: From Past Princesses and Refugees to Present-Day Community*, edited by Aïda Boudjikanian, 59–94. Beirut: Haigazian University Press, 2009.

———. 'The Cilician Armenians and French Polity, 1919–1921'. In *Armenian Cilicia*, edited by Richard Hovannisian and Simon Payaslian, 539–55. Costa Mesa: Mazda, 2008.

———. 'Des camps de réfugiés aux quartiers urbains: processus et enjeux'. In *Les Arméniens 1917–1939: La quête d'un refuge*, edited by Raymond Kévorkian, Levon Nordiguian and Vahé Tachjian, 113–45. Paris: Réunion des musées nationaux, 2007.

———. '"Repatriation": A New Chapter Studded with New Obstacles, in the History of AGBU's Cooperation in Soviet Armenia'. In *The Armenian General Benevolent Union: A Hundred Years of History 1906–2006, Volume 2*, edited by Raymond H. Kévorkian and Vahé Tachjian, 291–309. Cairo: AGBU Central Board, 2006.

Tashjian, Yeghia. 'The Origin, Success and Failure of the Lebanese–Armenian "Third Force" During the Intra-communal Cold War (1956–1960)'. In *Armenians of Lebanon (II) Proceedings of the Conference (14–16 May 2014)*, edited by Antranik Dakessian, 181–98. Beirut: Haigazian University Press, 2017.

Tchilingirian, Hratch. 'The "Other" Citizens: Armenians in Turkey between Isolation and (Dis)Integration'. *Journal of the Society for Armenian Studies* 25(4) (2017): 123–55.

———. 'The Catholicos and the Hierarchical Sees of the Armenian Church'. In *Eastern Christianity: Studies in Modern History, Religion and Politics*, edited by Anthony O'Mahony, 140–59, London: Melisende, 2004.

Hagop Tcholakian, 'Kessab as a Diasporan Community'. In *Armenian Communities of the Northeastern Mediterranean, Armenian Communities of the Northeastern Mediterranean: Musa Dagh–Dört-Yol–Kessab*, edited by Richard Hovannisian, 409–52. Costa Mesa: Mazda, 2016.

Thompson, Elizabeth. *Colonial Citizens: Republican Rights, Paternal Privilege, and*

Gender in French Syria and Lebanon. New York: Columbia University Press, 1999.
Tölölyan, Khachig. 'The Contemporary Discourse of Diaspora Studies'. *Comparative Studies of South Asia, Africa and the Middle East* 27(3) (2007): 647–55.
———. 'Elites and Institutions in the Armenian Transnation'. *Diaspora: A Journal of Transnational Studies* 9(1) (2000): 107–36.
———. 'The Nation-State and Its Others: In Lieu of a Preface'. *Diaspora: A Journal of Transnational Studies* 1(1) (1991): 3–7.
Touryantz, Hagop. *Search for a Homeland*. New York: issued privately, 1987.
Traboulsi, Fawwaz. *A History of Modern Lebanon*. London: Pluto Press, 2007.
Tufankjian, Scout and Atom Egoyan. *There Is Only the Earth: Images from the Armenian Diaspora Project*. New York: Melcher Media Inc., 2015.
Tyler, Patrick. *A World of Trouble: The White House and the Middle East – From the Cold War to the War on Terror*. New York: Farrar, Straus and Giroux, 2009.
Varnava, Andrekos. 'French and British Post-Imperial Agendas and Forging an Armenian Homeland after the Genocide'. *The Historical Journal* 57(4) (2014): 997–1025.
Walker, Christopher. 'World War I and the Armenian Genocide'. In *The Armenian People from Ancient to Modern Times (Volume 2) From Dominion to Statehood: The Fifteenth Century to the Twentieth*, ed. Richard Hovannisian 239–74. London: Macmillan, 1997.
———. *Armenia: Survival of Nation*. New York: St Martin's Press, 1980.
Watenpaugh, Keith David. 'Armenians, Alawites, and the Alexandretta Crisis (1937–1939)'. In *Armenian Communities of the Northeastern Mediterranean: Musa Dagh–Dört-Yol–Kessab*, edited by Richard Hovannisian, 193–206. Costa Mesa: Mazda, 2016.
———. *Bread from Stones: The Middle East and the Making of Modern Humanitarianism*. Berkeley: University of California Press, 2015.
White, Benjamin Thomas. *The Emergence of Minorities in the Middle East: The Politics of Community in French Mandate Syria*. Edinburgh: Edinburgh University Press, 2011.
Weiss, Max. *In the Shadow of Sectarianism: Law, Shi'ism, and the Making of Modern Lebanon*. Cambridge, MA: Harvard University Press, 2010.
Williams, Elizabeth Rachel. 'Cultivating Empires: Environment, Expertise, and Scientific Agriculture in Late Ottoman and French Mandate Syria'. Ph.D. diss., Georgetown University, 2015.

Yaghoubian, David. *Ethnicity, Identity, and the Development of Nationalism in Iran*. Syracuse: Syracuse University Press, 2014.

Yaqub, Salim. *Containing Arab Nationalism: The Eisenhower Doctrine in the Middle East*. Chapel Hill and London: University of North Carolina Press, 2004.

Yeghiayan, Buzand. *Zhamanakakitsʿ Padmutʿyun Katʿoghikosutʿyan Hayotsʿ Kilikioh 1914–1972* [The Contemporary History of The Armenian Catholicosate of Cilicia]. Antelias: The Catholicosate of Cilicia, 1975.

Yousefian, Sevan Nathaniel. 'The Postwar Repatriation Movement of Armenians to Soviet Armenia, 1945–1948'. Ph.D. diss., University of California, Los Angeles, 2011.

Zahr al-Din, Salih. *Min Jabal Musa ila Hawsh Musa – ʿAnjar: malhamah Armaniyah bayna al-mawt wa-al-hayah*. Beirut: Dar Hamaskaʾīn lil-Nashr wa-l-tawziʿ, 2015.

Zake, I. ed., *Anti-Communist Minorities in the U.S.: Political Activism of Ethnic Refugees*. New York: Palgrave, 2009.

INDEX

Note: references to images are in *italics*; references to notes are indicated by n.

1957 election, 167, 172–5, 176–7, 178–80, 183, 188–9, 200
1958 conflict, 11–12, 167–9, 177–8, 180–2, 200
  and aftermath, 187–8
  and Beirut, 183, 184–7

Abdallah of Transjordan, King, 46
ach (gold mound relic of St Gregory), 127, 144–51, 162n76, 163n82
Adana Massacres, 35n57
Aghbashian, Hovhannes, 110
Aghtamar See, 146
Alawites, 47
Aleppo, 90–1, 97–8, 112–13, 116–17
Anatolia, 2, 3, 4, 13, 119n13
Anjar, 49, 61, 62–3
Ankara, 87, 88, 89
Antelias, 60, 94, 102, 132, 159n34, 162n76, 174–5, 181; *see also* Cilician See
anti-communism, 131–2
Arab League, 47
Arab nationalism, 5, 48–9
Arabic language, 61–4, 80n79, 92–3
Arabs, 56–8, 79n57
Araks (newspaper), 105–6
Ararad (newspaper), 6–7, 45–9, 51, 58, 172
  and Soviet Union, 65–6, *67*, 68–72
Aravelk (newspaper), 116
Armenian Catholic Church, 62–4, 63n79, 183
Armenian Church *see* Armenian Catholic Church; Armenian Protestant Church; Catholicosate of Cilician See; Catholicosate of Echmiadzin See; Istanbul Patriarchate; Jerusalem Patriarchate
Armenian Evangelical College, 183, 201
Armenian General Benevolent Union (AGBU), 69
Armenian General Union and Scouts (Armenian General Union of Body Culture), 175, 184n94, 190n37
  and athletic games, 53–6, 78n38, 111–12, 113–14
  and resignations from, 117, 125n152
Armenian Genocide, 2–3, 6, 9, 16, 17–19
Armenian National Council of the Americas (ANCA), 69, 70
Armenian Protestant Church, 183
Armenian Scholars' Organisation, 112–13

221

Armenian Socialist Soviet Republic
  (ASSR), 4, 7–9, 11–12, 58, 61–2
  and Cilician See, 72–4
  and Lebanon, 68, 74–5
  and media, 45–6
  and politics, 176–7
  and repatriation, 84–6, 87–9,
    98–105
  and Soviet Union, 65–6, 68–72
Artavasd, Archbishop of the Cilician See,
  63–4
assimilation, 13, 18
ASSR *see* Armenian Socialist Soviet
  Republic
Ataturk, Kemal, 3
Azerbaijan, 105, 106
Aztag (newspaper), 6–7, 45–9, *50*, 51
  and 1957 election, 170–3, 175–6,
    178–80
  and *ach*, 145–9
  and Arab states, 56–8
  and ASSR, 69–71
  and athletic games, 53–6
  and Beirut, 184–5
  and ceasefire of 1958, 188
  and Cilician See, 129, 138, 141,
    142–3
  and imperialism, 52–3
  and language, 62
  and politicians, 60–1
  and repatriation, 111, 114
Aztarar (newspaper), 111–12, 114–16

Baghdad Pact, 5, 131–2, 167
Batumi, 105–6
Bedros (Batanian), Patriarch of the
  Armenian Catholic Church, 62–3,
  80n79
Beirut, 2–3, 24, 49
  and Armenian neighbourhoods, 85, 87,
    89, 182–7
  see also Bourj Hamoud; Corniche al-
    Nahr; Karantina; Mar Mikael; Sin
    el Fil
Bourj Hamoud, 2, 12, 53, 132, 135, 169,
  179, 181–6, 200
Britain *see* Great Britain
Bulgaria, 87, 88

Catholicos, 60, 94–5, 174–5; *see also*
  Cilician See; Echmiadzin See;
  Karekin; Khoren; Vasken; Zareh

Chamoun, Camille, 5, 9, 10, 131–2, 177
  and 1956 Catholicos election, 127, 128,
    139
  and 1957 election, 167, *168*, 171–2,
    173–5, 178–9
  and Catholicos Vasken, 137–8
  and Catholicos Zareh, 140, 141–2, 143
Chehab, Fouad, 168, 175, 185–6
chrism, 149–50, 162n77
Cilicia, 2, 13, 28n10, 52; *see also* Cilician
  See
Cilician See (Cilician Catholicosate), 4,
  5–6, 72–4, 130–1
  and 1956 Catholicos election, 9–10,
    126–30, 136–44, 199–200
  and *ach*, 144–51
  and USA, 152–3
citizenship law, 3, 6, 21
class, 12, 14, 51, 182
Cold War, 1, 2, 4–5, 8–12
  and Armenians, 196, 198, 199–200
  and Cilician See, 127–8
  and histories, 22–3
  and repatriation, 85–6
communism, 4, 12, 131–2, 178–9
Corniche al-Nahr, 12, 169, 182–3, 200
Cyprus, 15, 101, 149

Daily Star, The (newspaper), 142, 158n31,
  168
Damascus, 92–3, 98
Dashnak Party, 3, 4, 5, 9–10, 127
  and 1957 election, 173–5, 176–7,
    188–9
  and 1958 conflict, 177–8, 180–2,
    187–8
  and Archbishop Leon Tourian, 151–2
  and Beirut, 184–5
  and Catholicos, 131, 132, 140
  and repatriation, 110–13, 116–18
  see also *Aztag*
Deeb, Lara
  *An Enchanted Modern: Gender and
    Public Piety in Shi'i Lebanon*, 19–20
demonstrations, 70–1
Der Matossian, Bedross, 18
diaspora studies, 12–17, 20–1, 23–5
Diran (Nersoyan), Archbishop and Prelate
  of the Eastern Diocese of North
  America, 148, 149
Dro, General (Drastamat Kanayan),
  125n145

Druze, 20, 47
Dulles, John Foster, 168

Eastern Europe, 13, 14, 34n36, 87, 88
Echmiadzin See (Echmiadzin Catholicosate), 9, 69, 145–6, 152–3
and 1956 election, 126–7, 129–30
see also Kevork VI; Vasken I
Eddé, Raymond, 180, 181, 186–8
Egypt, 9, 18, 46, 105–6, 161n67
and Cilician See, 127, 141
and media, 46, 105–6
see also Nasser, Gamal Abdel
Eisenhower Doctrine, 167, 178

Faisal II of Iraq, King, 22
France, 3, 6, 9, 18
and Cilician See, 127, 141, 143
and citizenship rights, 21, 29n11–12
and imperialism, 47–8, 51–2
and Légion d'Orient, 27n8
and Soviet Union, 68
see also Paris
Friends of Soviet Armenia Association, 103–4

Gemayal, Amin, 204n15
Georgia, 105–6
Great Britain, 9, 18, 68
and Cilician See, 127, 140, 143
and imperialism, 47–8, 52–3
see also London
Greece, 15, 87, 88

Hajin, 2, 180–1, 183–6, 192n68
Hariri, Rafiq, 202
al-Hawadith (newspaper), 90–1
historiography
Armenian, 12–19
Cold War, 22–3
Lebanese, 19–22
Hitler, Adolf, 95, 110, 116
HMEM games *see* Armenian General Union and Scouts (Armenian General Union of Body Culture)
Hnchak Party, 4, 183, 186
and 1957 election, 174, 175, 176–7, 178, 179
and 1958 conflict, 187–8
and repatriation, 131
see also Ararad

homeland (*erkir*), 12–13, 17, 96–8, 101, 106–7
Hovannisian, Richard
The Armenian People from Ancient to Modern Times, 13–14, 17

identity, 9, 14–15, 170–82
imperialism, 47–8, 51–3
Iran, 15, 18, 90
Iraq, 15–16, 168
Isahakyan, Avetik, 102–3, 110
Istanbul, 13, 24, 75n1, 87, 88
Istanbul Patriarchate (Armenian Patriarchate of Istanbul), 130–1, 146, 157n23, 163n83
al-Ithnayn (newspaper), 46–7

Jerusalem, 148–9, 150
Jerusalem Patriarchate (Armenian Patriarchate of Jerusalem), 6, 36n61, 130, 157n25; *see also* Diran (Nersoyan), Archbishop and Prelate of the Eastern Diocese of North America; Yeghishe (Derderian), Patriarch of Jerusalem
Joghovourti Tzain (newspaper), 6–7
and repatriation, 84, 85, 89–96, 99–101, 102–5, 106–8, *109*, 110–18
Jordan, 9, 22, 178–9
and Cilician See, 127, 141, 150

Karami, Rashid, 180
Karantina, 85, 93, 99–100, 106–7, *108*, 182
Karekin I (Hovsepian), Catholicos of the Cilician See, 46, 68, 72–4, 101–2, 126
Karekin (Khachadourian), Patriarch of Istanbul Patriarchate, 146, 148
Kars, 31n22, 69, 81n86, 89
Kevork V (Soureniants), Catholicos of the Echmiadzin See, 131
Kevork VI (Cheorektjian), Catholicos of the Echmiadzin See, 73, 87, 101
Khat (Achabahian), Archbishop of the Cilician See, 145
Khoren (Muradpekyan), Catholicos of the Echmiadzin See, 73
Khoren (Paroyan), Archbishop of the Cilician See, 129–30, 132, 136–8, 153
and 1958 conflict, 181–2
and *ach*, 146–7, 151

al-Khouri, Faris, 59, 62, 64
al-Khoury, Beshara, 49, *50*, 60–1, 63–4
Khoury, Camille, 204n15
Kilis, 96, 98
Kozan *see* Sis

Lahoud, Emil, 49
land, 69, 70, 103; *see also* homeland
language, 3, 7, 131, 158n27, 199; *see also* Arabic language
Lausanne, Treaty of (1923), 3, 29n11
Lebanese army, 12, 138–9, 168–9, 180, 184–5
Lebanese Civil War, 200, 201–2
Lebanon, 1–6, 18, 19–23
   and Armenians prior to independence, 1–6, 18, 20–1, 44–5
Légion d'Orient, 27n8
Lenin, Vladimir, 66
London, 87, 88

Madeian, Harutyun, 92, 98–9
Makdisi, Ussama
   The Culture of Sectarianism: Community, History, and Violence in Nineteenth-Century Ottoman Lebanon, 19
Manouchian, Mélinée, 90
Manouchian, Misak, 90
Mar Mikael, 12, 169, 182, 183, 185, 200
Marash, 2
Marmnamarz (newspaper), 78n38
Matni, Nassib, 167, 179
media, 6–7, 45–9, *50*, 51, 88, 90, 184–7, 196–7, 198–9; *see also Ararad*; *Aztag*; *Daily Star, The*; *Joghovourti Tzain*; *L'Orient*; *Marmnamarz*; *al-Nahar*; *New York Times*; *Zartonk*
Miasnikyan, A., 66, 68
minorities, 20
al-Muqattam (newspaper), 46, 47

al-Nahar (newspaper), 142, 193–4n88
Nasser, Gamal Abdel, 5, 22, 143–4
Nazism, 110, 116
New York Times (newspaper), 152, 166n109, 166n111
newspapers *see* media
Nixon, Richard, 153
non-Alignment movement, 22

Orient, L' (newspaper), 147
Ottoman Empire, 2–3, 4, 35n57, 98, 130–1; *see also* Turkey

Palestine, 18, 36n64, 46–7
Panossian, Razmik
   The Armenians: From Kings and Priests to Merchants and Commissars, 14–15
Papyan, Matsak, 66, 68
Paris, 87, 88
Payaslian, Simon, 16–17, 129
Poland, 14, 18, 34n36
politicians, 58–61
politics, 3–5, 8–9, 11–12; *see also* 1957 election

al-Quwatli, Shukri, 141, 142, 143

Ramgavar Party, 4, 95, 131
   and 1957 election, 174, 175, 176–7, 178, 179
   and 1958 conflict, 187–8
   and Beirut, 184, 185, 186
   see also Zartonk
refugee camps, 2
relics *see* ach
religion, 4, 5–6, 19–20, 63–4, 182–3, 199; *see also* Armenian Catholic Church; Catholicos; Cilician See; Echmiadzin See; Istanbul; Jerusalem
repatriation movement, 31n22
   and ASSR, 102–5
   and Beirut, 85, 87, 89, 93–4, 99–100, 106–8, *109*
   and Catholicos Karekin of the Cilician See, 94–5, 101–2
   and Georgia, 105–6
   and history, 95–101
   and media, 69–71, 89–94, 110–18
   and Lebanon, 7–10, 94–5
   and Soviet Union, 84–6, 87–9, 199
Right Arm of St Gregory *see* ach
Romania, 87, 88
Russia, 14; *see also* Soviet Union
Russia (ship), 85, *86*
Russo-Persian War, 18

Salam, Sa'ib, 58
Salibi, Kamal
   A House of Many Mansions, 20, 128
sectarianism, 3, 4, 6, 19–20, 200–1, 203n2

Shi'ite Islam, 19–20
Sin el-Fil, 12, 182, 183, 201
Sis, 2, 5, 130
socialism, 4, 5
Solh, Sami, *50*
song, 19, 100–1, 113–14
Soviet Union (USSR), 4, 5, 7
    and ASSR, 65–6, 68–72
    and Cilician See, 72–3, 74, 126–7, 129–30
    and Cold War, 198, 199–200
    and glorification, 110
    and Iran, 18
    and repatriation, 84–6, 87–9, 96–7
    and USA, 151
    see also Armenian Socialist Soviet Republic; Stalin, Joseph
Soviet–Turkish Treaty of Neutrality and Friendship, 88
Stalin, Joseph, 65, 66, 68, 73, 87
    and Armenian support, 177
    and repatriation, 104–5
Suez crisis, 178
Sulh, Sami Bey, 58–9
Suny, Ronald Grigor, 14, 18
Syria, 4, 7, 16–17, 18
    and athletic games, 55–6
    and Cilician See, 141, 142
    and imperialism, 52–3
    and independence, 48–9
    and language, 64
    and media, 46, 47
    and politicians, 58–61
    and repatriation, 89, 90–4
    and Turkey, 57–8
    see also Aleppo; Damascus

Taif accords, 200, 201, 202n1
tanzimat reforms, 5–6
TASS (Soviet news agency), 71, 84, 87–9
al-Telegraph (newspaper), 167, 179
Tourian, Archbishop Leon, 151–2
Traboulsi, Fawwaz
    A History of Modern Lebanon, 20, 128
Transcaucasian Socialist Federative Soviet Republic (TSFSR), 151
Transylvania (ship), 85
tsarism, 14
Turkey, 3, 51–2, 111, 191n58
    and Cilician See, 143
    and Genocide, 18–19
    and land, 69, 70, 103
    and repatriation, 31n22, 115, 117–18
    and Syria, 57–8
    see also Istanbul

Ukraine, 14, 18
United Arab Republic, 22
United Nations, 51, 57
United States of America (USA), 4, 5, 9, 59, 88
    and ANCA, 69, 70
    and Cilician See, 127, 141, 143
    and Cold War, 198, 199–200
    and Lebanon, 168, 178–9
    and sees, 151–3
    and Soviet Union, 68
USSR *see* Soviet Union

Vasken I (Baljian), Catholicos of the Echmiadzin See, 9, 10, 143–4, 145–6
    and 1956 election, 126, 127, 128, 129–30, 136–41
    and Lebanon, 132–3, *134*, 135–6
Veratsnuntd (newspaper), 117
violence, 11n26, 20, 35n57, 165n109, 166n111
    and 1958 conflict, 32n26, 167, 180, 183, 184, 186–7, 188
    and Genocide, 16, 17
    and Lebanon, 197, 198, 201

women, 19, 139–40
World War I, 18, 95–6
World War II, 65; *see also* Hitler, Adolf

Yeghishe (Derderian), Patriarch of Jerusalem, 148–9, 154n5, 154n7, 164n93

Zareh I (Payaslian), Catholicos of the Cilician See, 126–7, 138–43
    and *ach*, 145, 146, 147–8, 149–50
    and National Order of the Cedar, 174–5
Zartonk (newspaper), 6–7, 142, 172, 184, 186, 191n58
Zeytun, 98

EU representative:
Easy Access System Europe
Mustamäe tee 50, 10621 Tallinn, Estonia
Gpsr.requests@easproject.com